Aligning Performance

Aligning Performance
Improving People, Systems, and Organizations

Danny G. Langdon

Jossey-Bass
Pfeiffer
San Francisco

Copyright © 2000 by Jossey-Bass/Pfeiffer

Jossey-Bass/Pfeiffer is a registered trademark of Jossey-Bass Inc., A Wiley Company.

ISBN: 0-7879-4736-9

Library of Congress Cataloging-in-Publication Data

Langdon, Danny G.
    Aligning performance: improving people,
    systems, and organizations/Danny G. Langdon.
    p. cm.
    Includes bibliographical references (p.) and index.
    ISBN 0-7879-4736-9 (alk. paper)
    1. Performance technology. 2. Performance standards.
    3. Employees—Training of. I. Title
    HF5549.5.P37L36 2000
    658.3'14—dc21 99-6755

Printed in the United States of America

Published by

JOSSEY-BASS/PFEIFFER
A Wiley Company
350 Sansome St.
San Francisco, CA 94104-1342
415.433.1740; Fax 415.433.0499
800.274.4434; Fax 800.569.0443

www.pfeiffer.com

Acquiring Editor: Matthew Holt
Director of Development: Kathleen Dolan Davies
Developmental Editor: Maryanne Koschier
Editor: Rebecca Taff
Senior Production Editor: Dawn Kilgore
Manufacturing Supervisor: Becky Carreño
Illustrations: Richard Sheppard

Printing 10 9 8 7 6 5 4 3 2

 This book is printed on acid-free, recycled stock that meets or exceeds the minimum GPO and EPA requirements for recycled paper.

"On earth, before anything is created materially, it has to be created mentally, doesn't it? When matter is put aside, all creation becomes exclusively mental, that's all. You'll come, in time, to adopt the power of the mind."

RICHARD MATHESON, "WHAT DREAMS MAY COME,"
© 1978 BY RICHARD MATHESON, *WHAT DREAMS MAY COME*,
P. 92. NEW YORK: TOM DOHERTY ASSOCIATES, 1998.
REPRINTED BY PERMISSION OF DON CONGDON ASSOCIATES, INC.

CONTENTS

FIGURES

Chapter 4

Chapter 5

Chapter 6

Chapter 7

Chapter 8

Chapter 9

Chapter 10

ACKNOWLEDGMENTS

In the course of writing seven books, one should certainly have thanked everyone who has had an influence on his professional and personal life. As I sit here tonight in Edinburgh, Scotland, at 3:00 A.M. I am remembering them all. I do want to especially thank my good friend Mel D'Souza for many of the illustrations used throughout this book. And Matt Holt of Jossey-Bass/Pfeiffer for believing in me.

However, at the pinnacle of my career, there are three people who stand out.

First, as always, was the woman, as both mother and father, who emulated the virtues of human life and work. I am but the son whom she crafted. You would have to have been there to see how this person ran a scrap iron business by herself for forty years and raised eight children to truly understand how you could not possibly help but grow up to appreciate life and give to others.

Second is the one who can never be second in my life. She, as partner both in life and business, is certain to be always loved like no other has been loved. I am in awe of how she draws so many to her side by her kindness and compassion. I am lucky to be by her side.

And I thank my god and creator. Having read most recently a book about dreams and the afterlife, certainly the words to be found here must have come from elsewhere. I am grateful and certainly enjoy being the conduit for these words.

PREFACE

The original purpose of the model of performance presented here was quite elementary. I developed the "Language of Work" model because no common way existed for everyone in the workforce—from executives to managers to workers—to think, communicate, and resolve common issues while making business more efficient and effective. The model was designated a "language" not so much as a way of speaking, but rather as a systematic thinking process that would result from individual and collective use. However, since its inception the Language of Work model has become much more than was originally intended. The emphasis today is on how it has been used to produce remarkable results in organizations. Therefore, the purpose of this book is twofold: (1) to describe how the model can be used to achieve performance alignment in business and (2) to describe the role of the performance consultant in using it with everyone in the business.

Performance alignment achieves harmony in all dimensions of work so that customers are best served and business goals are achieved. While the end is achieving performance alignment, the intermediate goal is to learn a systematic way to approach performance analysis that will result in immediate improvements in the organization for the business as a whole, its core processes, individuals, and work groups.

The book is written for anyone who wants to improve his or her performance, the performance of work groups, or the performance of the business as a whole. Executives, managers, and workers will benefit from knowing and practicing what is said here. However, the level of detail presented here probably excludes all but the most diligent lay person from reading this book to achieve performance improvement and alignment. The book is primarily intended for the new and evolving specialist in business known as the "performance consultant" (specialist, technologist). This is the individual who facilitates the business audience—who does the work to make improvements in performance. This individual holds the model, ensuring that the audience follows the steps in an orderly way. There will be bits and pieces, even whole chapters, that the performance consultant may find appropriate to share with an interested executive, manager, team, or individual. But the book is really for performance consultants who want to increase their own skills—who want to learn an overall system for performance analysis, measurement, and improvement of business. The result will be performance alignment throughout the business.

The manner in which the performance consultant will use the information in this book may be different from past roles he or she has played. Traditionally, trainers or other interventionists have been the sole analyzers of tasks, definers of objectives, and developers of materials and solutions, and perhaps even implementers of training or other interventions. Becoming an internal or external performance consultant requires a paradigm shift.

The new role of the performance consultant will be that of a facilitator and holder of models for analyzing performance while others do the work. The consultant will have to recognize that those who do the work have the answers. What they do not know how to do is to formulate the question—the performance situation—clearly enough to see those answers and consider alternatives for solutions. This role recognizes that the performance problems are the audience's to analyze, solve, be committed to, and implement.

The performance consultant will not be the holder of the answers (although this person will need to know the solution or intervention options), but rather be the one who helps constituents see their performance needs clearly. To do this, the consultant will need a model that (1) reflects what performance is, (2) can be readily understood, and (3) can be rapidly used to paint performance pictures of what exists and what should exist—the proverbial gaps in performance that must be filled. The model presented in this book is one way to do this; it is fully capable of being used for every kind of performance problem, and at every level in a business.

Chapter 1 provides an overview of performance alignment and shows how to use of the Language of Work model in achieving that alignment. Achieving internal performance alignment begins with understanding how businesses perform. Their need for alignment is readily apparent. The Business Sphere model presented in Chapter 2 displays the levels of the organization that require alignment. Performance is multi-level and multi-layered. There are four layers of work or performance: its work behavior, standards, support, and human relations. Chapters 3 through 6 will present the behavior of business units, core processes, individuals, and work groups. Once these levels of performance are defined and aligned, we can layer in the standards the behavior is expected to achieve, the support the business must provide to allow optimal behavior and standards, and the methods for reducing the human noise that can get in the way of achieving performance. Thus, Chapters 7 through 9 are devoted to the remaining three layers: work standards, work support, and human consonance, respectively. The book closes with Chapter 10, a summary of the tenets of performance alignment that are the performance goals of business, as facilitated through the assistance of its performance consultants.

In this book, you will need to look for the simplicity, as well as understand the complexity and hard work that it takes to achieve performance improvement and alignment in any business. This is a rewarding field of endeavor because you are helping all employees, workers, managers, and executives to be the best that they can be. You are helping organizations to thrive and grow, to achieve their desired ends. You could spend a lifetime helping to identify and fix problems at random and through brainstorming. And these methods would be useful in fixing immediate problems. But until those problems are assigned to someone who has an understanding of business in all its performance dimensions, the whole of the business will not get to where it needs to be—a business that has achieved performance alignment. This book will allow you to offer an integrated set of solutions to your clients. You will have an integrated understanding of all the parts of the business and have a perspective on making improvements that will not be random, but systematic. You will be able to link performance needs from any part of the organization to any other part. And you will be able to facilitate the employees and executives in seeing this integrated approach. Their clarity will bring excitement to every project; their understanding will bring improvement to every encounter. Then I will have done my work, which is to make the implicit explicit, the complex manageable, the unknown known. My work is to enable the communication and discussion of work to occur throughout the world in clear, nonemotional terms for the purpose of improving and aligning businesses everywhere.

Danny Langdon
October 1999

CHAPTER 1

Introduction to
Performance Alignment in Business

Performance alignment assures that all the work in a business is in harmony so that the organization can achieve its common mission: surviving while meeting its client needs. Work alignment and performance alignment are the same thing. This book describes how performance alignment can be achieved inside a business. It describes the role of the performance consultant as a facilitator to help executives, managers, and workers achieve performance alignment. Alignment can only exist when the people who do the work understand it in all its dimensions. They must also truly want to achieve alignment. The performance consultant's job is not to achieve alignment *for* management and the workforce. Rather, the consultant facilitates—through sound methodology—the understanding, definition, and improvement of performance *by those who actually do the work.* The performance to be improved may be a problem to be resolved, a job to be changed in light of a process change, a group that is out of whack within itself or with other groups, or a situation in which the entire business needs to be reengineered or reorganized.

There are two related aspects of achieving business alignment. One is the alignment of the business to its external environment—to its customers, suppliers, and the competitive environment in which it operates. This is a kind of alignment that looks out from within the business to the external environment to see what kind of business it wants to be, how it will relate to its clientele, and how it will survive in the competitive marketplace. The literature is replete with methods for achieving "external" business alignment. Except in passing, such external alignment—looking from the inside of business to the outside world—will not be addressed in this book. The reader is referred to the great variety of business development books that currently address this kind of alignment. The author recommends in particular the work of Dr. Donald Tosti (1999) on "Global Fluency." He has a handle on external alignment that is noteworthy, particularly in light of today's global economy.

The second kind of business alignment is the look from the outside world to the inside of the business. This is known as performance alignment; it must follow after the external alignment has been defined and implemented. This type of alignment arranges all the work or performance *within* the business so that the goals set out in external alignment can be achieved. Thus, it answers the question: "How will the business organize and perform the work in order to deliver to customers and clients?" Performance alignment is the subject of this book.

Of the two kinds of business alignment, the internal performance alignment is the more difficult, for two reasons: (1) the lack of methods for aligning all the work that goes on in the typical business, and (2) every person associated with the business is involved in one way or another. External alignment is the work of a few select executives, whereas internal alignment involves everyone in the organization. Resources, rules and regulations, communication needs, and so on need to be attended to and aligned, in addition to all the employees, their managers, and executives. No wonder internal performance alignment is so hard to achieve. The focus in this book will be on the tools and techniques a performance consultant can use to help everyone internally in the business align and operationalize performance. This will require not only tools and techniques, but a fundamental understanding of what performance is and how to implement and continuously improve it. Although the book is not written for executives, managers, and workers, there is a need for them to understand performance, which this book can provide. Would-be students in management will find this book a valuable resource for understanding internal work performance. The performance consultant will also find occasions on which to share select examples and readings with clients.

Achieving internal performance alignment requires profound knowledge and lots of hard work. It requires disciplined practice. It is not one of those "programs du jour" or initiatives that can be attended to on occasion. At the same time, any attention to performance alignment on any scale will have immediate payoffs in improving work. However, improving the overall health of a business takes long-term attention and discipline. This is made easier when everyone comes to understand performance and makes it a continuous effort to achieve.

The real challenge of performance alignment is to have a methodology that literally anyone in the organization can use. The performance consultant will be the expert in performance, but not the one who defines and aligns the work. He or she is a facilitator of this effort—a teacher and a coach. In this way the consultant imparts a method that is learned by everyone—so that everyone becomes an expert in performance. The author has coined the term "the Language of Work model" (Langdon, 1995) for his method of performance alignment. The model provides a way for everyone to speak, think, and act together in understanding and achieving performance alignment.

To achieve performance alignment requires having methods for answering three questions:

1. Where is the performance that needs alignment located in the business?
2. How can you describe the performance so that nothing is overlooked?
3. How can we make the performance understandable and align all performance together so that each part supports the others?

The following will briefly answer these questions and provide an overview to the rest of the book. The details will come in each succeeding chapter.

FOCUSING ON WHAT THE BUSINESS NEEDS TO ALIGN

The first thing to figure out is where the performance that needs alignment is located within the business. Business is not one big performance issue, but is a combination of "levels" of performance that take place and need to be aligned. These levels serve different business needs, but are inextricably linked.

We need agreement on where and what the performance is so that we are all on the same worksheet, so to speak, in achieving alignment. We also need agreement so that we can take responsibility for those aspects of performance that we "own." Executives, for example, may perceive that they own everything, but the reality is that they can only directly handle the highest level of performance, as they have limited time and resources. Managers, too, have to understand and own their levels of performance and not try to do work best left to the workers. And in the same way, workers have to own and understand their levels of performance. Unfortunately, the prevailing, traditional view of business does not support understanding and aligning performance. A more functional, performance-related view is required. A major step in this direction was achieved by Geary Rummler and Alan Brache (1995). In this book we will build on their model, but first, let's take a brief look at the traditional view of business.

Traditional View of Business

The traditional view of business is the organization chart, which conveys the notion that key functions exist and that key people are responsible for them. We all know what they look like. There is a president on the first page, with his or her reporting relationship to the board of directors, and under that is a series of executive vice presidents who head up major divisions or groups that meet special needs, such as legal, civil affairs, finance, and so on. On the next few pages we find each division broken down into several subgroups, each with a vice president or director's name next to some functional group name (engineering, research and development, sales). Then (maybe) there are pages and pages of individual workers with their titles. In many instances the workers (who do the majority of the work or performance) are not on the organization chart, which is only a listing of major departments and functions with executives' names. That is about it! We won't even address whether the organization chart is up-to-date. That's how we communicate our view of the company to employees. Right? Where is the performance—how we really do things? Where is the process? The procedures? What tells us what the individual or group does? These charts really do not describe what the work is and how it is done.

Organization charts, which reflect the "silos," as Rummler and Brache so aptly labeled them, are mere hierarchies of how work is organized; they do not show how work is *performed*. The charts give names to work, but provide no operational sense of how the work is accomplished. It is like comparing a blueprint of a building with a wooden model of the same building. In the former, you get an idea of what the building will look like and where things will be. However, you can't see how the building fits together and how the rooms relate from one to the next and how each floor connects with the next.

Additionally, fewer people can read a blueprint than can understand a model. Organization charts name work groups, but do not show how the work groups relate with one another to achieve mutual ends. No processes, by which work is done, are presented. The charts are useful for communicating overall structure, but not performance. They are really useless for identifying work problems and seeing potential solutions. Management, workers, and performance consultants need better models of work and business in order to achieve the desired alignment of performance.

The Business Sphere: A View of Business for Achieving Alignment

The first step in achieving performance alignment was developing a perspective of business that accurately accounts for and reflects where performance occurs in business. This perspective of performance will be known as the Business

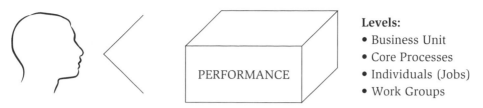

Levels:
- Business Unit
- Core Processes
- Individuals (Jobs)
- Work Groups

Figure 1.1. Business Performance.

Sphere, a four-level depiction of performance in business. The details of the Business Sphere will be provided in Chapter 2. For now, a brief introduction will show the value of the Business Sphere in achieving performance alignment and will form a foundation on which to build our understanding of performance in business.

The first level of performance is that which both establishes the external alignment and then determines what internal performance alignment is required. We will come to know it as the *business unit level of performance.* It is determined and administered by chief executives whose job it is to "run" the business. It is their job as well to see that every level of performance that follows is aligned to the business unit.

Business units are needed to plan, organize, and operationalize things. The business unit provides the link between the customers and their needs and the people whose work it is to meet those needs. Business units have their own special performance definitions, issues, and requirements. Indeed, these definitions form the foundation on which the rest of the performance alignment rests. Without them we can be assured that everything else in the way of performance will suffer.

The primary performance requirements that business units define is their outputs and consequences—what they will deliver to customers for specific results. These are based directly on the external alignment plan. To achieve these business needs, a second level of performance is needed. This performance level is the *core processes.* If business units represent the "what" of business and performance alignment, then the core processes represent the "how" of performance from an overall business performance perspective.

Core processes define the major performance steps that will be utilized by the individuals and groups who will actually produce (or service) business unit outputs. The core processes demonstrate the interdependency among the many levels of performance—namely people and their systems and resources. When the interdependency is not understood, work is fragmented, resulting in wasted time and money and, worst of all, a forgotten customer. If core processes are not defined, workers are left to figure out work on their own. Core processes must be identified and aligned to the performance of the business unit.

So, we have the "what" of business units and the "how" of core processes as our first two levels of performance. However, neither of these tells *who* will be doing the work and how they do it. Both business units and processes are nonhuman performance components. Each can be defined and aligned without any consideration of a human being. Humans (as individuals and groups) are in the next two levels of performance.

To achieve the core processes, we need *individuals,* who are assigned "jobs"—their performance—based on the core processes, which in turn are based on the business unit. To these ends, there will be jobs that directly carry out the steps of the core processes, jobs that support these direct jobs, and jobs that support activity and needs across the business, such as in benefits, legal, and so on. Then, there are jobs for managers and executives to facilitate the performance. All of these jobs require performance and need to be aligned to the business unit(s) and core processes. If these jobs are created by those who fill them—which occurs more often than we want to admit—we need to ask whether they are aligned to the core processes. If jobs are created without reference to well-defined processes, we have to ask why and determine the alignment issues that are presented.

The fourth and final performance level in any business is the various *work groups.* These may be organized in functional areas, such as engineering, in teams for special purposes, or brought together temporarily, as in matrix management systems. Work groups are needed in business because individuals must pool their individual work production with others to meet client needs; resources are always limited and need to be shared as well. In addition, basic communication, line-of-authority, and general administrative needs have to be met. Work groups have performance needs that are unique to them in a common, shared, and cooperative way. And they must often share with other work groups. Work group performance must be aligned with individuals, core processes, and business unit(s) performance.

In summary, the four levels of performance in a typical business are the business unit, core processes, individuals, and work groups, as illustrated in Figure 1.2. The business unit represents the "what" of performance, the core processes the "how" of performance, the individuals the "performance by whom," and the work groups the "organization of performance." With these four levels as a convenient and functional identification of where performance occurs in business, we can move on to determining the full dimension of performance at each level.

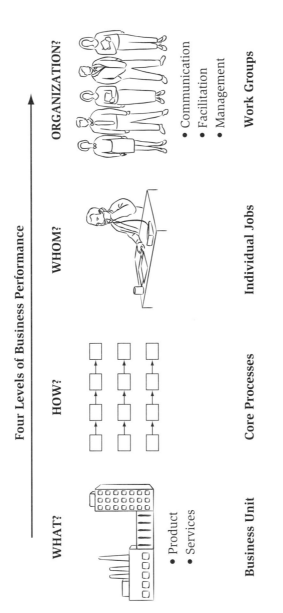

Figure 1.2. Four Levels of Business Performance.

THE DIMENSION OF PERFORMANCE
IN THE BUSINESS SPHERE

When we refer to performance or work at any one of the four levels, we think in terms of what is happening or is intended to occur. For example, the individual *does* certain tasks. The work group *produces* a plan or a product. The core process *satisfies* a customer need. The business unit has *determined* its products and services. All these instances are referring to the "behavior" (or actions and accomplishments) of these performance levels. However, performance or work is more than just a way of behaving (see Figure 1.3). Performance has several dimensions to it, which also must be aligned in the business.

Behavior (the act of doing things) is the first layer of performance. Individuals behave or should behave in a certain way to accomplish their job duties. We expect them to produce certain things, use certain resources, follow guidelines, processes, ask questions, and achieve desired results. This "behavior" is also present within work groups. And, although we don't often think of behavior applying to core processes and business units, it does. The fact that we can represent each level of a business by its behavior allows us to align that behavior, even if the behavior is not of humans. For example, the behavior in a core process requires alignment to the behavior of individuals and work groups.

Imagine a fish swimming. The swimming is the "behavior." Any level of the organization can be a fish swimming: be it the business unit(s), core processes, individual, or work group. But fish do more than swim.

All behavior must rise to certain *standards.* We expect individuals to not only produce a product, but to produce a certain amount, in a given time frame, to a certain level of customer satisfaction. There is an explicit or implicit standard. Standards are often discovered only when they are not met, but they certainly exist for individuals. In a similar way, work groups have standards, as should core processes and business unit(s). For example, we establish profitability standards for our business units.

Standards exist for a number of reasons. They protect the organization and its people. They project the activity level, cycle time, cost, volume, and so forth needed to keep the organization in business. Federal and state regulations cover safety standards, wages, and hours worked. Standards relate to production goals, which in turn connect to profitability. The question here is, "How high or fast must the 'fish' swim?" Standards are an integral part of performance and should be aligned throughout the business.

The next layer is *support* provided by the business. Without adequate support, desired behavior and standards are difficult, if not impossible, to achieve.

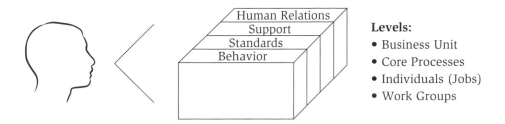

Figure 1.3. Performance Layers.

All performance needs support of one kind of another. Individuals need to be adequately paid and motivated. Work groups need mechanisms to have their ideas heard and accepted. Processes need adequate and timely resources. Business units need methods to keep on top of changing demographics, technologies, and shifting marketplaces. Every kind of performance needs support. And this support must be aligned in the business. We need clean and healthy water for the "fish" to swim in lest the behavior degrade and the standards suffer.

Finally, performance is highly impacted by *human relations.* Executives, managers, and co-workers can affect performance behavior by their attitudes, temperament, and prejudices. They may keep desired behavior from occurring, prevent standards from being reached, and circumvent the support that is in place. There is not a single person in the work environment who has not had his or her performance, others' performance, and the business as a whole impacted by other people. Obviously, other humans are an important part of our performance affecting all levels in the business. To follow the fish analogy, consider the degree that others polluting the organizational waters affect the behavior of the fish, its standards, and the very water itself. It doesn't take a fish long to find the safe place to hide out. This layer of performance, human relations, will be labeled "human consonance" in the Language of Work model, which is shown in Figure 1.4.

As seen in Figure 1.4, *behavior, standards, support,* and *human consonance* are the four critical layers of performance. All are found in and influence each of the four performance levels: *business unit, core processes, individual jobs,* and *work groups.* Each of these levels and layers must be aligned. But how? The answer lies in knowing what performance is, as well as in knowing how to define and align it.

The Relationship of the Layers of Performance

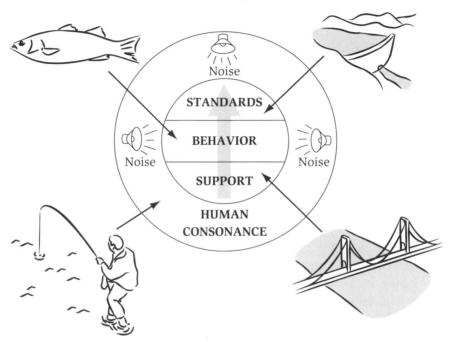

Figure 1.4. The Relationship of the Layers of Performance.

Defining Performance

When asked what their work or performance is, people typically answer in a revealing way. Rather than telling you what makes up their work and how they do it, they generally tell you *what* they do. "I produce this." "I sell widgets." "I am a marketing representative." You must probe to find out how they do their work, what they use to do it, who helps them, what resources they use, what rules they follow, and so on. When executives are asked what the business does as work, how the processes work, and what the work groups do, they too need to be probed for a complete answer. Today's business has no consistent way by which to describe work. The fact that we have no idea how to define work, change it, or obtain help from others explains our difficulty in improving work. The Eskimos are said to have twenty-seven words for snow. We have almost none for describing work. We have many ways to complain about it, but few to capture its essence. There is no common way to define performance, especially one that includes the various levels. We must have a common way to define work in order to align performance throughout the Business Sphere.

Proforma
    ...a paradigm for defining performance

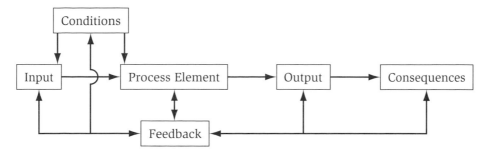

Figure 1.5. The Proforma Paradigm.

Language of Work Model

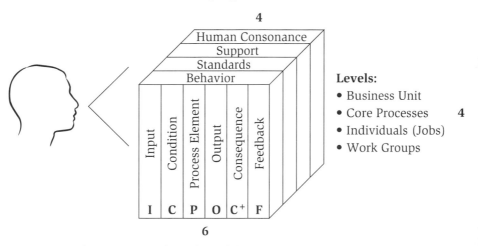

Levels:
- Business Unit
- Core Processes   4
- Individuals (Jobs)
- Work Groups

Figure 1.6. The Language of Work Model.

This exploration of the subject of performance alignment and how it might be achieved started with a consideration of exactly what performance is and how it is best represented. Initially, I observed that performance often reflected a kind of goal: "I produce this or make that." Although performance must achieve objectives or goals, it is not an objective itself. Rather, performance implies the action of *doing* things—using things, attending to conditions, processing, communicating, and achieving results. It is not a static concept, but active. It should be a "model" of what is occurring. However we define performance on paper, it should reflect what is happening (or supposed to happen) in as active terms as we can find.

If we look at the performance of any individual, group, core process, or business unit, we can see that performance has six key components. For the sake of simplicity, I have developed a proforma model to show the relationship among these key components, as shown in Figure 1.5 and Figure 1.6. The word proforma is borrowed from the finance field and means to "provide a prescribed form." The proforma model of performance will greatly aid everyone in the business to define and align the four layers within the four levels of performance in the Business Sphere.

The Proforma of Performance

All performance, first of all, produces an output (O), tangible work in the form of some product, service, or knowledge. Outputs are the "deliverables" we see from work groups, jobs, core processes, and business units. The outputs the business decides to produce at its business unit level must be capable of being traced throughout the business from that level through processes, individuals, and work groups. This is but one form of aligning the performance of the business: linking the output from the business unit to the other levels. Other elements of work will need the same consideration.

Output is the very first thing that needs to be determined. Output is the reason for existence as a business. Output is easiest to remember as the "deliverable" of performance. We need to know what the performance is primarily designed to do and achieve. The output is represented in Figure 1.6 as "O."

All output has a consequence (shown as C+), the result of the output being delivered. The consequence might range from profit for the business unit to personal satisfaction in one's work for the individual. Output and consequence relate directly to each other.

Now, to produce output and consequence we need some reason and resources, called inputs (shown as I). Both reason (or triggers) and resources are inputs because they are used to produce the output and achieve the consequence. First, we need the reason for doing the performance, which comes in the form of a request of some kind. For example, the business unit identifies a customer need. An order initiates a core process to deliver what the customer wants or a work group receives its assignment to meet this need. A manager asks individuals to do their part to produce the output. These are all (internal or external) client requests or "triggers" to start the performance.

Most of the inputs for performance are in the form of resources. We need materials, ideas, knowledge, equipment, and so on to produce outputs. We use these up, so to speak, in various ways to make or produce the product of service.

Performance is governed in all instances by certain conditions (shown as C). Business units have to follow external rules and regulations imposed by the government. These have a direct influence on how or what is produced—even on how the inputs are used. Similarly, the policies and procedures established by the business itself are conditions that govern core processes, individuals, and work groups. Thus far, the proforma shows that performance is composed of inputs, conditions, outputs, and consequences.

To use the input, under the conditions, to achieve the output and consequences, we need a procedure or process to follow. The process element (shown as P) of performance is composed of a series of steps we follow to produce the output. We call it the "process element" in the model to distinguish it from the "core processes," fully recognizing that it means a procedure to be followed in work behavior.

The final element of the proforma is feedback (represented by F). Feedback in relation to performance tells us: (1) that we have finished and (2) how we are doing along the way. First, feedback is necessary to tell us that we have finished the output and achieved the consequence. We often realize that an output is complete because we have enough experience to know, but when the output is new or unfamiliar, we may have to be told it is finished. Feedback on the result is also needed, such as when clients tell us that we have met their exact need. Suffice to say that we often need feedback from others to really know that work is finished.

The second type of feedback, while processing, is critical and integral to performance. This feedback may help us correct or adjust our actions so that we produce the desired output and achieve the consequence properly. We may and should ask for this kind of feedback to help ourselves in work, or it may come to us unsolicited by our supervisor, suppliers, or clients.

In summary, performance is inputs, conditions, process element, outputs, consequences, and feedback. This proforma can be used to define any performance level in the business sphere. The proforma also is of great use in defining and aligning the layers of performance that include behavior, standards, support, and human resonance. Figure 1.7 gives more detail about the proforma. It is a useful job aid as we define the concept further in the rest of the book and for you and others to use as you define and align your business.

ELEMENT	DEFINITION	TYPICAL SOURCES
Input	The resources and requests available or needed to produce outputs. What must be present for something (the output) to happen.	• Client Needs • People • Ideas • Equipment • Facilities • Funds • Information • Specific Requests
Condition	Existing factors that influence the use of inputs, processes, and feedback used to produce outputs.	• Rules • Policies • Environment
Process Element	The steps completed to use the inputs, under the conditions, in order to produce the outputs.	Steps are represented by action verbs such as: • Produce • Review • Edit • Etc.
Output	That which is produced as a result (product/service/ knowledge) of using inputs under certain conditions and through a process.	• Services • Products • Knowledge
Consequence	The effects that an output has on a person, product, service, or situation.	• Customer Satisfaction • Needs Met • Problem Solved • Opportunity Realized
Feedback	That which completes the work cycle; response to outputs that confirms success or indicates adjustment is needed. Also, response to processing, conditions, and feedback.	• Client Reactions • Information Needs • Reinforcements

Figure 1.7. Proforma Job Aid.

A 6:4:4 MODEL FOR ALIGNMENT

Essentially, we now have a 6:4:4 model, the Language of Work model shown in Figure 1.6. There are six elements that define performance (input, conditions, process element, output, consequences, and feedback); four levels of business (business unit, core processes, individual jobs, and work groups) performance, each of which can be defined and aligned to one another using the proforma; and four layers of performance (behavior, standards, work support, and human consonance).

The model creates a way for us to understand and improve performance. Throughout the pages that follow, you will achieve several benefits from the use of the Language of Work model. The model

- Combines the collective knowledge of people and the learning process developed by researchers in behavioral psychology with what we know about performance from such fields as organizational development, total quality, reengineering, learning organizations, and others.

- Extends beyond the individual and groups to the whole organization in a systematic way that helps to achieve and align total performance at all levels of the business.

- Captures the gaps in performance to show deficiencies clearly in order to decide what interventions will best solve performance needs.

- Defines and displays performance as a whole, so that the behavior, standards, needed organizational support, and human relations are accounted for.

- Embodies the human (individual and work group), non-human systems (core processes), and organizational side (business unit) that must be aligned if a business is to work in harmony (alignment).

In the chapters that follow, each of these will be described in more detail. We begin with a more in-depth study of the Business Sphere and its four levels of performance in Chapters 3 through 6.

CHAPTER 2

The Business Sphere

Where to Apply Performance

In Chapter 1, we introduced the four levels of the Business Sphere, the four layers of performance, and the six elements of the proforma. By slicing performance in these ways, we can locate the performance that requires improving. The Business Sphere will help keep us focused on how best to define, measure, improve, and implement, as well as achieve the ultimate goal of aligning internal business performance. This chapter provides additional detail on the nature of performance at each of the levels of the Business Sphere. In addition, we introduce two perspectives for the Business Sphere: defining and changing performance and implementation of performance.

DETAILS OF THE BUSINESS SPHERE

Four levels of operations are involved in accomplishing work in business. As illustrated in Figure 2.1, each level of the business can be represented as a level within a sphere, beginning with the external environment and moving to the business unit, core processes, individuals, and work group. These levels are described next.

Level One: The Business Unit

Whether for profit or not, business units produce outputs, in the form of products, services, or knowledge, for the purposes of achieving designed consequences. A typical business unit has a prescribed set of outputs the business wants to produce, the inputs it needs to produce these outputs, the conditions it will adhere to overall as a business, the consequences to be achieved, the process element in the form of an organizational working relationship between work groups, and feedback that will aid in production and measurement of satisfaction. Business units can comprise a few workers and managers or thousands of people. The words *business unit* may be used to designate the major level of a business that produces a significant output; they may also be used to designate the business as a whole.

In the case of large corporate business units, the corporation itself is the primary business unit, but there are other major business units within it, such as divisions, regional offices, branch offices, franchises, and so forth. Each of these produces significant outputs for external clients, although other business units of the corporation may receive them as well. The distinguishing feature of a business unit is that it produces common outputs of significant size that requires various core processes, through individuals organized in different work groups aligned to achieve work. One additional distinction is that business units are the entities that interact with and service the business clients or customers.

For example, XYZ Corporation is a business unit that also has other significant-sized business units that produce outputs and consequences for clients. It has interests in construction, mining, engineering, design, environmental services, operations and maintenance, and other profit units. Because these units are considered important business entities in the total context of a corporate "business," they must be examined for how they themselves can be improved effectively and efficiently, as well as be aligned as businesses. From a performance improvement perspective, to treat these divisions as anything less than a business unit would be misguided. In the grand scheme of producing meaningful outputs, divisions are complete business units that need definition of their own—if only because of their uniqueness of operations and focus on specific client needs. Indeed, the divisions may be more meaningful than the total business—each contributes profits to the whole and its specific outputs have unique inputs, conditions, process elements, feedback, and overall consequences.

Level Two: Core Processes

Core processes are the approaches that are used to produce major business outputs and their related consequences in the business unit. They may produce the output directly to an external client or pass off their output to other work groups as input for processing. When and where necessary, these core processes

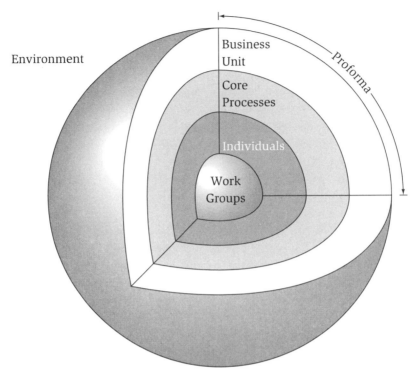

Figure 2.1. The Business Sphere: Changing and Aligning Performance.

interrelate at common points. Processes often cut across two or more work groups.

Typical processes are engineering, accounting, manufacturing, selling, researching, prospecting, and training. For example, proposal writing in a training company is a process that may be shared among several work groups, each of which contributes to the process, as shown below:

Work Group	*Contribution to Core Process*
Proposal Development	Writing the proposal
Project Management	Project content, staffing, some writing
Sales	Client knowledge, presentation practice
Training	Presentation preparation
Human Resources	Resumes
Reprographics	Printing, binding

Another example at a higher level in an engineering or construction company would be "constructing buildings." This core process would involve the following:

Work Group	Contribution to Core Process
Proposal Development	Writing the proposal
Legal	Preparing the legal contract
Project Management	Preparing the technical specifications
Engineering	Scoping the building
Design and Architecture	Designing the building
Construction	Building the building

Perhaps the clearest definition, other than our own action label for the core process, is that offered by Hammer and Champy (1993), who suggest labeling processes by the "starting" and "finishing" points. For example, a typical process might be labeled "concept to finished product," while another is labeled "preliminary design to prototype." The engineering/construction example above would be "proposal to construction." These boundaries define the beginning and ending points of the core process and clearly communicate to those doing a core process exactly what they must be concerned with.

Any process that is composed of systematic steps, stages, or phases can be said to be a technology. Processes that include specific, repeatable steps with predictable results are technologies. One of the goals of any core process should be that it eventually reach the status of a technology.

Technologies are very desirable in relation to alignment. Engineering, for example, has systematic steps that the engineers follow from the beginning of a project to the end. But many processes do not require individuals to follow systematic steps. In professional jobs, for example, individuals carry out the process in any way they choose. Even many trainers, also professionals, develop a training program using what they think will work the best, rather than a technology such as "instructional technology."

Both systematic technologies and nonsystematic processes produce outputs. However, one is better than the other in maintaining the effectiveness and efficiency for improving work—an important distinction. It is precisely because systematic processes use a defined procedure that is repeated over and over that the individuals using them tend to learn from both their successes and their mistakes; the next time they apply their technological process, they will do the job equally well or better. Also, individuals using technologies tend to associate in professional groups that research and share information to find ways to improve their technology. This, in turn, benefits the businesses that employ these individuals. By contrast, processes without systematic phases are more prone to failure and do not grow, except to a minor degree, by individual experience.

For the average business, once the "experienced" individual leaves, so does a great deal of or all of the process. The business is left to hire another "experienced" individual. By contrast, businesses built around technologies need only find another person who understands the technology, and any added experience the person brings is a bonus.

Fortunately for business and individuals, there are many nonsystematic processes that can be converted to systematic processes. Performance consultants can play a role in identifying and systematizing processes that can become true technologies. For example, in the process of marketing, usually people use personal "logic" (a nonsystematic approach) to do their work.

Level Three: Individuals and Their Jobs

Individuals are, of course, the ones who do the work. This level includes individual workers, managers, and executives. Individuals use core processes or support the core processes within and between work groups for the good of the business unit.

In business today, individuals need a greater understanding of their own job role, its relationship to other job roles, the process they work to achieve, the work group they function as a part of, and their relationship to the entire business unit's outputs and consequences. The proforma model described in Chapter 1, used on the individual level and aligned with the other three levels of a business, helps create the understanding needed. At the individual level of the Business Sphere, we can refer to work definition as *job modeling*. By using job models we can help individuals analyze their present understanding of their work, detect weaknesses, and make improvements. We can also help them make the transition more easily to fast-moving, ever-changing work environments. When people define their own job models and read others' job models, they understand what they and others are responsible for in the workplace. This alone is a significant alignment of work.

Level Four: Work Groups

Work groups are sets of individuals who are administratively organized to work in common process-related disciplines to produce outputs. Other work groups use these outputs for the good of the defined business unit. The outputs go—immediately or eventually—to external clients.

A business unit typically contains several major work groups. Work groups use inputs, operate under certain group conditions, use specific process elements to produce outputs, and have consequences that affect their livelihood. Collectively, work groups contribute to the ultimate outputs of the business unit. All work groups exist for the common purpose of serving the whole business unit's needs, as well as those of its individual members and their jobs.

Work groups are identified on organization charts and named after their process-related discipline (for example, proposal development, marketing, sales, human resources, design, legal, engineering, civil affairs, public relations, or finance). Usually several work groups make up the typical business unit.

Some businesses include work groups that can be put into a special category: "ways of doing business," for example, groups whose work involves project management or construction management. Ways of doing business are attempts by the business to promote or form a "concept" (that is, a team) approach to work through a formal organizational structure within the business unit. Traditional work groups, such as those cited previously, are structured by common task, process, or function. All accountants, for example, are grouped together into the accounting work group, all lawyers into the legal department. By contrast, ways of doing business work groups usually have workers and managers from different disciplines. The accountant and engineer find themselves organizationally in the same work group on a temporary, project basis.

"Ways of doing business" are not commonly identified on an organization chart. Nonetheless they function in the same way as the more common work groups. In defining a business using the Language of Work model, you will be able to specify and measure to improve these ways of doing business. The assistance we give work groups is called "work group alignment" here. The work group is simply "out of whack" and could benefit from the help of a performance consultant. How this is done will be described in Chapter 6.

THE FOUR LEVELS OF THE BUSINESS SPHERE AND THE PROFORMA

The Business Unit Level and the Proforma

Applying the proforma to the entire business unit is quite easy. All businesses produce *outputs.* We generally call them products and services (or knowledge in some instances). Businesses use *inputs.* We call inputs, in the general sense, resources, raw materials, funds, client needs, and even ideas. The *conditions* of the typical business unit are the rules the business has to live under, such as government, tax, ethics, public demands, and competition. The *processes* are how the work groups interrelate and "get the work done." Representative *consequences* include opportunities for the business unit to achieve client satisfaction, leadership in their service or products, and, of course, the all-important "profit" consequence. *Feedback* is the way the business checks on customer satisfaction, keeps employees informed, seeks their help in quality improvement efforts, and many other ways of communicating, measuring, and reinforcing work.

The Core Processes Level and the Proforma

Core processes are the procedural steps that the business intends to follow in actually producing or achieving the business outputs. In manufacturing, it is easy to identify these core processes and subprocesses. In service businesses, it is a little harder, but nonetheless possible. Whether it is a product, service, or knowledge process, all core processes can be defined and understood more readily using the proforma.

Because core processes are systems of work based on business unit definition, the processes utilize the *output* of the business as their focus point for definition. Thus, given any business output, we can define its related *inputs, conditions, consequences, process elements,* and *feedback.* Unlike traditional core process definition involving usually only the identification of "steps" (similar to the process element only) in the core process, the proforma expands our understanding of work to a more concise and complete definition of core processes and how they are best achieved, improved, and aligned to other performance levels. Of very significant importance, such definitions greatly aid in the subsequent definition of individual work.

The Individual Level and the Proforma

One of the more illuminating exercises that managers can conduct is to ask workers what they do and how they do it. This exercise results in a great variety of answers, most of which support the assertion that few of us really know how to describe the work we do. It's not that we don't do work! And yes, we can describe technically what we do in our particular occupation. But if we cannot describe our work accurately, in terms that clearly convey how we do it, then others cannot fit into our processes, help us improve, and communicate with us effectively about work. This really is not surprising, as no one has taught us how to describe our work. No one has ever sat down and said, "Let me show you how to describe your work as performance, so that you understand it better and can help your supervisors and co-workers understand what you do better." If this were a standard practice, business life would be much better, but it is not.

We can begin communicating better about work by using each element of the proforma to clarify for ourselves what our work is. As you look at your own work, ask yourself what outputs you produce. Is your major output a product or service or both? Be specific so that someone else would know too. What inputs do you utilize? What conditions must you understand and apply throughout the execution of your work? What are the process elements you use? And when finished with an output of your job, what consequences result. Whom do you communicate with for feedback? It is easier to describe your job to someone else using the proforma of inputs, conditions, process element, output, consequences, and feedback! It does help you communicate at a much higher and more meaningful level.

The Work Group Level and the Proforma

Work does not simply move through an organization because there are individuals and processes. Rather, the business is organized into various work groups either as individuals who share similar jobs or as teams that have a special way of doing projects. These are commonly identified as departments, sections, self-directed work teams, functional work units, and so forth.

Work groups relate to one another in several ways. One way is by the output that one work group provides another work group as its input. The quality of such an output will have a direct effect on the ability of a subsequent work group to use it to produce its own quality work.

Work groups also relate in terms of their understanding of other work groups. For example, when one work group wants something from another work group, how does their need relate to other work groups that have similar or competing needs? Where do their process elements intersect with one another? These need to be managed—or better, facilitated.

The proforma can be used to define different work groups using the same paradigm and therefore make it easier to see the similarity or differences between work groups. The proforma makes it quite clear where one group's output becomes the input to another work group. The proforma goes beyond the organizational structure view by defining how people actually accomplish their work and how they need to relate that work to the work of other work groups.

THE BUSINESS SPHERE: TWO ORDERS, TWO USES

Thus far, the Business Sphere has been presented as a place to define performance, improve performance, and ultimately to align performance. The order shown in Figure 2.1 allows one level to build properly on the next. However, this is not the order in which work is implemented or flows through an organization. As performance consultants we need to be aware of how work actually flows and explain the problems that using the wrong order present when improving business performance. Here is a comparison of the two orders and uses of a Business Sphere.

View 1: Changing and Aligning Performance

Figure 2.1 shows the Business Sphere as the relationship best used to change work for the goal of aligning performance. Thus, the *business unit* utilizes *core processes*, used by *individuals*, who are organized into *work groups*. Performance consultants often use this view, as is easier to use to define or redefine and reengineer, change, and align the work in a business.

However, this order runs contrary to executives' and managers' prevailing view of what performance is and how to change it. To follow this order, then, the performance consultant will need to do some teaching and be patient and tenacious. For example, in a recent enterprise-wide change effort, the vice president of finance in a major corporation announced to his staff that no change in the work could be done until he had reorganized his department—in other words, changed the work groups. By contrast, the Language of Work model calls for the work group to be the very last performance level to be defined and changed. One could hardly announce to the group that the vice president was wrong. Rather, patience and clarity were needed until the vice president saw the value of defining processes and jobs first.

View 2: Implementing Work

A different view, the implementation view, of the Business Sphere is shown in Figure 2.2. The variation is slight, but very significant. The work group comes between the individual and the core processes. This is a more hierarchical perspective, in which the business core unit, through executives, manages the core processes, work groups, and individuals. This is a perspective of work "implementation" or flow and not to be confused with the order for change described above.

Note in Figure 2.2 that the core level represents individuals—workers, managers, executives—showing that individuals are the keys to attaining business success. In terms of actually getting work done, individuals are more important than any of the other three levels—core processes, work groups, or the business unit. Without competent individuals, all other levels are worthless.

The statement "People are our most important resource" fits this view of the Business Sphere. We place *every* individual, including the average worker, in the role of understanding, improving, and implementing the business. For example, all individuals will be able to make quality improvements on their own and change their own jobs first. This is quite a contrast to the more traditional organizational views of business, in which managers and executives are the key resources and decision makers and decide what will be improved and how the work will be implemented. It is a view more consistent with self-directed work teams, but expanded to include self-directed individuals. It means the individual has to learn to define, measure, and improve his or her own work. This capacity to help oneself can be expressed as, "Quality Is Me!"

In the implementation view, the work groups aid the individual to do his or her work through teamwork while management *facilitates*. Or the self-directed work team self-directs activities and individuals. The work group is important, but not central. It exists to help all individuals and to bridge the use of the core

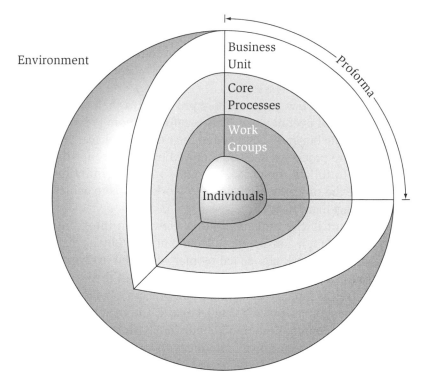

Figure 2.2. The Business Sphere: Implementing Work.

processes, rather than individuals and groups going off on their own. Indeed, it assures that core processes are followed, but can be improved when and where needed. The work of the individual must be aligned with the work group, as well as the reverse.

It is the implementation view of the work group before the individuals that gets us into trouble when the work group is changed (for example, reorganized) prior to aligning the individuals to the core processes. Although work groups do have a role helping individuals implement work and make changes, it is the individuals' jobs that must be defined before the work groups. Understanding this critical difference is important both when making changes and when achieving alignment. One must also understand that the Business Sphere is first a system for "change and alignment," then "implementation."

Core processes in the implementation view of the Business Sphere (Figure 2.2) are in close relationship to work groups, rather than to individuals. Basic is the understanding that core processes were defined (as in the change view) as the best means to accomplish the outputs and consequences of the business unit. This may seem obvious, but in the traditional organizational view of business, individuals and work groups are often left to determine their own process element of some undefined core process. Then, collectively their individual processes become the de facto core processes for the business. This is especially true in service-oriented businesses.

The implementation view positions core processes in their proper place for the accomplishment of overall work. This means that core processes must be defined to achieve the business outputs and their consequences. During implementation these core processes must be followed by work groups that facilitate their individuals to follow the processes. Only then can individual jobs be aligned to achieve the processes and aided by work groups to achieve communication and management needs.

The business unit in the implementation view is an integrated entity of aligned levels of work; not a disparate collection of individuals, disjointed core processes, or alienated work groups led by managers and executives. Instead, we see the business unit as a series of major outputs with their associated consequences, resources as inputs, work groups that process together, business conditions that influence inputs, process, and feedback, and major feedback needed to maintain constant communication with individuals and clients. The business is, or should be, an aligned entity in harmony with itself and the external environment.

There might arise some confusion regarding the Business Sphere. Some people might think that the four levels are composed of unlike parts; specifically, the business unit and core processes (which are not composed of people) do not belong with the other levels. However, one cannot view an organization as composed exclusively of people. The business unit and core processes function from a purely performance basis as entities not composed of people. Rather, they are systems, in a sense. Individuals and work groups, on the other hand, are people who do the work of core processes to meet the goals of the business unit.

A second confusion concerns whether work groups come before or after individuals in the Business Sphere. Individuals appear in both positions, depending on whether the sphere is being used for change or to describe implementation (execution). Individuals come after, or follow, the core processes in the Language of Work model when we are defining, reengineering, or reorganizing business performance. This is because individuals are assigned to jobs that are needed to complete the core processes. Then, in the performance-based setting, individuals can be clustered into work groups for meeting collective needs, facilitating, and coordinating with other work groups. This view of work groups and individuals runs counter to the prevailing notion that it is the work of executives to arrange work groups to do the work of the business unit. That approach may work in the military or in politics (both of which are power-based), but if optimum performance of people in organizations is desired, work groups need to be developed as the final step. When it comes then to implementation of the Business Sphere, the work group will be before, or above, the individuals and facilitate their work.

When we have a correct view of business, the following are more likely to occur:

- Individuals will be seen and utilized as the core strength of the business. Without individual skills, knowledge of one's job in relation to core processes, general contentment, individual and collective contribution to quality, emphasis on being customer-driven, and the like, a business is less likely to succeed.

- Core processes will drive accomplishment, rather than individuals driving the core processes.

- Work groups aid individuals in doing their work, rather than serving as barriers to communication and implementation. Managers and supervisors facilitate accomplishment, rather than supervise and control individuals.

- Executives learn to manage their business units and facilitate everyone else to use the core processes, make the work groups facilitate individuals, and value individuals in accomplishing performance.

- Business learns to look for needed improvements in core processes and individuals before changing the organization through realignment and reorganization of work groups.

- In light of its defined goals and mission, the business unit sets the overall direction through careful definition of business outputs and consequences and by providing the required inputs, conditions, processes, and feedback to produce them effectively and efficiently. It cascades these through the core processes, individuals, and work groups when defining/changing, but implements from individuals through work groups, core processes, and for the business unit.

ACHIEVING PERFORMANCE ALIGNMENT: THE ULTIMATE VIEW OF WORK

Every business needs ways to align the work at every level if it is to be a vital organization. It's one thing to have done a proper change, but it takes alignment to see that all is working in harmony. Most businesses conduct their work with very little performance alignment. They depend more on organizational structure and "key" individuals to make everything "work together." When things don't work, they make more changes than necessary—often resulting in less improvement than they wanted. This wastes time and resources, rather than moving the business ahead. Alignment is a way to understand all of the work of a business and make it function in harmony and to the benefit of its clients (customers) and, of course, its stakeholders and stockholders.

The details on defining, measuring, and improving performance at the four performance levels and their four layers is described and illustrated in the next seven chapters. Within these chapters you will learn your role as a performance consultant in making performance improvement and alignment happen. In the final chapter we will see how performance alignment is achieved in your Business Sphere using the Language of Work model.

CHAPTER 3

The Work Behavior of the Business Unit

The What *of Business*

The first level of performance to be defined is the business unit. At this level the translation begins of the business's desired achievement in the external environment through the work as it will occur in the internal business environment. The business unit is the foundation for defining and aligning the core processes, individuals, and work groups. In this chapter you can expect to learn a methodology for assisting executives to define their business in a form that communicates what the business performance is supposed to accomplish in light of its mission to the external marketplace.

Define Australia First

Suppose you know that you must travel somewhere, but instead of first determining the destination you decide the mode of transportation you will use to get there. You select your favorite type of car, buy it, and later feel quite satisfied with your purchase as you drive through Los Angeles, the city in which you live. Then you determine that your destination (goal) is Australia. However much you like the car (your process), you suddenly wish it were a boat or a plane. However long you look at it, hoping to transform it into a mode of transportation that can take you across the Pacific Ocean, it remains a car—and worthless for achieving your goal. *You did not define Australia (the goal) first.*

This happens again and again in business. We define work groups before knowing what the process will be to achieve the goal. We hire people without knowing exactly what their jobs will be because we haven't defined the processes. We set standards in arbitrary, group-think ways, rather than using the work elements on which they should be based. And there are many other examples.

Any time it is necessary to emphasize what needs defining or consideration first before other things, we will use the phrase "Define Australia first." First apply the phrase to defining the business unit.

Order of Analysis in the Business Sphere

In Chapter 2 you learned the order in which business analysis should be undertaken. Anyone employed for very long has most likely experienced management's reversing the order to improve the efficiency and effectiveness of work. This "reverse order analysis," as we might call it, likely did not produce the kinds of results anticipated. The four levels of business *must* be analyzed in the proper order. Consider the following instances of "reverse-order analysis":

- Overanalyzing processes before determining whether there is anything wrong with the primary outputs of the business. One sees this in many reengineering efforts where far too much detail is defined. This can also be the case in many attempts to meet ISO standards.

- Analyzing what is wrong with individuals (workers, managers, or teams) without having determined whether there is something wrong with the core processes they employ. This happens when we believe the employees must be at fault, rather than understanding that the fundamental processes they are obliged to follow may be the source of the problem. As Dr. Sivasailam Thiagarajan (Langdon, Whiteside, & McKenna, 1999) put it, "In relation to processes, when things go wrong, everyone blames the people rather than the process."

- Reorganizing a work group before determining whether the right process and individuals are present to achieve the defined business outputs. This common form of reverse order analysis is seen in reorganizations and in the cyclic move from centralization to decentralization and back again.

- Hiring individuals before defining and communicating what processes they will be expected to employ to achieve the primary outputs of the business. This is simply hiring the wrong people, largely caused by the lack of a clear definition of the position, the necessary skills and knowledge, and desirable attributes. People are hired on personality, with only some vague idea of what's really required of them to perform.

In general, reverse-order analysis represents the easy way out: you take symptoms and form projects from them, hoping for improvement. But more problems emerge. Hope is the operative word. Quite simply, it makes no sense—yet businesses often fail to recognize this fact. For example, it is clearly senseless to analyze processes before deciding whether the overall output is satisfactory, and yet this is often done by managers on their own or, in some instances, in the implementation of total quality management.

Recently an executive lamented about having to define all the processes to meet ISO 9000 (the European) standards in his company. The problem was not that he objected to defining the processes, nor did he object to ISO 9000 standards. Rather, he objected to the processes being defined in great detail before the overall goals (outputs and consequences) had been defined, measured, and analyzed. The business was analyzing all the processes to meet a standard rather than to *improve* the processes relative to specific outputs. They were also doing a process analysis that was void of any tangible evidence of client dissatisfaction with the products and services.

In another case, a CEO of a large corporation decided to reorganize the work groups without first investigating whether there was any problem with the processes or the individuals who produced the primary outputs. He knew there was something wrong with achievement of the business goals (his outputs), and he assumed the problem was with the work groups (the organization structure). In this case, he needed to measure the primary outputs, then look at the processes and individuals, and, finally, the organization chart. He applied his financial language, rather than an understanding of performance, to an existing problem. In this instance, I asked the CEO to look at process before reorganizing the work groups the next time. He agreed that this would make sense. Alas, within six months he had reorganized the work groups again without having looked at the processes, reverting to his comfort level. Does this sound familiar? If you have ever been reorganized, chances are you have experienced a reverse-order analysis of this type.

In the performance analysis approach described in this book, the four levels of business are analyzed in a logical sequence. The unique position and interrelationships among the *levels* are fully recognized, as well as their interdependencies—their performance alignment. One *level* is analyzed and measured to create a basis of knowledge for business improvement prior to conducting analysis at other *levels*. Certainly, an analysis using the proforma for performance described earlier can begin at any business level, but the preferred order is systematic. To summarize, here is the cascading process to improve performance and achieve performance alignment:

First: *Business unit* analysis defines and measures the overall business outputs and consequences in light of a defined business strategy/plan. This is the *what* of business.

Second: *Core process* analysis defines and measures the processes needed to achieve the business outputs and consequences. This is the *how* of business.

Third: *Individual* analysis defines, selects, and measures individual jobs needed to use the core processes to achieve the business outputs. This is the *work by whom* of business.

Fourth: *Work group* analysis defines and measures the best organization and communication of individuals to use core processes to produce the business outputs. This is the *organization of work* in business.

DEFINING AND MEASURING THE BUSINESS UNIT

Many people initially find defining and measuring the business unit difficult to do. This difficulty can be eased by introducing the proforma for the first time at the individual level—simply having people define their own jobs. The difficulty many experience in defining the business unit points out a major problem in business: many workers and managers (including executives) have little idea how to analyze and improve their business. Most will admit it and welcome learning a systematic method.

As executives work on a definition of the business unit, however difficult that is, they soon discover previously unknown relationships, lack of emphasis on consequences and feedback, and the need to define processes, among other things. They may even wonder how the business was ever run with any degree of effectiveness and efficiency. Through this analysis they will head up the path to real improvements, but their analysis of the business has just begun: core processes, individuals, and work groups lie ahead.

While conducting a business unit analysis, one of the exciting discoveries is the important contributions and relationships between work groups involved in producing the business outputs and consequences. Some of these relationships will be defined in the process element of the business unit. In the absence of such analysis, management often overlooks the full potential of some of the work groups and their value to the overall success of a business. For instance, in a particular business, the training work group could have improved business operations through the utilization of a variety of interventions, but it was only used to provide occasional training at the discretion of managers. No plan existed to support the processes that produced primary outputs. For example, this work group could train marketing personnel in giving better presentations, writing proposals, and so forth—training that could add value to the business unit. Instead, those courses sat on the shelf; the training work group was not used the way it could have been. Good business unit analysis begins the process of rectifying these and similar problems.

The root of many such business unit problems can be traced to a limited perception of work overall. Work groups are often viewed as mere symbols of routine activity or temporary fixes rather than as excellent resources that have been integrated (aligned) into the short-term or long-term needs of the business unit. The failure lies not in management's unwillingness to make the business better, but rather in the lack of a method for the executive and manager to look at work, analyze it, and then make it better. Business unit analysis, along with other levels of analysis introduced later, goes a long way in helping both management and workers broaden and deepen their perception of work, thus improving their jobs and their business.

BUSINESS UNIT ANALYSIS: USING A WORK MAP

A work map is a graphic way of depicting the work relationships among the six elements of work shown in the proforma. We can then tie any other related components to the basic map to give a clear performance picture of the business unit, core processes, individual jobs, and work groups. Work maps can be used effectively throughout all levels of the business sphere and help to achieve performance alignment.

The first value of mapping the business unit is that it gives us a common model for viewing the entire business. But mapping is a conceptual, graphic model. We can look at a work map, discuss its meaning, and use it to arrive at consensus on the definition of the business. The layout of a map gives us a comprehensive view of the six work elements, their specific content, and how they interrelate with one another. The map is a mirror of the work the business wants to perform and how it will do the work necessary to achieve the desired performance. Finally, a map allows a very complex entity to be simplified, providing greater understanding, discussion, and consensus. For example, we can easily see all the inputs and outputs of a business and how the process elements flow (by using arrows) to complete the outputs, using the inputs. It allows us to talk about, refine, and understand what the work of the business is or will be. Performance maps keep us focused, while also reducing the emotions that get in the way of understanding and moving ahead to enlightenment about our business. We will look at how a typical work map is developed and used for analyzing a business unit. We will begin with a generic, although real, business and then describe a typical business case.

Football as a Business Unit

In this and the next three chapters, we will use the American game of football as an illustration of the proforma model of four levels of the business sphere. You do not need to have knowledge of nor interest in football. In fact, the example was developed in partnership with a person who was antipathetic (her words) about this game. The illustration helps to make quick sense of the proforma and provide an understanding of football to novices and veterans alike. You can then see the implications when applied to a larger, real business case. Football is, after all, as much a business as any other.

The *business unit level* of professional football is the franchise. In the National Football League (NFL), there are approximately thirty franchises located in as many cities throughout the United States and Canada. These franchises together, like any business, comprise a competitive environment in which each vies to be the best and tries to make a ton of money. Figure 3.1 illustrates a typical football franchise as a business unit.

We note first that the business unit has several outputs that it delivers to its customer (fans). These include, but are not limited to, the team, draft choices, equipment, concessions, and parking. To produce these outputs, the franchise needs certain inputs, including vendors, players, owners, stadium, staff, and fans. The franchise operates under certain conditions, including the salary cap (for wages), NFL rules, the teams and owners, funds, and to some degree their team's standing in the league. The franchise desires certain consequences such as fan satisfaction, profit, being in a playoff and perhaps Super Bowl status, the owner's ego, and the personal satisfaction of the players. Furthermore, a generalized process is indicated that includes managing, scouting/drafting, marketing, selling, and player relations. Finally, we have certain feedback the franchise depends on to assess its success or make for a more efficient operation through communication and fulfillment of client needs. In its most elementary form, this is a performance description of a business unit that everyone can understand and agree to. If additional clarification is needed, more detail can be sought about any of the elements. Let's see what this has to do with a "real" business.

Developing the Work Map for a Sample Business

Figures 3.2a and 3.2b form a typical two-page work map for a business unit. In Figure 3.2a, the outputs always appear on the right, inputs on the left, conditions at the bottom, process element in the middle between inputs and outputs. Figure 3.2b shows the consequences and feedback. These are an integral part of the business unit map.

The business unit represented on the work map in Figures 3.2a and 3.2b is an engineering organization that uses a project management approach. This is often the case in design, construction, and engineering businesses. The example is from an actual engineering business that is a significant business unit (division) of a Fortune 500 corporation. The wider corporation is itself a business unit and could be defined also, but for now we are looking at only one business unit.

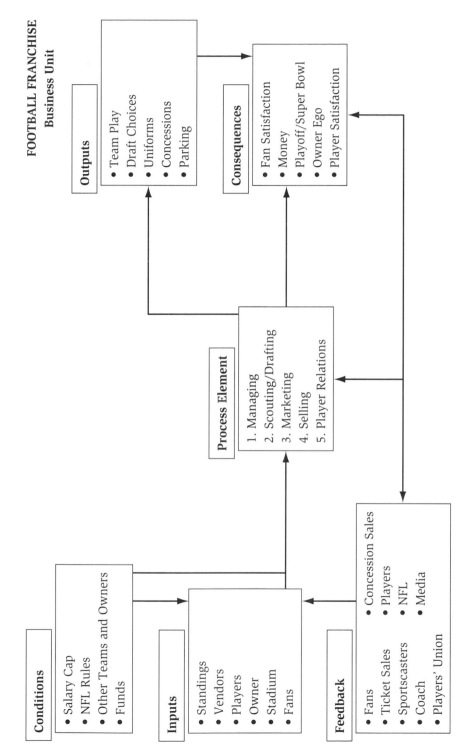

FOOTBALL FRANCHISE
Business Unit

Conditions
- Salary Cap
- NFL Rules
- Other Teams and Owners
- Funds

Inputs
- Standings
- Vendors
- Players
- Owner
- Stadium
- Fans

Process Element
1. Managing
2. Scouting/Drafting
3. Marketing
4. Selling
5. Player Relations

Outputs
- Team Play
- Draft Choices
- Uniforms
- Concessions
- Parking

Consequences
- Fan Satisfaction
- Money
- Playoff/Super Bowl
- Owner Ego
- Player Satisfaction

Feedback
- Fans
- Ticket Sales
- Sportscasters
- Coach
- Players' Union
- Concession Sales
- Players
- NFL
- Media

Figure 3.1. Work Map of a Football Franchise Business Unit.

Figure 3.2a. As-Is Business Unit Map.

As-Is Business Unit Map

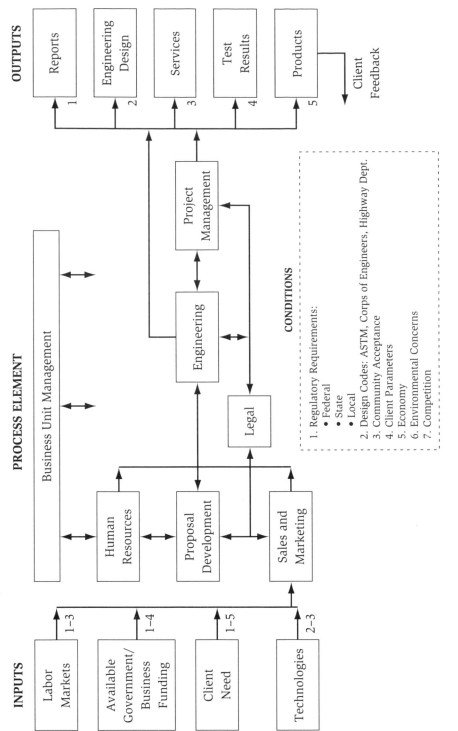

COMPANY: Environmental Safeguards Inc.

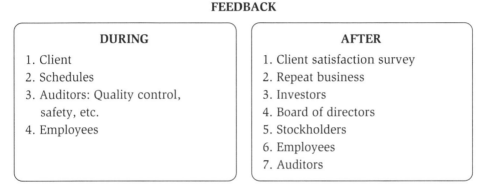

As-Is Businesss Unit Map   **COMPANY: Environmental Safeguards Inc.**

CONSEQUENCES

1. Cost-effective engineering designs, services, test results, and products (Outputs 1–5)
2. Complete and accurate reports that reflect the attainment of client requests and industrial standards (Output 1)
3. Safety (Outputs 1–5)
4. Positive community relations (Outputs 1–5)
5. Customer satisfaction (Outputs 1–5)

FEEDBACK

DURING
1. Client
2. Schedules
3. Auditors: Quality control, safety, etc.
4. Employees

AFTER
1. Client satisfaction survey
2. Repeat business
3. Investors
4. Board of directors
5. Stockholders
6. Employees
7. Auditors

Figure 3.2b. As-Is Business Unit Map (continued).

The division is defined as a business unit because it produces primary for-profit services and products for external clients, functioning as a "profit center." Indeed, profit centers are a convenient way to determine what is and what is not a business unit. In our case study, the sample business unit's clients typically include companies or governmental agencies that need to clean up, dispose of, or have tested environmental problems and materials within their operations. The following scenario describes how a team of executives, managers, and others formulated this map. They were faced with the task of analyzing and improving their business unit; a performance consultant facilitated as they worked through the Language of Work model. It is an eight-step process of analysis and definition, as described below.

Case: Engineering Business

Case Description. An area office of a large environmental service corporation provides engineering services to local government and private businesses related to clean up and prevention to meet federal environmental regulations. Some months ago the corporation adopted the Language of Work approach in order to improve everyday work communication to better align its business operations. They also wanted to use the model on a continuous basis for a variety of work functions, such as writing job descriptions, selecting new hires, giving task assignments, doing performance review, planning work, solving problems, team activities, and the like. Based on this effort, other business offices, scattered throughout the United States, would also be defining their individual business units.

The president of the business unit selected a team of managers and workers from within the business to draft a version of the business-unit work map. The team included three local managers representing engineering, project management, and office management. Four representatives from a cross section of the business joined them: an accountant, a marketing and sales representative, an attorney, and the head of quality assurance. In this way the team represented a cross section of others in the business, including nonsupervisory workers.

As a practical matter, the definition of the business unit should be undertaken by a team of senior management and others representative of different levels of the business, but no attempt should be made to represent every department or level. Too large a team can be counterproductive. About five to eight business representatives is just right. For larger corporate business units, the team is composed of executives (CEO, president, direct reports) and some workers.

The goal of the business unit team is to define an initial draft of a work map for the unit. They will share this draft with others for refinement and "buy-in." Other members of this team should include, if feasible, representative stakeholders (suppliers and clients, if possible), an outside expert in the business, and a facilitator in the Language of Work model. The following eight steps describe the overall approach to mapping a business unit.

○

Step 1: Orientation

Rather than providing a lengthy explanation of the proforma, a brief ten-minute illustration is recommended to get the group started.

The facilitator conducts an orientation to explain what the team will do, how it will do its work, and how it will be organized. A ten-minute discussion introduces everyone to the Language of Work model and the definitions of outputs, inputs, conditions,

A sample business unit map may also be useful, but is not necessary and may present some problems in copying what others have done rather than thinking through the issue.

process element, consequences, and feedback. A job aid defining these six work elements and typical sources of the elements is provided, as well as a sample business map. The goal of the task force is to define a work map that depicts their business unit, to confirm the definition with others in the business unit, and then, having reached consensus, to measure the business and make needed changes that will produce performance improvements.

Step 2: Define Outputs

Use the Proforma Job Aid.

Define Australia first: You have to agree on the targets (outputs) of the business first.

The team, facilitated by a performance consultant, begins by defining the major outputs of the business. These are listed on flip-chart paper. The outputs for the business case, shown below, include reports, engineering designs, services, tests, and products. Thus, this business unit is predominately a service business, although there is some product. These are fairly typical outputs of engineering business units. The flip-chart paper containing these outputs in tacked to the far right side of the wall. See the sample figure here.

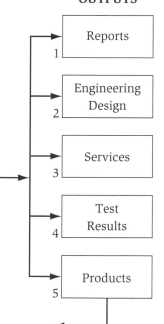

Figure 3.2a-1. **Define Outputs.**

Step 3: Define Inputs

The key questions to be answered here are: (1) What triggers the work of the business unit? and (2) What are the primary resources used in the business?

The team then defines the major *inputs* that are used by the business to produce the outputs defined in Step 2. These are best defined one by one as related to each output. Thus, the inputs for Output 1, reports, include labor markets, available government/business funds, and client need. Inputs are recorded on flip-chart paper and tacked to the wall on the far left. The team will find it easier to look at one output at a time and decide what inputs are needed to produce the output; this way they will not overlook any major input. Each input is numbered to correspond to its output(s).

Client need is the most common input of all businesses. These needs are usually made known in engineering by direct sales calls and in requests for proposals (RFPs), which are written documents provided by prospective clients. Thus, the engineering business unit writes a proposal outlining its response to specific client needs, such as a project to clean up a waste site. This kind of input provides the "trigger" that initiates the business unit to produce one or more of its outputs.

Other inputs for this sample business include the labor market for staffing jobs the business unit will perform, funds needed to do the work, and technologies (for example, a way to burn pollutants) that will be used to meet the client needs. These are, in contrast to the trigger inputs, the resource inputs the business will need to produce/service the business unit outputs. These, as with trigger inputs, are also numbered to the corresponding outputs. It is not uncommon for any given input to serve the needs of several different outputs. See the figure.

INPUTS

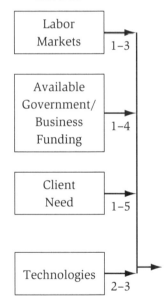

Figure 3.2a-2. Define Inputs.

As illustrated below, an interesting and informative addition to the inputs is the inclusion of a brief label of the purpose of an input. To the right of each input, a short statement can be included to identify what the input is used for. For instance, next to the "technologies" input in the sample case, we specify "New or Existing Services" to meet client needs. In this example, new or existing technologies are important as an input that keeps the business in line with, or ahead of, the competition (a condition that will be identified in the next step of analysis). See the sample labels in the figure below.

Figure 3.2a-3. Label Inputs.

Step 4: Define Conditions

Ask:

What external rules and regulations are to be followed?

What internal policies and procedures apply?

What are the conditions (high-level definition) for the use of inputs, process, and feedback?

Do not include judgments of why things don't work, such as "not enough time" or "multiple platforms." These come later when making improvements. See the next figure.

Conditions are the rules that must be followed to produce the outputs from inputs. The team defines all the conditions that affect the use of the inputs, processing, and use of feedback aimed at attainment of outputs and consequences. *Conditions* are of two types: *external and internal.* Typical external conditions include government regulations, which range from very specific requirements that affect some processes to more general requirements (for example, health and safety regulations) affecting all of the business. For example, the sample engineering business unit must observe numerous federal, state, and local government environmental regulations and local codes. Also, the business must take into consideration the public's concern for environmental issues, the economy in general, and competing corporations. These are all external conditions to which the business must pay attention in executing process, attending to the use of inputs, and when and how it must provide feedback in reporting its adherence to work.

1. Regulatory Requirements:
   - Federal
   - State
   - Local
2. Design Codes: ASTM, Corps of Engineers, Highway Dept.
3. Community Acceptance
4. Client Parameters
5. Economy
6. Environmental Concerns
7. Competition

Figure 3.2a-4. Define Conditions.

In addition to the *external conditions,* the business itself defines its own *internal conditions.* These are the company policies and procedures. In the more general sense, conditions relate to mission, vision, and other qualities the organization desires to be fostered. Without losing importance and impact, the business unit analysis team will have to decide for itself which of the conditions are important to list and which can be assumed to be universally known.

Conditions are different from inputs in that conditions are much harder to change and are not "used up." That is, they continue to exist and must be adhered to. Also, inputs relate only to outputs, whereas conditions impact inputs, process, and feedback.

Business is generally slow to change internal conditions, such as its policies, and external conditions (such as a state law) are often impossible to change, although an environmental business may ask the government to change or append regulations for a specific project. However, the business should not adopt the attitude that change is impossible. This is not a good business practice.

Once the team has defined all the conditions, it goes to the next step. Of course, as the team works through the business-unit map and gains additional insights into the business, it may (and usually does) return to any previous step(s) and modify what it has specified. For instance, defining a condition may well suggest that a particularly important input has been inadvertently overlooked. Because performance mapping is an iterative process, additions, corrections, and deletions can be made during initial development and also during later reviews.

Step 5: Define Consequences

Look for consequences for clients, the business, and the workforce. There should be at least one or more consequences per output.

State consequences in positive terms, never negative.

Once the team knows the outputs, inputs, and conditions, it needs to define the desired results that the business wants to achieve, stating them in the form of positive consequences.

Representative consequences for a business unit generally fall into two categories: (1) those that relate to client satisfaction, and (2) those that the business wants to achieve for itself (for its own satisfaction). Consequences are, or should be, a direct reflection of the mission of a business. The following are representative consequences for a business, most of which apply to the sample environmental engineering business.

Sample

Client Consequences
- Client satisfaction
- Return policy guarantee—"No questions asked"
- "Best price"
- Within budget

Business Consequences
- Profit
- Percentage of market share
- Employee satisfaction
- Growth

Of course, consequences will need to be more specific than those stated above. The team defines the consequences for the business unit, writes these on flip-chart paper, and tacks them to the wall to the right of the outputs. See Figure 3.2a-5. The following is a typical list of consequences that were identified for the case example:

CONSEQUENCES

1. Cost-effective engineering designs, services, test results, and products (Outputs 1-5)
2. Complete and accurate reports that reflect the attainment of client requests and industrial standards (Output 1)
3. Safety (Outputs 1–5)
4. Positive community relations (Outputs 1–5)
5. Customer satisfaction (Outputs 1–5)

Figure 3.2a-5. Define Consequences.

You will note the sample *consequences* represent the results that are expected from the outputs. Thus each consequence is referenced by number to the output(s) that help achieve it. In defining consequences, therefore, it is wise to look at each output and the associated result it is expected to achieve.

While there should be at least a corresponding consequence for each output, a given consequence can share more than one output. Client satisfaction, for instance, is usually related to every output the business produces.

Another important feature of consequences is that they are the positive attributes one desires, rather than the negative possibilities. People, due to their life experiences, sometimes associate consequences with the negative. In defining the business unit, as with core processes, jobs, and work groups later on, we are interested in the positive results the business is to strive toward attaining. As business unit analysis is not a time to vent emotions and criticisms of ongoing operations, leave the negative considerations to a later time devoted to how to improve the business.

Step 6: Define the Business Unit Process Element

Define significant-sized work groups and connect with arrows in direction of work flow.

The *process element* links inputs and outputs and is affected by business conditions and feedback. At the business unit level in an existing business, the process element defines what work groups exist and their relationships to one another, to process the inputs to the outputs. [*Please note:* At the core processes, work group, and individual levels, to be described later, defining the process element is different. There it means the individual steps (defined using action verbs) needed to produce each output, under conditions and aided by feedback.] At the business unit level the *process element* is defined as a series of work groups between which work flows and interacts. In the business case example, as illustrated here, we see work from inputs, first through sales and marketing, then proposal development, human resources, engineering, and the complete project management cycle. Over these is the management that facilitates, guides, and interacts with the various work groups in the process element. Therefore, in the illustration of the process element shown below, process element encompasses all that is between inputs on the left and outputs on the right. See the figure below.

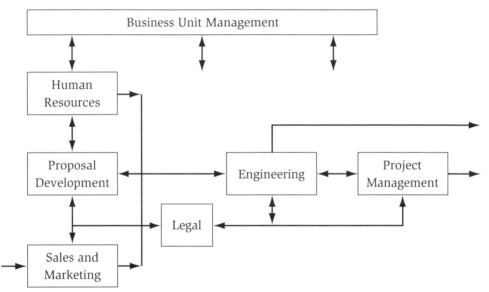

Figure 3.2a-6. Define the Business Unit Process Element.

Level of detail

Typically, performance analysis teams quickly come to an understanding of what level of detail makes sense and is therefore needed. Keep in mind that the very detailed analysis and definition of the rest of the business will emerge during subsequent analyses of the core processes, individuals, and work group levels.

Note in Figure 3.2a-6 that arrows are used to link work groups and show which way the process element flows. For example, client needs (as an input) first come to sales and marketing, who then decide whether proposal development will write a proposal. Proposal development works with engineering, legal, and human resources, and may be guided by management as needed. The essential requirement is that for each output, there should be a logical flow from input(s) through a process element to achieve the outputs. At the business unit level, this is done through defining the process in terms of work groups. [*Cautionary note:* In "reengineering work," as compared to definition of what currently exists as a business unit, the process element of the business unit must be defined after core processes, individuals, and work group levels are defined and agreed on. Whereas in an existing business we know the work groups that comprise the business, in reengineering we won't know them until after they are defined following core processes and jobs. More will be said about this later.]

When the team has finished defining the process element, it places that list between inputs and outputs and in sight of conditions and consequences on the wall. To complete the map, the team defines the supporting feedback to the business unit.

Step 7: Define Feedback

Questions to ask: How will the business unit decide whether clients are satisfied?

How will the business unit decide whether the workforce is satisfied?

Feedback to the business unit is the variety of client, other external communication, and internal communications that tell the business it is doing a good job of producing its product and services, as well as helps correct work while processing and using inputs.

The team defines two major types of feedback for its business unit map. This feedback occurs during and after the work of the business unit. There are two ways feedback is typically shown in a work map:

- Arrows

- Descriptions

Arrows, in addition to showing direction of work flow, are also used to show where feedback should occur. Arrows are the least definitive way to illustrate feedback, but nonetheless useful in ways the descriptive form does not allow. Basically, the arrows, as shown in many parts of the business unit map, indicate work flow (arrows in one direction) and when information should be "fed back" and forth (arrows on both ends of lines).

As illustrated in Figure 3.2a-7, one arrow is used to indicate that client satisfaction will be obtained after the outputs are delivered.

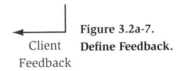

Client
Feedback

**Figure 3.2a-7.
Define Feedback.**

This client satisfaction arrow from below the outputs extends back toward the rest of the map and is intended to illustrate that such feedback will be planned and provided for. Some of the types of feedback are shown in Figure 3.2b-1. This indicates that the business seeks client information on outputs and consequences to determine whether clients are satisfied. This provides feedback to those in the process element. If positive feedback, it reinforces good use of the process element. If negative feedback, it tells the business it needs to correct something in its process element (or other work elements) and to respond to the client in ways that will restore satisfaction, or to do both. Various means can be used to collect this feedback, such as client satisfaction surveys, an 800 number, direct everyday contact, mail-in feedback cards, and so forth. These should be specified in the descriptive form of feedback that is part of the work map.

The second type of arrow in a work map indicates feedback within the process element. These arrows link work groups to indicate the flow of information—the feedback is that most often used within and between the work groups to improve processing, utilization of inputs, and adherence or attention to conditions. Such feedback arrows have two points, each pointing in a different direction. For example, you see a double-pointed arrow between proposal development and sales and marketing in Figure 3.2. This means that when developing proposals, the proposal writer seeks information and feedback from sales and marketing. You also see this kind of arrow between proposal development and engineering, where information is exchanged on the accuracy of the technical data in the proposal writing effort. Or, it could mean that engineering seeks information from the proposal development group to clarify a proposal that the project manager is now using to execute. Other feedback arrows link proposal development and legal, human resources and project management, and a number of other work groups. A number of feedback loops connect management (at the top of process element) to other work groups within the process element. The details of this feedback are specified either in descriptive form or as part of other work maps for processes and work groups.

As to the descriptive form of feedback in a work diagram, the following figure is an illustration of feedback to our sample engineering business.

FEEDBACK

DURING	AFTER
1. Client	1. Client satisfaction survey
2. Schedules	2. Repeat business
3. Auditors: Quality control, safety, etc	3. Investors
4. Employees	4. Board of directors
	5. Stockholders
	6. Employees
	7. Auditors

Figure 3.2b-1. During and After Feedback

Here we note that the feedback has been divided according to that which is used during or after the business unit work. Typical *"after" feedback* includes client satisfaction surveys or informal communication with clients. It also includes repeat business, investor confidence and participation, feedback from the board of directors, stockholders, employees, and more formal auditing. By contrast, the *feedback "during"* processing includes use of inputs and adherence to conditions. Typical examples include feedback from clients, schedules, auditors, employees, and such. The same sources may be used both during and after the work, although the nature and kind of the feedback may vary, as in the case of client feedback during and after.

Step 8: Reach Consensus/Achieve Commitment

In light of the input from others, keep the definition of the map at a high level. Too much detail will defeat the purpose. Such detail comes later.

With this step, the business unit analysis team shares its map to date, collects additional input, and completes the business unit map. The team divides the business organization in a logical way (for example, by area of work expertise or assignment). Members then take the draft of the work map to others in the business and ask for their comments on all aspects of their business unit definition. This can be typically accomplished in one to two weeks. These comments are brought back to the analysis team as a whole and used to refine the first draft. This is one of the several ways, as we cascade our way through other levels of business doing work mapping, that we help reach accuracy, completeness, and commitment. It also serves as a means of orientation and training to the overall business performance improvement effort.

The sample business unit map that has been illustrated here was produced with consensus by an actual analysis team. As described later in this chapter, the team has additional steps and tasks to perform in using the business unit map to institute performance improvements and use it for performance alignment.

IMPROVING THE BUSINESS UNIT: WHAT NOT TO DO!

Improving performance at the business unit level must be approached carefully and in the context of what is possible. In other words, businesses—namely their executive management—are prone to improve the overall business (units) in ways that are traditional but not necessarily effective. Examples will be highlighted below. A second consideration is that business unit success *in the behavioral sense* is the result not of the business unit's behavior in some way, but rather the combined effort of the other three levels of the business sphere—core processes, jobs, and work groups. Note carefully the qualifier in the "behavioral sense." It is important to distinguish between the behavior of the organization and other performance improvement efforts instigated by what the business chooses to be as a business—that is, improving performance in such ways as acquisitions, market differentiation, financing, and so forth. How would we approach improving business unit performance using the Language of Work model once we have defined its business unit map? Many efforts, while popular, do not provide true results in work improvement. Let's discuss these briefly so no future effort will be wasted.

What to Stop Doing

Three commonly used interventions for trying to improve overall business unit performance have been consistently used and just as consistently proven to be ineffective. Business leaders use these three daily; they need, however, to be refocused for their best use in business improvement efforts. A clearer understanding of work and performance from reading this book will help. The three common practices that need to be rethought are the use of reorganization, the employment of new leadership, and "business article program du jour."

Reorganization. Executives need to stop reorganizing when it is inappropriate. Reorganization is a final step, not an initial intervention. Reorganizing—meaning reconstituting, renaming, combining, or eliminating work groups—is a daily occurrence throughout American industry. The net result of this reshuffling is negligible for improving any overall business performance. Instead, employees become anxious about their positions, seek new alliances to protect themselves and get their work done, fear layoffs, and wait until the next time. Managers and supervisors jockey for power positions, protect those whom they feel they need or want, and are generally silent until they are sure of their own situation and survival. Reorganization may be needed, but there is an optimal time to use it for improving business performance.

Reorganization is best done after the business unit has been defined (and improved in the ways to be described here), after core process definition and improvement, after individual level definition and improvement, and as part of the work group level definition and improvement effort. As previously noted, the *process element* of a business unit is the relationship between the various work groups that constitute an existing business. On the other hand, if we were defining an entirely new business or reengineering an existing business, we would have no process element for the business unit until such time as the core processes, jobs, and work groups had been defined. Reorganization in this context is the definition of the right work groups (based on core processes and job definitions) and the relationship that those work groups would have to one another to form the business unit process element. Therefore, to reorganize without consideration of needed changes in core processes, jobs, and individual work groups is to get, as they say, the "cart before the horse." It's another case of needing to "Define Australia first!" And, in this instance there are several Australias before work groups can be defined and reorganized.

Leadership. If reorganization is not chosen as the weapon of rapid business improvement, then new leadership is often selected. This is a kind of military solution. If the troops are not marching in the right direction, find a new person to give the orders. There is some merit to this, but this solution is often applied for the wrong reason and based on poor decisions.

No one is foolish enough to conclude that leadership is not important. That is not the issue here. Rather, the issue is the use of leadership change as the way to stimulate business unit improvement. First, the performance problems are not generally at this level. Well-functioning businesses, based on solid processes, with workers performing well-defined jobs, combined into well-defined functioning work groups can nearly run a business on their own. Some have gone so far as to claim that good companies are really run by individuals who happen to be in the right place at the right time. We won't go that far; we recognize that business is not a leadership issue, except perhaps in setting where the business goes and the model of leadership. Rather, it is, as they say, a "well-oiled machine" going in a known direction, with good processes, individuals who care and do their work, and with self-directed work groups. So where and when does leadership come into play?

First, when choosing a leader, we need to know the nature of the business and then match the individual to it. As with reorganization, this means defining and knowing the business unit, the core processes, the individuals, and the work groups first. What are the core processes the individual will lead? How are the work groups currently working together to achieve business goals? Who are the incumbent individuals, their jobs? Having identified these, then we can ask what kind of leader will be needed, what his work will be, and what work groups will report to this leader so that this person's skills can be most effectively used.

"Program du Jour." There is no question that business leaders can be fascinated by the most current "program du jour." If Jack Welch used it at GE, then imagine what it will do for us! Executives then ask their staff to look into and implement the same program. These programs are the quick fix. As they say about investing, "If it sounds too good, it probably is."

Improving business performance is hard work. There are no quick fixes. No surefire ways. Rather, there are interrelated elements of behavior, standards, support, and human relations that constitute the dynamics of business operating at different levels of performance (work). Just setting a mission and vision and plastering it on walls won't do. Reengineering the business alone won't do, nor will a quality program. Nor will "work outs" and "town halls," "the seven habits of whatever" or any single effort you can imagine do it. These efforts fool some of the people, but fewer each time.

So what will we concentrate on to improve performance at the business unit level? There are two primary areas: (1) in terms of what the business is currently doing and (2) what the business should be doing.

IMPROVING WHAT THE BUSINESS IS DOING: AS-IS PERFORMANCE ANALYSIS

As-Is performance analysis involves three critical steps:

1. Define what the business is.
2. Measure what the business is doing.
3. Determine what needs improving.

Few businesses begin their improvement efforts by understanding what their business is from a performance point of view. Rather, they say, "Let's identify what's wrong and fix it!" Then they brainstorm a laundry list of items and decide to begin with a particular problem. This is a "hit-and-miss" approach. Worse yet, they may begin with a solution (such as reengineering, training, or a program they read about recently), and say, "Let's try this." This process has been aptly expressed as the "Ready, Fire, Aim" approach to business improvement.

After the business has been defined, the second step is measurement.

Measuring What the Business Is Doing

Remember, as performance consultants our task is to define performance gaps. Therefore, we need to know how we will define the gaps in performance at the business unit level. Guessing what to measure in order to know where to improve performance in a business is far less useful and accurate than careful measurement of the right things. We need to determine where and when to use accurate measurement techniques, versus personal assessments that are translated into suggestions.

Brainstorming what to measure is also inappropriate and will result in opinions, not facts. Collective wisdom does not necessarily translate to more accurate assessments or solutions. The following exercise, which you can conduct in your own business, will demonstrate the difficulty of knowing what to measure.

1. Select a group of twenty or more workers and managers, and divide them into groups of five to seven.

2. Ask each group to devise a set of questions that they would use to measure any one of the major work groups in your business. For example, have each group write a set of questions that could be used to measure whether they believe human resources is performing at the quality level it should be. Each small group should write questions that apply to the same work group.

3. Have each group report what it would measure. Review the results. Be prepared to find that each group comes up with completely different sets of questions or items to measure.

This exercise clearly points out two things:

1. Most workers (and managers) don't know specifically what to measure in someone else's work group, let alone their own; and

2. What they do measure is usually a specific and often small aspect of performance that is personally bothering them or of special interest.

The latter is useful information for other purposes, but not for measuring the overall work performance of a specific work group, business unit, process, or individual. A better way of learning what to measure and how to measure it is called for. Fortunately, if we have defined the business unit as a business unit map, then the map tells us what to measure. Performance measures should be defined in relation to the six elements of the proforma on a business unit map: inputs, conditions, process element, outputs, consequences, and feedback. We only need to determine the best and useful order in which to measure these elements of performance.

With a proper frame of reference, performance measures can be defined with relative ease. A brief description of all six elements, in their proper order, on the proforma for a business unit will help define performance measures for the business unit, and for each subsequent performance level of the business sphere. We divide the six elements into two major groups that serve two related needs.

Measure Consequences and Outputs First

Begin by defining performance measures for the outputs and consequences that have been defined. Because these two elements represent the reason we are in business, they are the starting point. They are achieved by the execution of the other four elements of work. This is a question of cause and effect. The effect is the output and consequences. The cause is the combined behavior of the interaction between inputs, conditions, process, and feedback. Thus, *the initial measurement of any performance (at any level) must first be the outputs and consequences.*

Whether to measure outputs or consequences first is kind of a chicken and egg thing. You produce a bad output; you get bad consequences. You get a bad consequence; chances are you have one or more bad outputs. What is really critical here is whether you have one or both of these problems. You need to measure both. You could receive an overall positive customer satisfaction consequence, but not realize that one of the several outputs that relate to that consequence is not what it should be. Or you could experience a negative consequence, and not determine which outputs caused it.

If these two elements cannot be measured simultaneously, then start with consequences because they are the ultimate reason for being in business, but you will still need to measure the outputs to evaluate whether or not they have reached their ultimate level of performance.

Performance measures for consequences should center on the extent to which there is satisfaction for the end user—customer, clients, stakeholders. Consequences need standards of acceptable performance in terms of quantity, quality, timeliness, cost, or a combination of these. Details on how to set these standards for measurement are given in Chapter 7. A sample consequence from our engineering case study will serve as an illustration for now.

The second consequence in the case study of the Safeguards Inc. business unit states: "Complete and accurate reports that reflect the attainment of client requests and industrial standards."

This particular consequence, as are most consequences, is quite simple as far as performance requirements that need measurement. A variety of such reports are available to be evaluated. Further, these reports can be evaluated against

- The original client's request (usually in a written proposal or letter)
- Client surveys or interviews
- Industrial standards of some kind

Of course consequences can be more or less complex than the one illustrated here. Nonetheless, the guiding principles are to keep it simple and to the point. Do not make measurement any more complex than it needs to be.

Like measuring consequences, measuring outputs is mainly a matter of measuring quantity, quality, timeliness, and cost. For example, relative to Output 1, reports, in the sample engineering business, the following measures could be used:

- "Did the reports address the specific needs and requirements specified in the contract?" Quantity
- "Is the report data accurate?" Quality
- "Was the output delivered on time?" Timeliness
- "Was the output produced within budget?" Cost

Having measured outputs and consequences and perhaps found one or more problems, measuring for the root cause is next. Once the cause or causes have been identified, they can be fixed and measured again. [*Note:* Although the questions posed here seem to have yes/no answers, this is not meant to imply that measurement is this simple. The complexity of how to achieve accuracy of response to measurement is left to other resources, for example, Hale (1998) for excellent guidelines. We are concerned here with *what* to measure, *when and why.*]

Measure the Inputs, Conditions, Process, and Feedback

Next find the root causes for not achieving desired outputs and consequences.

Defining performance measures for inputs is mainly a matter of measuring for two things: (1) inputs as the trigger to performance, and (2) their availability and development for use in processing. Recall that there are inputs from clients that request action. These are *trigger* inputs. Then, there are *resource* inputs that must be available when and where needed to produce the outputs through processes, aided by conditions and feedback. Let's look at each of these types of input.

Here are some typical performance measures for the *trigger inputs,* client needs:

- "Does a systematic plan for identifying client needs for marketing purposes exist and produce satisfactory results?"
- "Are client needs clearly defined before projects commence?"
- "Are client needs being developed for future work as the project is being executed?"

These measures address what is available as well as what needs to be developed in the business. Without identifying these measures and actually measuring them, the business may (and often does) overlook needs and opportunities to improve and maintain itself.

Resource inputs are a little easier to measure because the typical measurements have to do with the four standards: quantity, quality, timeliness, and cost. Using the case business as an example, ask input resource measurement questions such as

- "Are the number of resources needed available for processing?"
- "Are there enough personnel for the first input?"
- "Is the input of such a quality that it can be processed (or produce) to a quality output?"
- "Are personnel skilled and experienced for the first input?"
- "Is the input available on a timely basis?"
- "Are the personnel available when we need them?"
- "Is the input cost-effective?"
- "Can we afford the personnel for the input?"

Performance measures for conditions have unique requirements. Unlike the other work elements, many conditions are pre-set for the business and cannot be changed. Of course, the internally established conditions from business policies can be changed, but it often takes much effort. Consequently, conditions probably do not need to be measured to see whether they exist, unless you have reason to believe that some conditions, such as company policies, might be missing. Most businesses first need to measure their individual awareness of the conditions and then determine whether the conditions are being attended to during input, processing, and feedback stages. Similarly, it is useful to test whether the conditions are being reinforced when attended to or whether they are ignored altogether. The business has control over worker and manager "awareness" of the conditions (provided workers and managers cooperate) and over assuring that the conditions are met. It is surprising how many businesses are not fully aware of conditions, which leads to trouble. For instance, environmental engineering businesses may not pay enough attention to government regulations, public concerns, safety, the competition, or economic trends. The same may be said when individuals do not pay attention to company policies.

A sample performance question for a condition would be, "Are we collecting data on where our competition is winning our business?" For example, in the engineering case business, there is a condition (number 7) for competition, which relates to the "client need" input. The company might also want to know what means to use to measure the effect of government regulations on the process they are using. There are many questions that could be asked. For example, for the Business Unit Management work group, we could ask, "Is the business meeting EEO guidelines while doing its projects?" For the Engineering group we need to ask, "Are engineers being kept up-to-date and are they licensed in local and state codes/regulations?"

It is one thing to be aware of the conditions; another to ensure they are being followed. Workers have to apply conditions to inputs, the process used to produce the outputs, and to the feedback. Thus, a typical performance question for a condition related to input would be, "Do the inputs used in the business measure up to the standards applied by federal regulations?" Regarding the process, one question might be, "Are managers made aware of EEO guidelines in hiring practices?" And, for feedback, "Is the data being collected in a form and in a timely manner to assure safety standards are being met?"

Performance measures for feedback center on whether measures are being asked, reinforcement given, and information shared, and if so, in what form and on what schedule. Businesses that merely pass their outputs from one work group to another or do not follow up with external clients are not asking and measuring performance feedback. A typical feedback question is, "How efficient is our response mechanism to customer complaints?" Or even simpler, "How difficult is it for our clients to call us on the telephone?" A very important feedback question is, "Are our managers actively asking workers what kind of help they need with inputs and during processing?" and "Are our managers actively asking workers when, where, and how they need this help?" Any of these questions could be asked of the engineering case business.

One other consideration in relation to measuring feedback is that we have to be concerned with measuring both during and after performance. It is obvious that assurance is needed that our business produced what it said it would produce. This is feedback at the end of the performance. Feedback *during the processing* is more often overlooked and less frequently measured. A (counterproductive) business rule seems to be to provide "after" feedback in order to beat people over the head with it, rather than to measure performance during processing when performance problems can be avoided. More in-process feedback would help avoid eventual negative client reactions that may be irreparable.

Performance measures for process elements are especially hard to define for the average manager and worker. Therefore, some special attention to measuring the process element is in order. Remember that the process element of a business unit map is the only element composed of work groups. All others have procedural steps, or mini-deliverables. Work groups are the process element in the business unit because *the business unit processes work through a combination of work groups.* As you learn each of the other levels, the need for this distinction will become more evident and useful. The business unit process element is composed of interrelated and interacting work groups, as seen in Figure 3.2a. The question is, "How should the process element or work groups of a business unit be measured?"

As we saw in the performance measures exercise earlier in this chapter, if we ask groups of managers and workers to formulate a set of measures for their work group, we will receive dissimilar sets of measures. To avoid this, we need a systematic approach to identifying and defining a way to measure work groups. This means first defining the outputs of the various work groups that comprise the business unit process. Let us take one of the work groups from Figure 3.2a, see what is meant by "work group outputs," and determine the metrics we would formulate to measure these outputs.

Two kinds of measurement are needed for the process element of a business unit. The first measures each work group in the process element separately, and the second measures the interaction between work groups. Only a brief description of measurement *within* work groups will be provided here, as it will be discussed in detail in Chapter 6. The measurement *between* work groups, which Rummler and Brache (1995, 98) label the "white space" is discussed below.

Figure 3.3 lists sample outputs for work groups and corresponding performance measures for these outputs, using the work groups from Figure 3.2a. For purposes of illustration, look at the outputs and corresponding performance measures for the human resources work group, since this is a work group with which most of us are familiar.

The first question in Figure 3.3, "Are in-house resumes available/updated?" is a performance measure related to the human resources output of "resumes." This question is important in an engineering company because resumes are used both for proposal writing and to find the right people to work on approved projects. Thus, the human resources work group is responsible for, and partially measured in its overall success by, meeting the requirements of this question. Should the answer to this question demonstrate that human resources is not providing timely or complete resumes, a needed change (improvement) would be in order for this work group.

Formulating the proper question requires first determining the output, then determining how the output is utilized, usually by asking what the internal or external client does with the given output. In the example, the client is an internal one (such as a project manager) who uses the output (resumes) as his or her input (qualified candidates) to do the work (to fill project positions, leading eventually to the execution of the project). The question, "Are in-house resumes available/updated?" is pertinent. Let us look at another example and have you determine the performance question.

The proposal development work group is expected to produce cost proposals for projects. What question should be asked to measure this output? Think in terms of the critical question of what cost proposals represent to the business unit. How will a client use the "cost proposal"? Remember, at this time we are considering the business unit, not the individual. Which of the following would be the best performance question to ask and use to measure cost proposals?

- "Does the cost proposal include all the critical components to make it a complete cost proposal?"

OUTPUTS	PERFORMANCE QUESTIONS

Human Resources

- Resumes
- Performance review plans

- Training program/
  performance improvement

- Career development plans

- Compensation package
- Salary ranges
- Flexplan

- Recruiting program

- Employees hired

1. Are in-house resumes available/updated?
2. Are workers provided meaningful performance reviews annually?
3. Are the workers receiving needed training and other performance improvement programs to establish or maintain skills and to obtain the knowledge to perform future job needs?
4. Given growth plans, are workers provided career development opportunities?
5. Are compensation expectations clearly defined?
6. Are salary ranges fair to competition standards?
7. Is the "flexplan" meeting work needs for health care relative to business ability to provide?
8. Are we able to recruit skilled employees to meet general business and project contract requirements?
9. Are skilled employees hired?

Proposal Development

- Proposals
- Proposal reviews
- Oral presentations

- Visuals for proposals

1. Are winning proposals developed?
2. Are proposals legally correct?
3. Are individuals and teams prepared to give winning oral presentations?
4. Are visuals prepared that enhance proposal communication and oral presentation?

Sales and Marketing

- Marketing plans

- Market research
- Competition reviews
- New market studies

- Manpower studies

- Marketing orientations

- Resource plans

1. Is a marketing plan prepared and reviewed annually?
2. Does marketing conduct market research?
3. Is the competition evaluated on a regular basis?
4. Are new market opportunities evaluated semi-annually?
5. Do marketing opportunities match staffing/planning?
6. Is office staff given orientations to marketing plans?
7. Once market areas are identified, are resources made available to develop them?
   - Operations support personnel and equipment
   - Salespeople
   - Brochures, etc.

Figure 3.3. Sample Performance Questions on Output.

- "Are our cost proposals competitive with others to win new projects and realize a reasonable profit?"

Both of these are good measures about cost proposals; however, when measuring output you need to consider what purpose the output serves for the business unit (or individual or work group). In this case, the second question is the relevant performance question for the business unit. The first question is relevant to the process of producing cost proposals, and thus useful at the process level. But if our cost proposals are not competitive with others, then the business unit can neither win new projects nor profitably carry out new projects. *Remember: When formulating performance measures for process elements, first define the output for a work group; then, frame the question in terms of how that output is used by the client of the work group.* The same can and should be done for consequences to be achieved by the work groups.

As to performance measures between work groups, the essential questions are (1) "Where are the handoffs between work groups?" and (2) "Are the measures of handoff a question of quantity, quality, timelessness, and/or cost?" For example, one of the handoffs between proposal development and other work groups would be measured through a question such as

- "Does proposal development seek the input of all the necessary parties in a timely manner in the business unit to develop good cost proposals?"

Handoff questions are most often related to one group's output that becomes another group's input. Thus, the proposal development group must seek another group's output as the input to the proposal-writing effort. This handoff should be identified and measured with a pertinent question. Work maps at all levels of the Business Sphere are especially useful in identifying where these handoffs occur, and thus what should be measured.

TO-BE PERFORMANCE ANALYSIS

Most performance improvement is of the as-is type already described. The business unit exists and needs to improve its current, or as-is, status. Therefore, we define the as-is business unit, measure its elements of work, and decide how to improve it. However, there is another kind of performance analysis that helps identify other performance gaps. It is called to-be analysis. Here, the definition of the as-is business unit is taken one step farther into the future: define the to-be state, and compare it to the as-is definition, which will identify other performance gaps that need to be filled. This kind of analysis would be typical of reengineering and reorganization efforts.

Later, in Chapter 5, there is a description of business improvement that concerns the "how" of business from the position of "strength." This includes arenas such as its competitive edge, competition, and the like. Here, we will examine what the business decides it wants to be in the future. The assumption is that the business has looked at what it currently does (as-is performance analysis) and has decided that certain basic changes are preferred. These might be new outputs, consequences, or basic changes in inputs, conditions, process element, and feedback. The emphasis is on new, not fixing what exists. Although new outputs would be obvious instances of such desired change, new technologies affecting process elements, new kinds of inputs, new regulations, and new measures of feedback would be other instances needing "to-be" analysis. Let's compare to-be analysis with how such changes are usually treated in business.

For example, say executives decide to enter a new line of work—to produce a new output. The next thing you know they are wanting to organize work groups, get a person to head up this or that, disrupt some other ongoing work, start special projects, allocate resources, make a budget, take people off an ongoing, critical project, and on and on. They seem to leap from here to there and back again. One thing is usually certain. There is rarely an organized plan or, even when it seems organized, the order confuses one activity with another and causes any number of subordinates to scramble.

Instead, at the business unit level, they should deal with only the "what" of business, not the "how" (core process), "who" (individuals), and the "organization" (work groups). These will come later when prior levels have been analyzed. Don't be a "business-level buster"—one who can't wait to get to some other level of performance improvement before the previous one has been defined, committed to, and made the best it can be.

This is best illustrated with an example. Suppose our case business, Environmental Safeguard Inc., decided it wanted to have a new output: site cleanup. Thus, the business not only would produce reports, do engineering design and services, test results, and produce products, but it would actually go to client sites and clean up hazardous waste. This new output is shown Figure 3.4.

A performance gap exists in "establishing" a new desired performance that did not exist previously. In the "to-be" case it will exist. Similarly, our case business could have decided it would no longer produce "test results." This would be a performance change called "extinguishing" performance at the business unit level and represent a performance gap between the as-is and to-be as well. We will use the establishing example above, rather than the extinguishing example.

Naturally, as an output changes, there are changes in related consequences, inputs, conditions, process elements, and feedback to the output at the business unit that will occur. Some of these are reflected in Figures 3.5a and 3.5b. For instance, although there is no fundamental change in input categories,

OUTPUTS

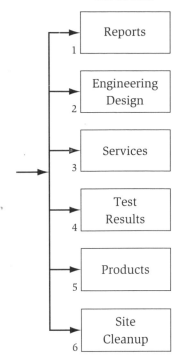

**Figure 3.4. Additional Business
Unit Output.**

details in the inputs would need to reflect technology and identification-of-client-need inputs that would be required to meet the new site cleanup output. In the process element a new work group, construction, needs to be added to take care of site cleanup. Additionally, an external agency (located on-site at the cleanup) is added to the process element to monitor existing engineering and project management as they relate to site cleanup. This is necessary because there are many more regulations to be attended to, as well as general public concerns. This agency's presence was mandated by a new condition imposed by a federal regulations; that condition also influenced new feedback in the form of quality reports. See the figure for these additions. A new consequence was also defined reflecting the company's desire to achieve results that they would be willing to live with as a group of people; not just as a company seeking a profit and other consequences.

Given either the establishment or extinguishing of a business performance output, one can see the result in new consequences, perhaps changes in input,

To-Be Business Unit Map

COMPANY: Environmental Safeguards Inc.

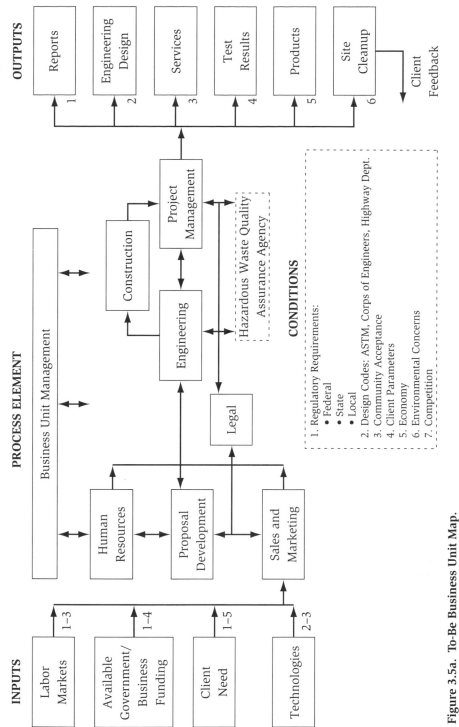

Figure 3.5a. To-Be Business Unit Map.

To-Be Businesss Unit Map   **COMPANY: Environmental Safegaurds Inc.**

CONSEQUENCES

1. Cost-effective engineering designs, services, test results, site cleanup, and products (Outputs 1–6)
2. Complete and accurate reports that reflect the attainment of client requests and industrial standards (Output 1)
3. Safety (Outputs 1–6)
4. Positive community relations (Outputs 1–6)
5. Customer satisfaction (Outputs 1–6)
6. Environmental safe standards that our company family would live with (Output 6)

FEEDBACK

DURING	AFTER
1. Clients	1. Client satisfaction survey
2. Schedules	2. Repeat business
3. Auditors: Quality control, safety, etc.	3. Investors
4. Employees	4. Board of directors
5. External quality reports	5. Stockholders
	6. Employees
	7. Auditors
	8. External quality reports

Figure 3.5b. To-Be Business Unit Map (continued).

certainly new conditions, new process elements, and perhaps new feedback. Each of these would present new performance gaps between as-is and to-be. These would require appropriate interventions to come into or out of existence to meet these gaps. And to keep from "business-level busting," these needs are best determined when the core processes, jobs, and work group performance analyses are done— not deciding what to do at the business unit level. These kinds of fundamental changes in a business unit demonstrate the fundamentals of to-be performance Analysis and how it differs from as-is performance analysis. Additional details would be defined and accounted for as one cascades the performance analyses to other levels of the business sphere. To-be performance analysis involves projecting the as-is analysis into the future. When we get to applications of to-be analysis for processes, work groups, and individuals, other considerations of performance change will come into play.

Grey Bar: Business Unit Level

Kathleen Whiteside

Partner, Performance International

The newly appointed president of a failing division of an insurance company asked us to use the Language of Work to help him change his entire organization. There were two hundred employees, $200 million in revenue, and falling market share. Because the CEO was new to the role and to the work, he saw himself as the leader of a jazz quartet rather than the conductor of a large orchestra. In other words, he had a vision and was prepared to collaborate with his staff to turn the vision into reality. An orchestra conductor, on the other hand, knows exactly which note will be played by whom and when. Our jazz leader wanted everyone to have a complete picture of the current situation from which he and they would forge a completely new organization.

He assembled a staff of knowledgeable experts and put them to work, utilizing the *proforma* as his blueprint. To begin painting the picture of the current situation, the staff used the Language of Work to define every job in the current organization; eighty-one separate jobs were defined. The staff then developed maps of all current processes and work groups. This order was useful at this stage because it moved from the smaller to the larger segments. (It would have to be done in the reverse of the order for creating a new organization.) The senior management team then reviewed every map. A number of efficiencies were identified immediately and changes were implemented. These included several instances where handoffs were incomplete or unnecessary. The number of jobs was excessive as well, so blending and combining of jobs occurred. In accounting, for example, a senior clerk, a clerk, and an assistant clerk produced the same outputs. The difference in job titles indicated levels of seniority and therefore speed and skill in execution. The result was that work could sit on a desk for weeks because the one person assigned to it was occupied elsewhere or on vacation. Combining the job into one title brought needed efficiency to the operation.

Once a complete picture of the current situation (as-is) was available, the senior management team discussed what the future organization would be able to do. Experts in insurance products and profitability in the industry were engaged to transfer their knowledge while broadening the thinking of long-time residents of the old organization. A strategic plan was developed that identified the new direction, new products, new technology to be used, and the competitive edge to be created. The senior staff then went to work defining the new business unit. An external facilitator was crucial here because of remaining investment in the old system. This was demonstrated in resistance to the internal facilitator's suggestions, internal arguments, and challenges to the new president's authority. After being called in to help, the external facilitator with no history in the organization was able to move the team off dead center and into creating a map of the outputs and consequences of the new business unit. Once the map of the business unit was complete, the four major core process maps were created. A two-day pause in activities was called to review and understand both the business unit and the core process maps, and to determine implications for staffing. This pause was useful in helping the senior staff think through how they would proceed. Again it was determined that an external facilitator would be helpful in processing the mapping of the jobs. Based on the process map, it appeared that about twenty-five jobs would be needed to meet the needs of the new business unit.

The mapping of the jobs was done in a hotel conference room. Twelve people, all managers, participated. The human resources manager participated as well, and arranged for two compensation specialists to be in a nearby room and simultaneously grade the jobs. This allowed twenty-five jobs to be modeled, defined, and graded in a four-day period.

Finally, with the jobs all mapped, it was an easy task to see how the work groups should be organized. In this case, each of the four core processes (selling, proposing, implementing, and maintaining) required a manager and a staff. The size of the staff depended on the amount of work each major process required, so implementing and maintaining were staffed with a number of experts and a number of clerks. Selling and proposing had fewer people, but their skills and expertise were greater. The accounting folks were surprised to be reduced to a small role in the new scheme. While not an easy transition, it was accomplished with relatively little tension because the decision had been made in full sight of all players, and for good business reasons. No back room dealing occurred.

As a result of this process, the staff learned a systematic way to change an entire organization quickly. They reduced staff from two hundred to one hundred twenty-five and cut $2 million in inefficiencies out of the budget. Another $20 million in savings resulted from the reductions in staff. It should be noted that the employees were kept informed throughout the process. They were advised to look for jobs in other places in the company as well as outside the company. Every employee was provided support in terms of time off for interviews, preparation of resumes, counseling by HR personnel, and information about deadlines and expected decision days. It took an elapsed time of just sixty-five days to complete the initial work definition of the as-is state and reengineer to the to-be state of work.

CHAPTER 4

The Work Behavior of Core Processes

The How *of Business*

The core processes represent the link between "what" the business unit wants to achieve in the form of outputs and consequences and the individuals and work groups who do the actual work. The core processes are the "work flow," if you will, that shows how the performance is to be accomplished from a business perspective. They are operationalized by people—individually or collectively. Therefore, it goes without saying that if you do not define the core processes you have no framework on which to base jobs. Leaving individuals to define their own way in how the business will achieve its ends is foolhardy. While individuals can be allowed to bring their creativity and experience to work, the business must decide how it wants to achieve its ends. In this chapter you will learn a systematic method, using the proforma, to define, measure, improve, and align core processes to business units, which will serve as the basis for defining individual jobs and work groups in the succeeding chapters.

In this chapter we expand the application of the proforma from the business unit to the process core level. We move from the *what* to the *how* of work. The key question is, "How will the business carry out its core processes in order to accomplish the primary business unit outputs and consequences to its client base?" This is not an organizational issue, but rather describes the specific process delivery steps that cut across the business to achieve its major aims.

Core processes are the procedural events carried out by individuals through work groups to produce outputs. As with the other three levels of the Business Sphere, core processes can be mapped, explained, managed, measured, and improved most effectively through using a commonly understood and applied proforma. Much of this effectiveness comes from an expanded view of the true composition of a process. More traditional thinking has viewed process as merely a set of steps to be followed. The Language of Work proforma recognizes that core processes of the Business Sphere are composed of outputs, consequences, inputs, conditions, the process element, and feedback. Core processes in business must be defined as such; otherwise they are planned and executed in an incomplete and inaccurate form.

Changing core process is probably the most frequently used means of business improvement after changing the organization chart (that is, rearranging, creating, and eliminating work groups) and changing the leadership of a business unit. At first glance, changing core processes makes more sense than changing either the organization chart or the leadership, but there is one very important thing to consider before contemplating changing core processes. It is inadvisable to change the core process before measuring the output(s) and consequences the core process is designed to achieve. That old saying, "If it ain't broke, don't fix it!" fully applies to core process. Don't change it unless you find out that something is wrong with the output. This is important to emphasize because, in general, many business improvement techniques are unwittingly used to measure for the sake of measurement without examining the overall output and consequences. For instance, workers and managers are taught to do a lot of measurements to identify problems with core processes and fix them before examining existing satisfaction with the output. There is a sense that some type of improvement is necessary—without the knowledge of exactly what is wrong. Also, the measurement of an output should be a true measure of the output, not just someone's opinion that there is something wrong. This is why doing a business unit analysis *before* a core process analysis is so important. Remember: *Define Australia first!,* that is, define the business intent first. In this case, the first goal is defining business outputs and consequences. The goal of business should not be process change in and of itself. The need for change should be based on real business problems.

Football as a Core Process

To continue the football analogy from Chapter 3, the next step after the business unit (franchise) should be the core processes for producing one or more of the business unit outputs. The core process we will use to illustrate will be the "team play" output—the playing of football as a sport. This is shown in Figure 4.1.

Figure 4.1. Work Map of a Football Core Process.

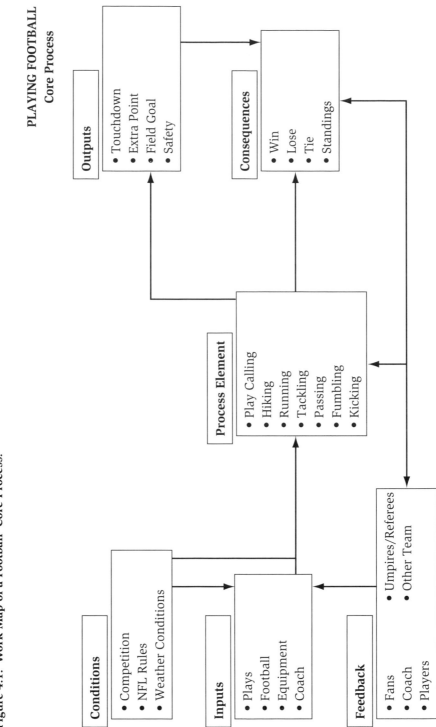

In the figure, playing football, as a core process, has four major *outputs,* the "deliverables" of the game. They are touchdowns, the extra point kicked after a touchdown, field goals, and safeties (tackling opponents in their end zone). To produce these outputs, plays will be needed for running and passing the ball. Of course, you need a football and equipment. The coach will have his own input. There are other *inputs,* such as the time clock, but we will assume these to exist for the sake of simplicity.

The *conditions* are the rules of the game. We will assume that the National Football League (NFL) sets the rules. Then, there are conditions such as competition and the weather.

Consequences of the process include the results of winning, losing, tying, and one's standing in the league against other teams. The *process element* includes a variety of steps, play calling, hiking, running, tackling, passing, fumbling, and kicking—each of which could be further "drilled-down" to subprocesses.

Finally, the *feedback* comes from fans, coaches, players, umpires/referees, and others, such as the team one is playing against.

Process in the General Sense

In the very general use of the term "process" in business, every performance level from the business unit to core processes, individual jobs, and work groups has "process." The word process is—unavoidably—being used in the Language of Work model in two ways. This is not meant to cause confusion, but rather to make sure one is clear on what "process" we are talking about. Is it "process element" or "core processes"?

As illustrated in Figure 4.2, process is one of the six basic elements of the work proforma used in the Language of Work model. Thus, you find a process element within each of the four performance levels of business, along with its inputs (I), conditions (C), outputs (O), consequences (C +), and feedback (F). This is the little "p," or what we will distinguish in terminology as the "process element" to differentiate it from the "core process" (big "P") performance level of the Business Sphere. This chapter is about the big P—core processes.

THREE TYPES OF CORE PROCESSES

There are *three basic types of core processes: product, service, and knowledge.* We will first see how the proforma, through work maps, can be applied to product and service core processes. We will see as well how to measure and improve these two core processes. We will also look at systematic core processes, which increase effectiveness and efficiency of product and service core processes. Then, you will learn a rather unique application of the proforma related to using *knowledge* processes. This is especially useful to the performance consultant in

Big "P" and Little "p"

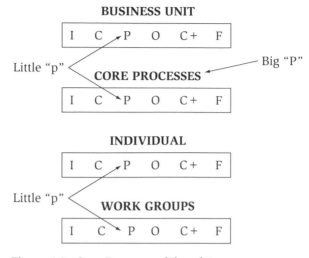

Figure 4.2. Core Processes (P) and Process Elements (p).

conducting a performance analysis to solve a client decision/goal/problem. Knowledge processes can also be used widely by teams and managers trying to solve business problems or take advantage of other opportunities for performance improvement. We will learn to use a work matrix, rather than a work map, to do knowledge analysis.

Product Core Processes

Product core processes lead to tangible product outputs (material things). The production line is a common product process. Product core processes may be human-led or machine-led. Automotive core processes are both human-led (as in assembly of an automobile), with some core processes (such a stamping body parts) entirely machine-led. In the construction industry, most of the core processes are human-led, with relatively few machine-led.

Usually, product core processes are readily observed and defined, and their efficiency and effectiveness can be changed by attending to them. The human element, if involved, is most often improved by a variety of motivational interventions, although skill enhancements are critical and may be needed initially and on a continuous basis. For example, improving the production line in an auto assembly plant is not mainly a case of enhancing the skill of the workforce. The workforce, unless brand new, already knows how to "assemble." Certainly, their skills will need to be kept up-to-date or perhaps improved in some manner, but we are not talking about incremental improvement. Rather, making the individual worker a part of a well-functioning team is usually far more effective in bringing about major improvements—a kind of motivational intervention. The Saturn Corporation has certainly proved this, although software and hardware technologies have played a critical role as well.

Traditionally, industrial engineering has played a key role in improving product core processes. It has enjoyed a notable degree of success with time studies, streamlining, work simplification, facilities layout, and the like, and its approaches are worth knowing about. Nonetheless, its preoccupation with microanalysis has kept many business improvements from happening. Using the Language of Work model in conjunction with business unit and work group analysis can help us see the bigger picture. When people play a larger or dominant role in a business, as in service core processes, the Language of Work model is most useful. The best approach is to apply the proforma to product core processes and improve them first; then consider the industrial engineering tools and techniques to fine-tune the processes. How to use the proforma is covered in the following description of service core processes.

Service Core Processes

Service core processes also result in tangible outputs, such as documentation (designs), questions answered, service provided, and so forth. Usually, machines and tools are not used as a major part of the process. Workers may use computers or pencil and paper, but these are extensions of the human mind, not machines. The service core process is one in which people play a dominant role in the business in serving other people outside the business. Thus, the call center, making hamburgers, telemarketing, and the like are service core processes.

Other service core processes do not result in tangible output, but may fulfill psychological and physical needs. There are professionals who use core processes to produce positive attitudes, understanding, or sensations. These would include those engaged in religion, therapy, counseling, and the like.

Service core processes may be very complex. For example, in our sample engineering business, the core processes of producing engineering designs and services are complex. Engineering, as an overall process, is very complex. The number of people involved, with varying talents and temperaments and experience, is extensive and hard to control—unlike pulling a lever to stamp out a part. In service core processes we rely on numerous individuals to "do their part"—to understand what must be done—and (as if that were not enough) to choose whether to do so or not and vary the degree of participation. Generally, we do not have to worry about the temperament or motivation of a machine, but the human machine is another thing. Because of this, an objective and concrete way to define and agree on service core processes so that we can improve them is paramount. Furthermore, because the human element can get in the way of service core processes by the "noise" (Chapter 9) created by fellow humans inside or outside the core process, it is even more critical that a systematic methodology (such as the proforma) be used to define, implement, and improve the process.

Now, the complexity of service core processes is not news! What may be *new* news is that those involved in service core processes cannot accurately tell you, other than through the technical language of their jobs, how they do what they do. They may be able to tell you what they are supposed to produce as an output (for example, a written proposal), but having them agree on the exact process used to produce it in a timely, cooperative way is another matter. And even when they can agree among themselves, how often does another work group or individual or manager have a similar understanding of that same process? Does John, the CAD (computer-aided design) engineer, understand and appreciate Lee's job as a proposal writer? Does Monica, the trainer, understand and appreciate either John's or Lee's process? If you do not think these are really problems in communication, just ask anyone with internal clients how well the client understands process and timing needs. For example, how well does a project manager understand what the proposal writer goes through? Or ask the print shop if the proposal writer understands the printing process and its timing requirements. Ask a trainer if he or she gets much respect from an engineer. These answers would be quite different if each person had a common work language in order to understand the other processes in order to use communication and collaborative efforts to produce a common output.

Knowledge Processes

In business, knowledge processes are most often associated with either decision making or problem solving. These knowledge processes are designed to produce tangible outputs, such as ideas to generate new business approaches, decisions on important issues, and solving problems that produce plans, strategies, and the like. They can as well be associated with what has become known today as knowledge transfer and creating knowledge.

Knowledge processes are used by individuals and groups of people. For example, a team working to answer a question such as, "How should we develop a strategic plan for our business?" would need to use a knowledge process. An executive's requirement that his staff develop a solution to a vexing problem would require a systematic knowledge process; otherwise, individuals are left to use their intuition, which sometimes works, or to guess, which works less often. Without a knowledge process, teams and individuals are left to their own devices. It is not uncommon, for instance, to see a group in a typical problem-solving meeting floundering around in search of an answer to the issue at hand. They gather some data, but it doesn't reveal how to solve the performance issue. The assumption that "more heads are better than one" isn't necessarily true. When no common thinking process is shared by the group, it is no wonder they are not effective in problem solving, let alone anywhere near as efficient as they could be.

The most commonly used knowledge process in business is a general discussion or brainstorming session, perhaps within the framework of a set of steps: define the goal, look for various options, weigh the potential results, and so on. This is one of those data-gathering methods referred to above. Typically, a group will simply start to discuss their individual perceptions of, and experience with, the "problem." They may even do some measurement and use what looks like sophisticated techniques such as histograms, nominal group techniques, and so forth. Out of this comes some decision or plan based on their collective logic. But even when groups follow such prescribed paths of collecting data, they do not necessarily know how to "process" the information to find the best solution. The group may jump to solutions or fail to arrive at any viable solution. Is this a good way to find answers for performance issues? Does it find us the best solutions? Would performance analysis based on modeling the problem or opportunity do a better job of getting at the solution? A matrix version of the proforma (to be described a little later) will greatly help in meeting knowledge performance needs. But first, a look at analyzing product and service core processes.

AS-IS PROCESS PERFORMANCE ANALYSIS

As-is performance analysis will be used by the performance consultant to define and improve product and service core processes. As we learned in the business unit, the order in which we define the elements of the proforma to create a work map is critical. Therefore, in analyzing core processes, we will build the work maps in the following sequence:

1. Outputs
2. Inputs
3. Conditions
4. Consequences
5. Process elements
6. Feedback

For illustration purposes, we will assume that we are continuing to define the business case example of Safeguards Inc. We know what the business unit is and the several outputs it produces, as illustrated in Chapter 3. One of these business unit outputs, you will recall, is "engineering designs." In describing how to define existing business core processes and improve them, we will use the "engineering design" output in this chapter and throughout the rest of the book. We will do an as-is core process analysis on which we can then conduct measurements and make improvements. This means we are analyzing an existing business to determine how to improve it by aligning the core processes to the business unit. Later in the chapter we will also see how to do a to-be performance analysis of this core process in order to make new changes. We begin our as-is analysis, as prescribed in the proforma, with outputs.

○

Step 1: Orientation

Introduce the proforma in ten minutes.

A sample map may also be useful, but is not necessary, and may present some problems if people are copying what others have done, rather than thinking through the issue.

Introduce the team to the proforma and purpose at hand.

Step 2: Define Outputs

Use the Proforma Job Aid.

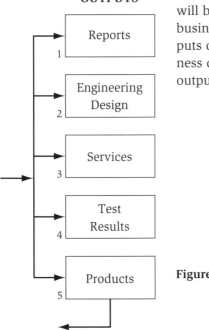

OUTPUTS

| Reports |
| 1 |

| Engineering Design |
| 2 |

| Services |
| 3 |

| Test Results |
| 4 |

| Products |
| 5 |

We start core process analysis with a fundamental question: "What are the outputs we will be building core processes for in the business unit?" They are, naturally, the outputs of the business unit itself. In our business case example (from Figure 3.2a), these outputs are repeated in Figure 4.3.

Figure 4.3. Business Unit Outputs.

Define "Australia First." You have to agree on the targets (outputs) of the processes first. Source for outputs: business unit.

In defining the core process for any one of these business unit outputs, we have to decide what degree of clarity and communication the definition of the core process will require. For example, Output 1, reports, may be several different kinds of reports, each using different inputs, following different conditions, consequences, process steps, and feedback. Would it be desirable to specify all reports and their unique core processes? Or would one core process do for all kinds of reports. The same might be true in the business case example for Output 3, services. But, Outputs 4 and 5, test results and products, might have different core processes for each of the kinds of test results and products. Thus, any given business unit output may, and often does, have two or more process outputs. Achieving consensus and communication are the guiding principles for deciding the level of definition needed.

In other instances, similar outputs may share the same process up to a given stage or step, then branch off in different directions. Which of all these possibilities is prevalent will best be determined when one gets into the mapping process and adjusts the mapping to fit the need and clarity of the definition at hand. See Figures 4.4a and 4.4b.

(Here, we will simplify our illustration of a business unit through only one of its core processes, producing engineering designs.) As shown in Figure 4.4a-1, there are core processes for each output, and these have varying levels of complexity. In defining the core process for engineering design, we would first specify the output of the engineering design and place it on the right side of our process map.

OUTPUT

Engineering Designs

Figure 4.4a-1. Output.

Step 3: Define Inputs

The key questions to be answered here are: What triggers the work of the process? and What are the primary resources used in the process?

After specifying an output, we define the inputs required to achieve that output. What is needed to produce the outputs? Inputs typically come from a variety of sources and fall into two categories. They include those inputs that trigger the work and those inputs as resources to be used in processing. As you have learned about business unit inputs, one source of trigger input is the client who requests the output. For example, in the sample engineering design process, clients are typically external clients who request, through documents called requests for proposals (RFPs) and by architectural specs and plans, specific drawings to meet their needs. Thus, you see in the list of inputs that follow, "client request/goal." This is the trigger input. If for added clarity it would be useful to specify the nature of client requests, such as architect specifications and plans, then do so. Do what is needed to assure understanding for those doing the analysis, as well as to whom it will be communicated and decisions made.

INPUTS

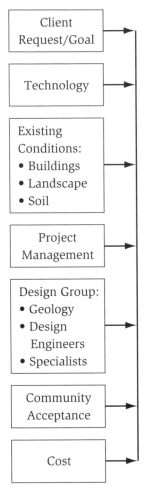

Figure 4.4a-2. Inputs.

The majority of inputs are resources for producing the engineering drawings. Here you see, in the case example, inputs such as technology, a variety of existing conditions, input from project management sources, and so on. Those who know much about engineering drawing will recognize many of these inputs; however, as is often the case, the specifics inputs for any given business vary by the nature and scope of that business. So, don't expect inputs, like any work element, to be universal by definition.

Also, we are trying to capture the business core processes while capturing elements against which to eventually benchmark.

Step 4: Define Conditions

Ask: What external rules and regulations are to be followed?

What internal policies and procedures apply?

What are the conditions (high-level definition) for the use of inputs, process elements, and then feedback?

Do not include judgments of why things don't work, such as "not enough time" or "multiple platforms." These come later when making improvements.

Inputs, process elements, and feedback are influenced by conditions that will be specified in our work map in the box labeled "conditions." Conditions are the external and internal factors that, although relatively fixed and hard to change, influence key elements of the core process work. These were just identified as inputs, process element, and feedback. Let's see what this means in terms of the core process conditions in the case of engineering drawings. The specific conditions specified for our case example include the following, shown in Figure 4.4a-3:

CONDITIONS

1. Regulatory Requirements:
   - Federal
   - State
   - Local
2. Design Codes: ASTM, Corps of Engineers, Highway Dept.
3. Community Acceptance
4. Client Parameters

Figure 4.4a-3. Conditions.

Certainly, community acceptance will influence how the business can and will use its technology. Having worked for an environmental engineering company, I can guarantee that community acceptance has quite an influence on how and when the business moved toxic waste materials over the streets of many cities. In the case example, the available technology that was used in an engineering drawing was influenced by the degree to which a community would be willing to accept a newly designed and proposed facility for handling (burning) toxic waste. You will note, by the way, that "community acceptance" is both input and a condition. It is not all that unusual to find a given work item to be both an input and a condition. Community acceptance guides as a condition how input will be used, what will be processed, and what it wants as feedback. Equally, community acceptance is an input to be processed in terms of specific content and circumstances. This is why engineering companies hold community discussion sessions. Indeed, smart businesses anticipate such community involvement and plan, rather than react to it. One way to do good planning is in doing process maps, such as the ones used here.

As to conditions that affect the process element, government rules and regulations are the most common and often stated conditions to business core processes. There is hardly a process, for example, that doesn't get touched by OSHA, safety, and health regulations. It isn't hard to imagine the government regulations to influence the engineering drawings of an environmental engineering business. Each industry tends to have a common set of regulations it wants attended to.

Finally, conditions that influence feedback often take the form of reports and information that must be made available or reported for compliance. Thus, in the engineering drawing process, local government might require updating on meeting local codes, permits, and even community meetings to access public input and reaction to proposed designs.

Step 5: Define Consequences

Look for consequences for clients, the business, and the workforce. There should be at least one or more consequences per output.

State in positive terms; never negative.

Consequences, you recall, are the results we expect from the outputs. In the case of core processes, this means the results expected from the outputs of the core process. They reflect what the customer desires, what the company wants to achieve in the way of standards, and, in general, what the core process will achieve overall. It is helpful to think in terms of quantity, quality, timeliness, and cost. For example, "cost effective engineering drawing." The consequences are shown in Figure 4.4a-4 below.

CONSEQUENCES

Output 1: Engineering Designs
- Cost-effective engineering designs
- Safety
- Designs within compliance
- Community acceptance
- Ease of construction
- Customer satisfaction

Figure 4.4a-4. Consequences.

One the things you will want to do in defining consequences, as with any work element, is use the previous performance level work definition, the business unit in this case, to identify and specify consequences.

In comparing the business unit to the core process consequences, the prior level has been used to define the later level. Thus, core process level consequence 1, "cost effective engineering design," is related to business unit consequence 1, "cost effective designs, services, test results, and products." Other process consequences are more detailed and, although they may not always use the exact wording as in the business unit, they are related. For example, "ease of construction" in the process is a critical consequence to client satisfaction in the business unit. One should never have a work element specified if it does not relate to some other level of work.

Step 6: Define the Process Element

Define the steps necessary to complete each core process output.

Now that we have defined the inputs, conditions, and consequences to the output(s), the next major step is to develop the process element in the core process map. The process element you choose to define may be a step-by-step process or it may have parallel and simultaneous steps. The examples here use linear steps for the sake of simplicity. As shown in Figure 4.4a-5, there are fourteen steps to the engineering drawing process element.

Level of detail

This is a very systematic core process that everyone involved in this engineering business is expected to adhere to and on which several jobs are based.

Process elements are composed of incremental steps that are followed to produce or serve a given output, using the associated inputs, governed by the conditions to be followed, using certain feedback, and designed to result in specified, desirable consequences. It is rather easy to specify a process element if you remember to focus on two things.

First, think of the first thing that needs to be done in response to a client request (as an input), keeping in mind that each step is a mini-deliverable. In other words, we do this, and then we do that, and it looks like this. It should take a form and be complete—a

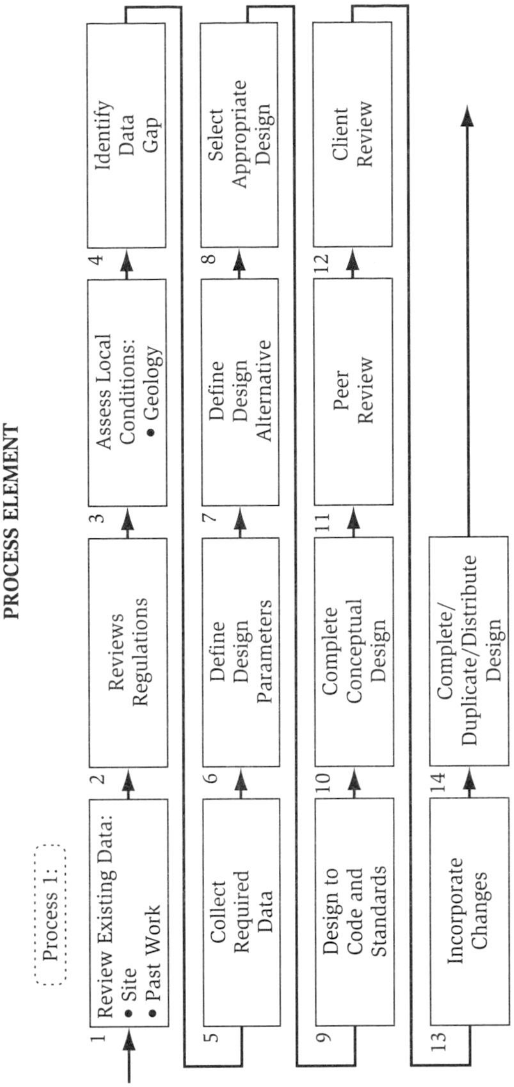

Figure 4.4a-5. Process Element.

deliverable. State each deliverable beginning with an action verb. Specify each step in the process, for example:

- Review Existing Data
- Assess Local Conditions
- Identify Data Gap
- Design to Code and Standard

The last and final step of the process element should result in, of course, a core process output.

Step 7: Define Feedback

Questions to ask:

How will the work group decide whether clients are satisfied?

How will the process check on its progress and know to make corrections?

The final step of core process analysis is to define feedback. Feedback by its very nature is the information needed to tell us when the product or service is finished properly. Is the engineering drawing done and correct? What tells us it is done and correct? Certainly the client (internal or external) is one source of feedback. Others might include external agencies, stockholders, or internal work groups.

A second use of feedback is information that tells us the process element is followed correctly. If it is not, can it be adjusted to do better work, fix the problem immediately, and/or provide the workforce and management with basic communication on what is going on.

A third use of feedback for core processes is information on inputs. Are the inputs correct and timely? If not, what effect will that have on processing? How can it be adjusted?

Finally, feedback is used for core process conditions. Are the conditions being adhered to?

The four uses of feedback described here serve three fundamental performance needs: reinforcement, communication, and adjustment of work. It is not only useful to know that an output has been produced (and appreciated), but feedback is needed during processing, using inputs, and assuring that the conditions are adhered to. Figure 4.4a-6 shows examples of the four uses of feedback in the engineering design core process:

FEEDBACK

<table>
<tr><td>DURING</td><td>AFTER</td></tr>
<tr><td>

1. Permits
2. Client: Conceptual stage
3. Project team
4. Regulatory agencies
5. Project manager
6. Architects and other professionals (construction, landscape, etc.)
7. Community

</td><td>

1. Client: Final design
2. Regulatory permits in place
3. Constructional personnel
4. Professional engineer signoff

</td></tr>
</table>

Figure 4.4a-6. Feedback.

Uses	Source in Case Example
After Output	Client: Final Design
During Process Element	Project Team
For Input	Client: Conceptual Stage
For Conditions	Permits, Community

When it comes to determining what feedback is necessary, one factor is critical in your planning. It has been shown again and again that feedback is not only a necessity, but among work elements is also perhaps the factor most often lacking in both quantity and quality. Would the firm simply want to give a client their engineering drawings and wait for their reactions and payment? Or, would the firm ask how they liked the drawings and whether they are up to the desired standards? In many instances, outputs are simply produced or serviced, but not measured for impact. This is a failure to plan, seek, and use information that would be useful in making core processes better. That is why in the business case example client feedback on the final design should be planned and executed—indeed, required.

Another form of "after" feedback is seeing that permits are in place to use the drawings. This feedback comes from construction personnel—one of the clients of the engineering core process. A third client is the professional engineer, who must sign off on the drawings before they are used by construction.

All these sources of "after" feedback provide information to the process element, inputs, conditions, and/or influence the consequences. Revisions would be made to improve processing the output so as to assure satisfaction of current and future clients. In large measure, we are trying our hardest to assure that clients will want to return for future work with us. We are also trying to make our core process more systematic by learning what we did right or wrong and fixing what needs fixing. This is deliberate and not left to chance. It is directed at improving the process element, inputs, conditions, and reinforcing consequences—not just the individual who gains experience, but the process itself.

As important as it is to collect information after processing, it is equally important to get feedback while processing, using inputs, and following conditions in order to assure we produce the best product or service before we ask the client or others. This is the proactive, rather than reactive approach to feedback (and business). In the engineering drawing process we find "during" feedback such as: permits, client, project team, regulatory agencies, and project manager, architects and other professionals.

As with "after" feedback, "during" feedback must be planned and encouraged, otherwise it will not be done to the extent needed. Human nature is such that people won't ask if they don't have to. Although it is contrary to human nature to go out of our way to seek "trouble" or to assert ourselves when we are shy, we need to encourage, even demand, voluntary feedback from internal clients in the Business Sphere. One way to increase the likelihood of feedback occurring is to actually plan for it. We need opportunities for managers and workers to see that the feedback is valued as positive consequences of their work. One way to do this, of course, is to build feedback right into the process element so that it is not missed. Hence, you see in the case example the opportunity for "client" and "project team" review built into the process element. In a much more general sense, much of the feedback at any performance level of business, while needing to be specified, really needs to be accepted as a cultural attribute of the business in general.

Step 8: Reach Consensus and Achieve Commitment

In light of the input from others, keep the definition of the map at a high level. Too much detail will defeat the purpose. Such detail comes later. Drill down until clarity, communication, and consensus are reached.

The complete core process map for the engineering design output of the business case example is shown in Figure 4.4a and Figure 4.4b. The map should be shared with others who were not involved with the team in the initial definition of the core processes. These range from executives to managers and certainly workers who use the core processes. Additional input should be obtained, if feasible, from both suppliers and customers receiving the output of the core processes. One might have the core process reviewed by an external consultant knowledgeable in the core process. Of course, many of these parties may have been, and should have been, involved during the initial definition of the core process map.

One additional and important aspect of the procedure for defining core processes, as well as other levels of performance in the business unit, is worth noting before moving to other considerations about core processes in general. This is the topic of "drilling down."

Figure 4.4a. As-Is Engineering Design Core Process.

As-Is Core Process Map

PROCESS TITLE: Engineering Design

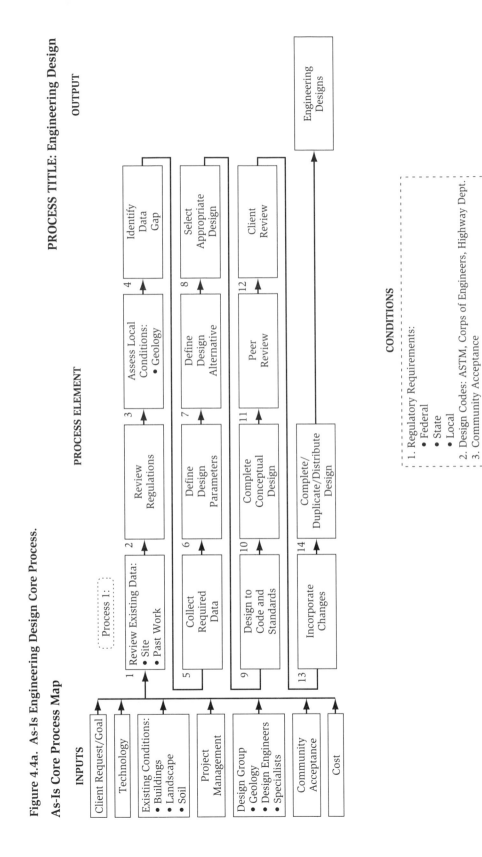

As-Is Core Process Map **PROCESS TITLE: Engineering Design**

CONSEQUENCES

Output 1: Engineering Designs
• Cost-effective engineering designs
• Safety
• Designs within compliance
• Community acceptance
• Ease of construction
• Customer satisfaction

FEEDBACK

DURING	AFTER
1. Permits	1. Client: Final design
2. Client: Conceptual stage	2. Regulatory permits in place
3. Project team	3. Constructional personnel
4. Regulatory agencies	4. Professional engineer signoff
5. Project manager	
6. Architects and other professionals (construction, landscape, etc.)	
7. Community	

Figure 4.4b. As-Is Engineering Design Core Process (continued).

O

Steps in the "Drilling-Down" Process Element

One of the more curious results of work mapping in general is that people think that once they have defined a map that they are done. The truth is, mapping is incomplete until understanding has been established. And understanding is not necessarily achieved with the first draft. It may require several iterations and sharing with many people in the business to obtain their input and their commitment. Therefore, one other mapping requirement may be needed. It is called "drilling down" to a level of understanding. This is said with the cautionary note that too much detail is as bad as too little.

As was emphasized previously, work mapping is a very iterative function. The "first cut" or draft is simply that. Most often done in a group environment with several experts, client and supplier representatives, the first draft should be taken into the work environment and shared, clarified, and agreed to. Further data, measurements, and opinions must be sought. The three goals to be attained in mapping are understanding, completeness, and commitment. An essential need is to decide where and when to "drill down" any process steps that need it. Keep in mind that drilling down provides understanding and completeness, but going into too much detail may confuse those doing the analysis and using it to improve performance. Too much detail also can be the death nail to any reengineering or reorganization method.

To "drill down" is just what it implies: defining another level of detail that will clarify what is not currently well understood. Some individuals may not see what others see. For example, as illustrated in Figure 4.5, suppose in the engineering business case example there is a lack of clarity around Step 6, "define design parameters," of the process element. What clarity is needed? For the particular group who defined this case example, it meant three additional steps. For another group, it might mean five steps; for another, no need for such detail. This all goes to say that "drilling down" has no hard-and-fast rules. It simply means including those steps that bring about understanding, completeness, and commitment. Doing any more leads to potential confusion over definitions and to a sense of wondering why we are doing what we don't need to do.

MEASURING AND IMPROVING CORE PROCESSES

Knowing how to measure core processes is another instance of "Define Australia first!" We must decide what to measure first, for what purposes, and what root cause so as to be able to fix the core process problem(s). Which work element(s) would you measure first? The answer is fundamentally the same as how you learned to measure when we discussed the business unit in Chapter 3. Measure output and consequences first; then if a problem or gap exists, look for root causes in the inputs, conditions, process element, and feedback that produce the outputs and consequences.

Measure Process Outputs and Consequences First

We begin with process output because it, along with its associated consequences, represents the reason we have the business. The core process is to produce a given output, and we want to find out whether that process did produce the desired quantity, quality, cost, and/or timeliness it should have. If it did not, then why not? Let's look at this in light of our business case example.

The process output we have mapped is the "engineering designs." It has several associated consequences (see Figure 4.4a-4).

We would want to determine, relative to each consequence, to what degree that consequences were achieved. How cost-effective are the designs? Is safety assured in each design? Have the designs complied with regulations and codes?

Process 1, Step 6:

5	Collect Required Data

6.1

Define Client Goal: • Number of People   • Etc.

6.2

Obtain Data from Assessment of Existing Conditions: • Weak soil

6.3

Assess Regulations

7

Define Design Alternatives

Figure 4.5. Drilling-Down a Core Process.

And so on. If any problems are revealed through measurement of outputs and consequences, we move to find the root cause. We are ready to measure the related inputs, conditions, process element, and feedback.

Measure for Root Cause in Core Processes

Measuring the various work elements within a core process is not significantly different from measuring the work elements previously described for the business unit. We still need to know how the conditions support the process. We need to see that the inputs meet standards and are ready in a timely way for processing. We need to make sure that feedback is solicited from the client when the output is delivered. Or is it, along with problems in input, conditions, and/or feedback, the process element of a core process where we need to look for root cause. Let's assume there was a problem identified with our engineering design output and a related consequence in customer satisfaction. Let's see where we might have problems in input, conditions, feedback, and process element.

Referring once more to Figure 4.4a, on the input side we can see that the root cause problems might be in the

- Clarity of client input
- The technology employed
- Data from existing conditions
- Or any of the other inputs

Did, for example, the client provide accurate and complete specifications for the engineering design, or perhaps make many changes as they were being processed, that in the end significantly affected the final output and consequences? Indeed, this is often the case in core processes when clients think they know what they want but make changes as things become clearer to them—inferring that is what they wanted all along and we just didn't understand.

For conditions, we look at the restraints imposed by regulations, design codes, what the community would accept, and other client parameters. These conditions can affect input, processing, and/or feedback. For example, simple delays in gaining community acceptance can often impede progress in processing outputs and achieving consequences. As another example, in producing environmental engineering designs, it is quite often the case that regulations impact the nature and scope of what kinds of drawing are approved versus what is possible. "Red tape," as we like to label it, can get in the way of many core processes.

In the process element, we might be looking for

- Steps that were overlooked

- Steps that were not effectively carried out, or

- The failure of other core processes that interact with the engineering design process to achieve their input to this process (This is another example of the "white space" that needs to be attended to.)

Any step in the process element may be an example of a process element gone wrong. Were the regulations accurately reviewed in Step 2? Were more acceptable alternatives available, but not considered in Step 7? And so on.

And then there is feedback itself—often the cause of many performance difficulties. Because we are looking at root cause, we are mainly investigating the problems caused by lack of or inappropriate feedback during processing. This is not to suggest that feedback after the fact is not significant. "After" feedback is often caused by not reinforcing good and acceptable behavior. In other words, if acceptable behavior begins to degrade, one can be fairly certain that *after* feedback has itself degraded.

"During" feedback relates to the accuracy, frequency, and availability of feedback to correct process element steps that are not producing acceptable outputs and consequences while the work is under way. This feedback can relate to inputs, process, and conditions. For example, was there adequate feedback to suggest that the designer had solicited all the relevant data needed? In the peer review (Step 11) of the process element, was there feedback on meeting compliance to all of the stated conditions? And for the process element, how adequate was the feedback from the project manager as the work was in process—a not so unusual shortcoming of management feedback?

Of course, there are other kinds of measurement that can and perhaps should be conducted that will not be addressed here. Descriptions of these are to be found in many other resources and include the wide range of metrics available to measure timeliness, cost, quantity, and quality. The point here is that these should be generally undertaken only when the measurement for consequences and output has been done. Then the root cause for other work elements can be ascertained and the available metric tools used.

Improving the Support to Core Processes

Process can be adjusted in a number of ways. We just reviewed how to improve core processes by looking for root cause in the work elements of associated inputs, conditions, process element, and feedback. But there are a number of other ways, such as speeding up the execution of steps, negotiating quality standards, using technology, adding input resources, and negotiating changes in conditions. In Chapter 8, we will put these improvements in the context of what will be called "work support," but a brief discussion is important here to establish that all improvement is not just in the six elements that define work performance. To understand how we might make adjustments such as these, let us assume there is a problem in the engineering design core process for our business case. A client has requested an engineering design and suddenly wants the business to submit the design five days earlier than originally indicated. What could be done to adjust the core process?

One of the first adjustments would be adding additional resources, something many businesses do when faced with a problem like this. Among the specific resource adjustments that could be made are more CAD engineers could be assigned to do the actual drawings, overtime could be authorized, and the engineering work group could bring in additional staff resources from outside the company. Another adjustment could be to eliminate (or modify in some way) Step 11, the peer review. This would cut down the steps and also members of the Peer Review Team could be involved in the actual design of the drawings instead. These adjustments would speed up the process. It is possible that using technology—e-mailing drawings between engineer and client—would speed up the process even more. Designing and building at nearly the same time is another technique often employed in an engineering/construction business.

Some of the more interesting adjustments in core process involve changing conditions and standards. Of course, core processes that are designed to lead to exacting standards or require strict adherence to conditions may not be able to take advantage of these adjustments—safety standards and exacting equipment specifications, etc. But there are instances that can be modified. For example, one can imagine negotiating with a client who wants the engineering design earlier to see what aspects of the design could be delayed or eliminated. A change in standards, such as budget limitations, might allow for changes in the materials and resources utilized in order to get things done faster.

MAKING CORE PROCESSES SYSTEMATIC

A good core process should produce an acceptable output every time it is used. Why doesn't it? Well, we know that the human element can be a significant contributor to varying outputs. People get tired, lose their motivation, have personal problems, and so on. These are subjects of human psychology/physiology. The Language of Work model can help improve consistent quality output by helping to assure that core processes are made more systematic. The need for more systematic processes was outlined in Chapter 2, but more details are given below.

Systematic core processes are characterized by the following:

- A defined set of steps that can be repeatedly applied.
- The use of feedback as the steps are applied. This assures that adjust-

ments are made to the process element so that it is more effective and efficient.

- The use of measurement to make sure the output is satisfactory. Measurement is also used to provide data on which revisions can be based to improve the output before it is finished.

- Consistent utilization that improves the process element for the purpose of applying it better the next time.

- Continuously seeking to find better ways and methods to improve the core process.

It is important to note that core processes are systematic only when all these characteristics are present. For example, virtually all core processes have defined steps, but this alone does not make the process highly systematic. It should continue to strive toward excellence. In particular, it is the presence of feedback and measurement that make a process systematic. Here we will look at core processes in the context of measurement.

Systematic core processes may include three important kinds of measurement: measuring output, feedback, and tryout.

1. Systematically Measuring Output. When we systematically measure output, we respond continually to the needs and desires of our clients—whether internal or external. We continuously attend to improving the inputs, conditions, process element, consequences, and feedback because we want the output to maintain a certain quality standard.

2. Systematically Attending to Feedback. Feedback is a way to keep others informed, as well as a way to collect information for ourselves. Unfortunately, lack of feedback is one of the principle failures in processing. When we structure feedback as a requirement in processing at specific steps, we make the process more responsive. You will recall that the structured feedback in the engineering design process required a peer review before delivery of the output. Without the requirement, the output can suffer. By systematically requiring or giving feedback at every critical step in our work, higher quality in the output is more assured.

3. Systematic Tryout. Most, but not all, core processes lend themselves to tryout, using the intended output on a real or simulated client in order to determine their satisfaction and utilization of the output. For example, the peer review in the engineering design process is a kind of tryout. When a trainer tries a new training program being developed on a sample group of trainees, tests what they learned, and makes improvements in the training program before it goes to everyone else, this is using a tryout. Tryouts can be built into many core processes that currently do not employ such a step. Practice tryout of a presentation before you deliver it to an audience is an example from a core process on preparing client presentations.

The alternative to a systematic process is a very random walk-through of the application of core processes, from which little learning occurs. As a result, we repeat old errors or create new errors rather than improve each time we apply the core process. Systematic core processes are very important to the success of businesses and individuals. We use the proforma to improve nonsystematic core processes by defining the process element steps, giving attention to measurement, providing feedback, and providing consistent utilization by users toward succeeding levels of repeatable exemplary performance.

TO-BE PROCESS PERFORMANCE ANALYSIS

You will recall that to-be analysis is looking to the future of work. It is not primarily about what already exists and improving it (that would call for using as-is analysis, measurement, and improvement). Rather, to-be analysis is looking to what needs to be added or changed primarily as a result of competition or change in business conditions. To-be analysis, like as-is analysis, involves identifying performance gaps in a different way. In the case of core processes, the new needs or change gaps are driven by business unit changes. Thus, for example, if the business decides to institute a new output, then a new core process will need to be defined. In the business case example we introduced earlier, the idea of the business unit deciding to get into the "site cleanup" service was a new output. A to-be core process would have to be defined and would follow the already described path of defining, in order, the output, inputs, conditions, consequences, process element, and feedback. The new core process for the new site cleanup output is illustrated in Figure 4.6.

As you can see, the definition of new core process (showing only the process element) to new outputs is pretty straightforward as far as core process changes go. What is more complicated are core process changes brought on by many of the other reasons core processes must change. In today's business, these changes relate mainly to what has become known as

- Enterprise-wide changes
- Regulatory changes
- Globalization
- Downsizing
- Restructuring

Site Cleanup Process Element

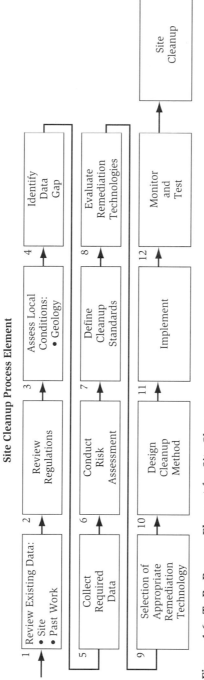

1 Review Existing Data: • Site • Past Work	2 Review Regulations	3 Assess Local Conditions: • Geology	4 Identify Data Gap
5 Collect Required Data	6 Conduct Risk Assessment	7 Define Cleanup Standards	8 Evaluate Remediation Technologies
9 Selection of Appropriate Remediation Technology	10 Design Cleanup Method	11 Implement	12 Monitor and Test

Site Cleanup

Figure 4.6. To-Be Process Element for Site Cleanup.

Each of these is a hefty change in and of itself, so we will only attempt to describe the first, enterprise-wide changes, in detail. It will help to make the point about core process to-be analysis.

Enterprise-wide changes refer to changes brought on by the introduction of computer information technology—particularly those that integrate the various software programs used in business to one common software that everyone in the business can use in tracking and completing customer needs. Some of the most common enterprise-wide change programs today include SAP, ORACLE, Bann, Peoplesoft, IBM. The ability of these software packages to track the client from the time he or she enters the system to delivery without re-creating the records over and over in various forms is rather remarkable. They also afford the means to work on many of the client's needs on-line rather than off-line. The use of these programs has affected many existing core processes, required new core processes, and changed many people's jobs (which we will describe in the next chapter). Let's see how we can use the proforma of the Language of Work model to aid in these kinds of core process transition needs.

Much of the change in the information technology side of implementing an enterprise-wide change quite naturally involves changing the existing procedures, forms, and policies to the new format. These changes are best described and performed by information technologists. But we want to see how an enterprise-wide change might affect an existing core process level definition and indicate what performance changes must be planned and implemented. In other words, we want to find the performance gaps in the core processes and what needs to be done to bring about the changes at this level (and then, how these changes will impact jobs and work groups). We will use the business case example to illustrate a to-be change in core process.

First, review Figures 4.4a and 4.4b for the existing engineering design core process; then we will take a look at changes that could be brought on by introduction of an enterprise-wide software package. We will call our enterprise-wide package EWS. We will approach this analysis in the same order and manner as any performance analysis using the proforma. We know the output—engineering drawings (which will not be changing), so we begin with looking at the impact on inputs. The enterprise-wide changes through the introduction of EWS on the engineering design process are summarized in Figures 4.7a and 4.7b.

Inputs.   There are two overall impacts on the inputs. First, two existing inputs, project management and cost, will be affected by the introduction of the EWS. Project management will be affected by doing more management input on-line, rather than in person. This will range from input data provided to how to check on progress. Similarly, cost inputs will also be on-line because the cost proposal will have been generated on-line and be directly accessible. Two *new* inputs are being added because all client history and all written proposals in the future will be on-line and directly accessible to engineering.

Conditions. There will be new conditions related to who has access to EWS based on a security need and, of course, the conditions established by the new EWS procedures and forms themselves.

Consequences. The change here is on-line use of all data and access by internal sources.

Process Element. Three steps of the engineering design process will be impacted by the introduction of EWS. The review of existing data generated from site and past work will be on-line. Engineers will not have to go to files and other sources searching for existing data. In fact, historical data from other projects will be in the system and be of direct use whenever desired. Further, in Step 2, all related regulations will be on-line, and when dimensions of the data are entered, the computer will do cross-referencing so that regulations are not overlooked. Finally, the assessment of local conditions will take on a new dimension. Field personnel, such as geologists, will be able to collect data in the field, do some testing there, and report their findings into a laptop or palm computer and download into EWS.

Feedback. The permits will be tracked on-line, feedback from the project manager, in part, will be tracked on-line, and a new form of feedback will be provided from EWS schedule reports to everyone on a real-time basis.

In summary, we can see from this to-be performance analysis where the changes—performance gaps—will occur when compared to the as-is analysis map. To this we can add the details (specified in attached documents) as to the nature and scope of each change and plan the appropriate interventions to assist in these changes.

Remember, this is one level of defining, clarifying, and determining performance change. In this case it is a core process level definition. Added clarity will occur when we go the next level of analysis—the individual level. Each performance level of analysis in the Business Sphere provides the basis for subsequent levels, while subsequent levels provide additional details to more fully understand previous levels and make decisions for needed changes.

The more detailed scope of each change may be specified elsewhere and keyed to the to-be core process map. As teams work their way through these changes, they can use the proforma to also do some of their planning and problem solving. The following description of knowledge processes will be of assistance in this regard.

Figure 4.7a. To-Be Core Process Map for New Software Installation.

To-Be Core Process Map
Introduction of EWS Software

CORE PROCESS TITLE: Engineering Design

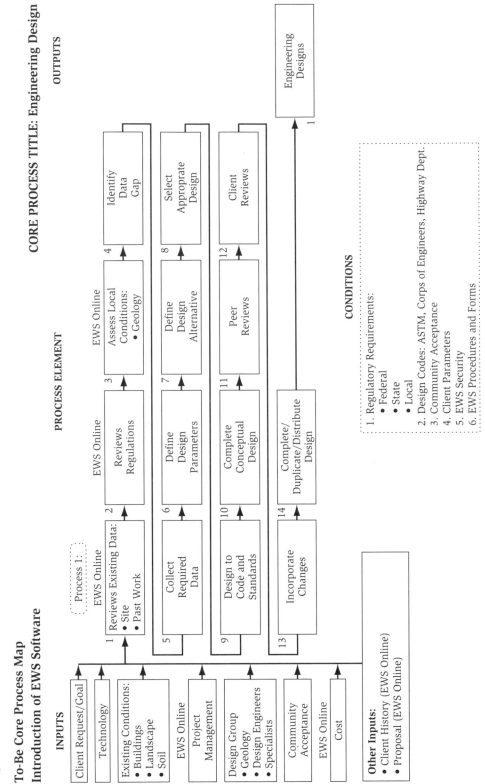

To-Be Core Process Map   **CORE PROCESS TITLE: Engineering Design**
Introduction of EWS Software

CONSEQUENCES

Output 1: Engineering Designs
- Cost-effective engineering designs
- Safety
- Designs within compliance
- Community acceptance
- Ease of construction
- Customer satisfaction
- Online use by internal sources

FEEDBACK

DURING	AFTER
1. Permits (EW Online)	1. Client: Final design
2. Client: Conceptual stage	2. Regulatory permits in place
3. Project team	3. Construction personnel
4. Regulatory agencies	4. Professional engineer sign-off
5. Project manager (EW Online)	
6. Architects and other professionals (construction, landscape, etc.)	
7. Community	
8. EWS schedule reports	

Figure 4.7b. To-Be Core Process Map for New Software Installation (continued).

KNOWLEDGE PROCESSES

Knowledge processes are used daily by managers, individuals, and work groups. Most often these are part of the ongoing daily activities designed to accomplish product and service core processes. Improving knowledge processes affords tremendous opportunities for improving several aspects of a business.

Knowledge processes deal with solution creation, problem solving/decision making, and knowledge transfer. Modern businesses are filled with knowledge processes, making this a key area in which performance improvements can be realized. In applying the proforma to these core processes, we will mainly address knowledge processes that call for intense study, often in groups, rather than focus on the simpler knowledge processes where common sense or experience tells one what to do. The more intense process is typified by the problem-solving analysis that a performance consultant often performs with clients. For instance, an executive may say that she has a new goal to achieve or a manager may say that his team needs help resolving a thorny issue. What approach will the performance consultant use to help the executive and manager arrive at a knowledge solution?

Knowledge processes are needed primarily to facilitate three kinds of knowledge needs in business: (1) creation of knowledge, (2) solving knowledge problems/needs, and (3) transferring knowledge to others (inside or outside the organization).

The *creation of knowledge* encompasses the need to devise knowledge that would be useful for the organization to do its work more effectively or efficiently, or for the purpose of enhancing its competitive edge as a business. For example, new knowledge in a computer application software would be of interest to clients the business serves in that it enhances their own business operations or service to their own customers. A new scheduling software might be one such example. In the former instance of improving its own operations, the creation of knowledge on a new way to clean toxic waste would aid the internal operations of the business case example. How is this knowledge best created? Can the proforma aid the creation of this knowledge?

Solving knowledge problems and needs refers to the common requirements of executives, managers, and teams to deal with the variety of goals and opportunities presented in their work. For example, an executive is presented with the need to put together a diversity program for his company or a line manager needs to improve a performance review program. A team may be solving a quality improvement item suggested by an employee or a performance consultant needs to improve the oral presentation of engineers and other technical personnel. These are all knowledge need opportunities.

Finally, *knowledge transfer* is the need to take what someone knows and effectively and efficiently instill that skill and knowledge in others so that he or she becomes proficient in its utilization. Thus, the knowledge created needs to be transferred to someone else—typically to a client outside the business who has purchased the knowledge. For example, the new scheduling software needs to be learned by the client it is sold to. This may sound like a simple training solution, but more often than not it involves a variety of interventions working in combination with one another. To simply define a set of typical learning objectives and provide a training program may not suffice. Rather, a more comprehensive analysis model is needed to identify all the performance needs (gaps) and their related interventions. The Language of Work proforma can be used both for the analysis and for the transfer of knowledge itself.

Knowledge Creation

To suggest that knowledge creation is an easy performance requirement and capable of being accomplished through a formula approach would be foolish. Knowledge creation requires not only knowledge, collaboration, and creative insight, but is often limited to those few individuals who seem to have the attributes and know-how to create intuitively. Nonetheless, certain techniques can help in their efforts. One such tool is the proforma.

The essence of knowledge creation is not only knowing your goal, but the process that will obtain that knowledge. Clarity of both the goal and process are therefore key attributes. Also, knowledge creation does not necessarily exclusively mean *new* knowledge. It can be the use of existing knowledge to create a different application.

Let's suppose that your business, or the environmental engineering business in our case example, is creating a business plan. This would be an example of typical knowledge creation task, although it is not the creation of a strictly new idea. Many knowledge creations are the reformulation of old ideas in new ways and contexts.

The typical approach to business planning is to define categories of information, as follows:

- General company description
- Present situation
- Objectives
- Product/services
- Market analysis
- Marketing and sales strategies
- Management
- Financial projections
- Executive summary

Business plans actually do a good job of capturing what will be planned and what it will cost. There are usually numerous goals and objectives for divisions and individuals to achieve. This is highly useful and necessary knowledge information. However, these plans often lack clarity around how the goals and objectives will be achieved and measured during development and what it will take to accomplish the plan from a work (versus resources only) standpoint. The proforma will operationalize the knowledge needed by executives, managers, and workers to achieve the business goals. The proforma will also improve the overall communication of how and what to measure if the things planned are indeed provided. Figure 4.8 provides a typical (albeit hypothetical) business goal and a definition of a proforma related to it that could be included in a business plan for our business case example.

Looking at the business goal, we first determine the specific *outputs* that will be needed to achieve the goal. The details provided by the other five elements of work will be useful in knowing how to execute and measure the business plan to wards these outputs—therefore achieving the goal. Let's see what this means.

The outputs, in this instance, are new products. Specifically, the new products include a new consulting process built on a new technology discovered by engineers in our business case company, and a new and related analytic report that can be used to identify the specific makeup of toxic waste faster and cheaper than currently available.

The *inputs* will tell us what needs to be collected, reviewed, and researched in order to develop the outputs. In this example, the inputs are the details of the new technology, a description of the new report, the literature on similar technologies, the legal department for patent office rules, funds for development, and knowledge about translating a discovery into a commercial product. The *conditions* force us to look at the laws, rules, and constraints required. Here, the conditions include patent laws, the guidelines for conversion to commercial product, and the competition. The *consequences* will capture what we want the new business goal to achieve for clients and contribute to the business. Here, we need profitability at a certain level by a certain point in time, new markets, and protection from expensive misjudgments of potential project cost and long-term viability for the company (also known as risk management). The *process element* causes us to decide who will participate in the development, what steps or models will be followed, the timeline, costs, and other details of getting to the output. In this case, we will follow a product development map that is detailed elsewhere and attached to this business plan. Finally, the *feedback* will tell us when and what form to use to measure the output, what to measure during processing, providing inputs, and following conditions. In this project, the key criteria for measuring *process* success will include time to market and cost to develop. *Input* measurement will include evaluating the leadership of the knowledge experts, the quality of the data provided, and the wisdom with which the funds are used. The *output* and *consequences* will be measured in terms of profitability and contribution to the viability of the company.

This entire description is part of knowledge creation that enhances the business planning effort. It creates the knowledge that others need to make the business successful. It communicates it an operational way like no other way.

If the knowledge to be created is truly new, think of using the Language of Work proforma to assemble the data in an orderly, systematic way. It is an

KNOWLEDGE CREATION

Business Planning Example

Goal: To commercialize scrubber toxic waste technology and sell its products (process & reports).

	Input	Conditions	Process Elements	Output	Consequences	Feedback
BUSINESS OPPORTUNITY	• Technology Specifications • 3-Level Specs. • Other Similar Technologies • Legal Department Patent Office Rules • Cost • Discovery-to Commercial Plan	• Patent Laws • Commercial Product Guidelines • Competition	See Attached Product Development Map	• Scrubber Toxic Waste Emulsion Process • 3-Level Toxic Waste Analytic Report	• Profit of $12M by 2001 • New Market Penetration: 15% • Risk Management of Less Than 10% Profit	• Timeline to Market • Budget • Knowledge Consultant • Development Schedule • Profitability • Viability Index
RESOURCES	• Engineering • Scientists • Legal Department • Budget Department • Marketing Department • 3-Level Consultant • Client Site	• Patent Office • Legal Dept. • Commercial Product Guidelines • Waste Mgmt. Institute • Association of Toxicologists	Project Planning and Management Information Technology Research and Development	NOT NEEDED	NOT NEEDED	• Project Management • Senior Management Council • Master Schedule (SAP) • Viability Index • Engineer • Science

Figure 4.8. Example of Knowledge Creation for a Business Opportunity.

excellent addition to one of the several creativity, brainstorming, or innovation processes currently available to performance consultants.

Solving Knowledge Problems

Solving knowledge problems, as difficult as they may be, are greatly aided by the use of the proforma. For instance, they can be used to solve performance needs and opportunities. The following is a typical case.

A quality improvement team was charged with devising a way for planning future work while also planning career development opportunities for employees within a performance review system. As shown in Figure 4.9, using the proforma the team created a matrix. On the horizontal axis you see the six-element proforma. On the vertical axis of the matrix you will find three headings: "What Exists," "What Should Exist," and "Solutions."

• *What exists* includes all information that relates to inputs, conditions, process element, outputs, consequences, and feedback for what currently exists in the business environment relevant to a performance need. The current situation described is a performance review program between a manager and worker that centers on a review of past job accomplishments over the past six to twelve months. By reading the information across the matrix, you can get a clear picture of what the current performance situation is. For a problem-solving team, having a clear idea of what currently exists is paramount to determining what should exist.

The value of this compilation of data lies in creating a common "performance" picture for the entire group. This picture and the way it is composed is similar to that of describing any as-is core process. Imagine a room full of cartoon people, each with a balloon figure over his or her head capturing what they think they know about a problem being analyzed. Although there is some duplication, there are also some unique bits of data. Now imagine these cartoon characters with a single, common unified view of the problem. Using a common paradigm—the proforma—to deposit thoughts and facts enhances communication, understanding, solution, and eventually commitment. As we often say in working with others, it provides the scaffolding of performance upon which we can build understanding and solution. The next step is just as critical to reaching that understanding and solution of knowledge processes.

• *What should exist* includes all information that relates to inputs, conditions, process element, outputs, consequences, and feedback for what should exist in the ideal situation to meet the desired business need. According to the information entered into the various categories of the work matrix in Figure 4.9, the new output would have two new features: (1) a performance plan for the next six to twelve months, and (2) a direct tie between responsibilities covered in performance review and the worker's current job descriptions, other jobs, and career development opportunities. Related changes, if any, are specified for inputs, conditions, process, consequences, and feedback as they relate to the new desired outputs. Note that the outputs are descriptions of desired character-

PROJECT: Work Planning and Development

	Input	Conditions	Process	Output	Consequences	Feedback
WHAT EXISTS	• Existing job descriptions • Job task list of past performance • Interview with others who know of worker's performance	• Schedule for review • Beginning of employment/six months/tied to salary review, etc. • Documentation	• Worker & manager use "Performance Review" Form	• Completed "Employee Review Program" Booklet • Review of past (six to twelve month) performance	• Worker understands past performance and why some opportunities were not feasible • Supervisor understands past performance achieved and reasons why opportunities for others were not possible	• Provide past performance reviews on specific tasks related to each accountability from supervisor and others • Job satisfaction in general • Periodic progress discussions during the year on current performance
WHAT SHOULD EXIST	• Projection of job task needs • Career development objectives	• Career development opportunities	• Need to reflect "Performance Plan" for next six months • Need to tie the job responsibilities to those in job description	• Peformance plan for next six to twelve months • Career development opportunities that are tied to specific job responsibilities of a new job description	• Understand areas for future improvement in present job • Understand what job responsibilities to work on for career development • Understand the relationship of their job responsibilities to other jobs they work with, for, or might grow toward	• Periodic progress discussions during the year on career development • End-of-the-year assessment of career development progress
SOLUTIONS	• Career Day: "Job Resilience" • Career Book • "Job Lunch"	• NONE	• Mgr and associates discuss future performance plan for specific responsibilities tied to current job description • They list new job accountabilities and how to achieve them	• Expansion of the existing form to include a plan for the next six to twelve months for current job responsibilities • A new section of the plan that has (a) new job responsibilities to work on, (b) specification of what job the responsibility relates to, and (c) plan for achieving the responsibility over next six to twelve months	• Understand areas for future improvement in present job • Understand what job responsibilities to work on for career development • Understand the relationship of their job responsibilities to other jobs they work with, for, or might grow toward	• Provide past performance reviews on specific tasks related to each accountability from supervisor and others • Job satisfaction in general • Periodic progress discussions during the year on current performance

Figure 4.9. Problem-Solving Matrix.

istics. This is because we do not know the form the output solution will take, so we describe its desired characteristics. By contrast, the outputs under "what exists" are very specific to what does exist. When a group involved in a problem situation describes all the elements for "what should exist," they have a clear idea of what the goal is.

When a problem-solving team has worked through "what exists" and "what should exist," the members have a clear picture of the current situation and the ideal situation. Specifications such as these are known as "performance discrepancies" (opportunities) and present a clear picture of what must be solved. What remains is then to arrive at a solution.

• *Solutions* represent what will be done to effect the change to a performance improvement from "what exists" to "what should exist." In this context, a solution is not just a single answer to "the problem"; it is a detailed explanation of what needs to be changed in one or more of the six work elements of the proforma. In the usual problem-solving situation, the solution to most people is the new output. In the example illustrated here, the solution is also envisioned as the new form. However, in the proforma view the solution is not just output. Rather, solution is what changes are needed in related process elements, inputs, conditions, feedback, and consequences that produce or result from the output. It is a variety of solutions. For example, the career development opportunities output as part of the solution in Figure 4.9 calls for additional inputs. Other solutions are called for in conditions, process, consequences, and feedback. The solution is all these solutions for various work elements together.

The manner in which a performance matrix is developed by a group is rather straightforward. A person acting as a facilitator guides the group in its analysis by directing attention first to the "what exists" definition of performance. The order of analysis is the same as already suggested up to this point—outputs, inputs, conditions, consequences, process elements, and feedback. Having painted the current state of performance, the group then defines the future state (what should exist) in the prescribed order of six performance elements in a proforma. Finally, the group analyzes for solutions between the existing and to-be states, and again in the preferred order of analysis for a proforma.

You can see that the matrix model of problem solving provides structure to group (and individual) problem-solving discussions. It also requires full exploration of all aspects of what exists, should exist, and the solution itself. When the matrix information is recorded on a whiteboard and used to focus data gathering, problem solving, and decision making, the group typically stays on course, rather than straying into random discussions. For knowledge process solution finding, the performance matrix is very effective and efficient.

Knowledge Transfer

Modern business requires enormous transfer of knowledge. This is especially true in the computer, information technology, scientific, financial, and many other businesses. Davenport and Prusak suggest in their book, *Working Knowl-*

edge (1998), that knowledge transfer involves transmission, absorption, and use of knowledge to establish behavior. Furthermore, they say, "People can't share knowledge if they don't speak a common language." While their model for how this is done suggests many other factors, such as common culture, the proforma as a definition of what constitutes performance (knowledge in this instance) is an added tool to help achieve knowledge transfer.

Some knowledge transfer occurs formally in training and orientation. Job aids, documentation, information technology, and electronic support systems all help transfer of knowledge. Some transfer occurs informally through experience transferred from mentors or coaches, managers and supervisors to employees, worker to worker, and programs like Ride-Along, where junior staff travel with senior staff to learn how to sell, service, problem solve, and so on. Our interests here, however, are two: (1) developing systematic, replicable ways in business to communicate knowledge informally and (2) codifying, packaging, and transferring knowledge into a product or service for others. Examples of the first would include communicating what your work is to someone else, explaining a procedure to someone, and general communication within and between work groups. An example of the second, a knowledge product, might be a book, software, or a patented technology. A knowledge service would generally include consulting or teaching and training.

An example of informal communication would be my need to explain my job to you because you and I are going to work on a project together. To accomplish this, I would use my job model (from Chapter 5) to explain my outputs, inputs, conditions, consequences, process, and feedback. I can put this in the context of common outputs you might be familiar with, as well as how our jobs interrelate. This would be a transfer of my knowledge about my work to you. I would furthermore want to check on whether you absorbed the knowledge and to what extent (for example, by asking you questions about my inputs, conditions, and so on). In cases in which the knowledge is not already structured in the proforma model, I can simply translate my knowledge into the six elements of work as I describe and we talk about the knowledge. Thus, if I needed to explain how to use a software application, I can explain the outputs you can produce from it, the inputs you will use, the conditions to be adhered to, the consequences you can expect to achieve, the process of using the software for various outputs (words, visuals, tables), and provide feedback as needed. From this overview, I can cascade to other levels of knowledge transfer, using the proforma as appropriate.

In a final example, the proforma was used to develop new products. A client organization had consulted with financial firms and had accumulated a great deal of knowledge through their consulting work. As part of the strategic plan, the firm needed to diversify from pure consulting into offering products for consumption. They needed a way to transfer the knowledge accumulated through consulting into purchasable products. In this case, they used the proforma to develop clarity on the knowledge to be transferred, that is, by determining the output or the deliverable, they have then been able to itemize the specific inputs required to create the output. They have mapped the process element they must follow, which is different from merely consulting, because they must prototype, beta test, price per piece, and develop the entire packaging and marketing scheme. They have to identify formally the conditions that affect them. They have identified the consequences in terms of profitability, viability of the company in the future, and reduction of travel for consultants. Feedback will come from measuring how well the inputs were used, the process element was followed, and the consequences achieved. As a result of following this model for planning, the team decided it needed to obtain more feedback from customers and provide a bonus if the aggressive deadlines were met and a quality product hit the marketplace on time.

Now that you know how the core processes of a business can be defined using the proforma model, how can you define the jobs need to execute these core processes? Chapter 5 provides the answer.

Grey Bar: Core Process Level

Kathleen Whiteside
Partner, Performance International

Performance technologists are sometimes faced with the prospect of analyzing a core process. Often core processes are given to the industrial engineers or even information technology specialists to map; however, it is quite appropriate for performance technologists to lead the way when the issue is primarily a human one.

In one instance, the new manager of the market support department of a high-tech firm needed a methodology for

1. Orienting herself to the new department

2. Team building with old and new staff

3. Examining the reasons the department was not well regarded

Her goal was to improve the performance of the department, and she needed to do it quickly. She chose the Language of Work model as the way to meet her goals. Her front-end work, critical to the success of the project, was to share her goals and objectives with the department members. They were aware of the importance of the project, understood that changes would result, but also knew that this was not a cost-cutting effort. Their jobs, if they chose to keep them, were secure. What might change would be the content of the job, the focus of the department, or the process to be followed. The manager, her internal performance technologist, and two new people joined the current staff in what was planned to be four days of meetings spread out over three weeks.

After first acquainting the group with the Language of Work model, the group analyzed its core process. The core process parameters were defined as "new product release to market support plan." The team needed to create a database on each new product, including determining the repair and replacement strategy, training requirements for field engineers, as well as identifying parts numbers and several other codes needed to support a high-tech new product. New equipment could not be released for sale until the database was complete; yet sales and distribution complained that this group was holding them up because market support was "too slow." As the major steps in the process were posted on the whiteboard by a Performance International facilitator, the group discussed the details needed for total understanding. This meant that the new manager was brought up to speed quickly on historical issues and was oriented to the difficulties in the work itself. At the same time, the new staff was receiving a superb orientation to the job.

After mapping the core process, the group mapped the job of market support engineer. Although no one understood at the beginning of the exercise that the job was identical to the core process being performed, the job mapping showed this relationship quite clearly. Although some individuals specialized in certain product areas, in fact everyone in the group did the same work and followed the same process. This was revealing to the group members and beneficial to all. The barriers to quality performance were identified during the mapping, giving additional insight.

Using the process map as the focal point for discussions, the group then attacked the problem of its poor reputation. The manager recognized the complexity of the work they did and the barriers to performance. It became clear that they were dependent on several other sources for input in order to complete their jobs. Their suppliers did not always trust them, resisted answering questions, and contributed to the length of time the task took. However, looking at the core process as a group helped members to form several questions about their own work. They developed, on the spot, an assessment instrument to measure their customers' satisfaction with their service and even tested it on a friendly internal customer. By the end of the second day of facilitation, they had mapped their own process, identified potential areas for improvement, developed a data gathering plan, and built an implementation plan.

In the next two weeks, they interviewed thirty of their internal customers. One person agreed to tabulate the data and develop a report for the group. The report showed that there were actually two different kinds of customers: those who needed the data a long time in advance of product release and others who needed nothing until six weeks before product release. Neither had been satisfied with the work of the department because it was either too late or too incomplete. Once they had customer feedback, the group re-examined its core process map. The members determined that the core process could be divided into two major parts: "long lead" and "quick start." The long lead group included the training department, which needed to obtain enough information about the product to determine what kind of training to provide. The quick start departments needed much more detail, but did not need the data until a week before the product was released. By classifying their customers appropriately, the team made minor changes to the core process maps, showing two different outputs. These became their to-be process maps. Once their plan was implemented, the department was able to meet customer needs, improve its reputation, and eliminate a great deal of worry. Finally, the team was able to meet the desired consequences of the position, core process(es), and work group. As an added bonus, the manager found that the team had been "built" using this core process: every person was comfortable with each of the others, personalities were able to emerge, and differences in opinion were treated as such and not as the beginning of a turf battle. The department was able to meet its customers' needs, which then satisfied the needs of the business unit and all the individual players.

CHAPTER 5

The Work Behavior of Individuals

Work by Whom?

There is an old adage that goes, "Where the rubber meets the road!" At the *individual* performance level of business is where the rubber meets the road. Here the individual's job must be translated from *what* (business unit) the business wants of each individual relative to *how* (core processes) the work is supposed to be done *by whom*. Any vagueness, short-sightedness, or inability to make sure the individual clearly understands what to do will cause a multitude of problems that could have been avoided. The challenge for the performance consultant is how to make sure everyone understands his or her role and what to do, as well as how to measure and improve work on their own—"Quality is me!"

The individual is the "Work by whom?" level, which translates the core processes into action and accountability to the business unit. This level, along with core processes, forms the understanding of how to organize the work groups.

The individual level should be one of the easiest to learn and apply. Indeed, the Language of Work model is easiest to learn at the level of individuals—your job and those with whom you work. Once you understand the application to yourself and others, it is far easier to see the potential for core processes, work groups, and the entire business unit. The individual level is a kind of shakedown period in which you learn, see what others do, and work out the subtleties (and there are several) to the proforma. Of course, the preferred order of development and alignment is first the business unit, then core processes, and then individual, but you can and will define individual jobs and apply various applications outside this preferred order for various reasons.

If there were one level of business in which large potential gains are possible, it is the individual level, which includes the jobs of executives, managers, and workers. The saying, "People are our most important resource" is true, even if business in general has not found particularly effective and efficient ways to utilize that resource. Unfortunately, individuals still seem to be viewed as just another "resource," like some piece of equipment. Lately, efforts such as integrated work teams and total quality management for continuous improvement have helped people feel more "important." Perhaps the problem is because businesses have not been able to:

1. Show the individual where he or she fits into the Business Sphere,

2. Provide reflective performance models that lead to true understanding and commitment to one's own work, and

3. Provide the means and motivation for individuals to undertake improvement on their own.

Of these three problems, the last is worthy of special mention. Individual initiative is, after all, a very powerful force for business improvement, if business leaders allow and encourage it. But few in management know how to encourage initiative in their facilitative role; and workers become discouraged when they have shown individual initiative, but others don't follow up or encourage their efforts. This chapter will show how to use the proforma to help restore initiative. Individuals will learn how to define, measure, and make improvements to their work. Individual effort is the heart and soul of initiative.

Football as an Illustration of Individual Performance

We previously defined both a business unit and the core process using a metaphor of playing football. It is also possible to define any position—an individual level of work—on the team. For our purposes, we will use the job of a quarterback. Figure 5.1 illustrates a quarterback's job using the proforma model.

The key *outputs* of the quarterback are to throw passes, give handoffs, run with the ball, call the play, and give the signal that begins a play.

To produce these outputs, the quarterback uses *inputs* such as information from the coach, preplanned plays, other players, a football, a playbook, as well as what is known as "reading the defense."

To do his processing and use the inputs, the quarterback attends to a number of *conditions.* Principal among these are the rules of game, in this case from the National Football League. Under other conditions, rules of the game could

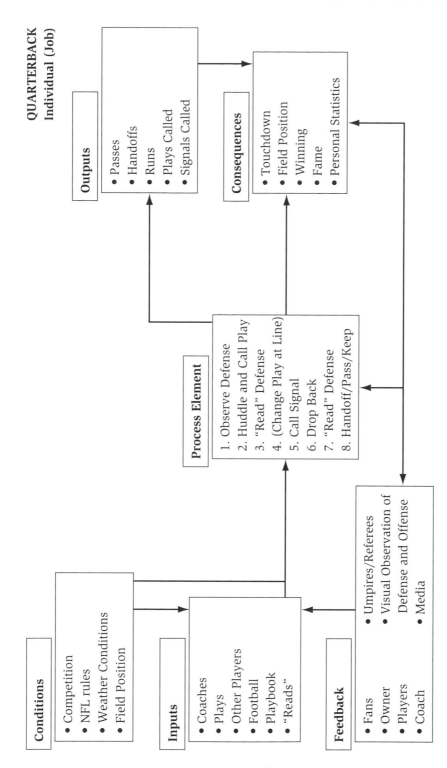

Figure 5.1. Work Map of an Individual: Quarterback's Job.

be slightly different. For example, when you play sandlot football, the players might agree that the quarterback cannot cross over the line of scrimmage where the play on the field starts from. Conditions thus determine the parameters for performance.

The quarterback's outputs result in *consequences*—in touchdowns, extra points, yardage gained, fame, winning, and personal statistics. These result from achieving outputs. It's a question of cause and effect—an important distinction.

The *process element* used is fairly standard, although variations are possible. Basically the process is to observe (read) the defense, huddle and call a play, read the defense again when at the line of scrimmage, change a play (if desired) at the line, call the signal, drop back, read the defense, and hand off, pass, or keep the ball. Of course, the quarterback could yell, and jump up and down, but this is up to him and not part of the process element of his job.

Finally, he uses a number of different kinds of *feedback* from fans, owners, players, coaches, umpires, and referees, from visual observation of the opposing team's defense and offense, and the media.

LEARNING TO USE THE PROFORMA ON THE INDIVIDUAL LEVEL

The same proforma used at other performance levels of a business and core process can be used in defining your own job. Some additions will enhance use at the individual level for a variety of training and other performance improvement and implementation needs. There are also many ways to use the proforma in implementing individual work.

When workers and managers want to learn how to apply the proforma, it makes sense for them to focus on their own work—what they as individuals do and how they do it. The job model, as we know it, is a particularly useful tool for helping workers and managers look closely at their current work and analyze future changes in their jobs. In this way, they can detect weaknesses in their understanding and make improvements without having to rely totally on management. Also, managers can know precisely what to look for to help make improvements as an output of their own jobs.

The following exercise will exemplify how to introduce the proforma into an organization.

An Exercise in Job Modeling

To introduce you to the use of the proforma for the individual, you will define your present job and compare it with a generic job, a proposal writer. A person in this position writes the documents used by an engineering company to communicate with a potential client the nature, scope, and cost for a proposed project, such as engineering designs (or any of the other major outputs of the business). For now, we will simplify the job model. Later, we will show a model of a more complex job.

Here's the exercise: On the right side of a piece of blank paper, list all the *outputs* that you produce in your present job. Outputs include various services, products, and knowledge. (You may wish to refer to Figure 1.7, the proforma job aid, for the definitions of terms used here.) Here is one helpful approach: Imagine that you had to carry or deliver your outputs to someone else. Label what they would look like. State them in the past tense, as if you had already delivered the output. For example, the outputs for the proposal writer would include the written technical proposal, cost proposal documented, oral presentation assisted, and qualification descriptions documented. These outputs would be written to the right of the job title.

Another useful approach for determining outputs is to focus on the customer. Think of who your customers are. Then ask, "What it is that they need, want, or expect from me in the form of a product, a service, or knowledge?" For internal clients, these outputs are typically things they need to do their own job. For example, an engineer would need the output of the proposal writing (for example, the cost figures on project items) to do his or her job as an engineer.

The most accurate and relevant source for your job outputs and any other work element will be the defined core processes of the business. The core processes are the "how" of work, and individual jobs are part of the "how." Unfortunately, many businesses have not defined their core processes, but have allowed the individuals they have hired to define core processes in a loose way to achieve business ends. Or, individual's jobs are defined on the basis of their "roles" in the work group. However, that is a reverse-order analysis, as work groups are best defined *last* to assist the workers to get their job done. Later in this chapter, a method will be proposed to convert defined core process maps to job models, thus achieving the proper sequence.

Now, let's return to the personal job model exercise. List to the far left of your job outputs any of the *inputs* you are provided or must obtain to do your job. Inputs typically include client needs, people, ideas, equipment, facilities, funds, and information. One convenient way to identify inputs is to think of those inputs that trigger your work, such as a client request, as compared to those that are resources, such as other workers, management, equipment, reports, and so forth. Another convenient way to identify all the inputs is to take one output at a time and identify its inputs. Some outputs will share the same inputs. Only define those that would not otherwise be assumed to exist. For example, a computer could be assumed to exist for the proposal writer position. However, it would be necessary to list inputs for this position such as client requests (RFP), proposal manager, client records, and client contact.

Next, list the *conditions* that would have an impact on your use of the inputs, *processes* you employ to turn your inputs into outputs, and the *feedback* you receive. Write your conditions in the upper left corner of your page. Conditions are the factors that influence the use of inputs, execution of process elements, and use of feedback. Fundamentally, you cannot change conditions. Rules, company policies, and government regulations are examples. For the proposal writer, conditions typically include business policies, government regulations, perhaps a proposal-writing style manual, and competition. Competition in the example of the proposal writer would influence inputs like pricing and methods for doing things to be suggested in the proposal.

As a point of practical consideration, restrict conditions to those that you must be directly concerned with in the execution of your job. Specify what is practical and needed, rather than identifying every possible condition. Conditions are not reasons why things are not being done. There may be reasons, but they're not the concern during job modeling, but during job evaluation. This distinction will be discussed more in Chapters 8 and 9, where such business conditions are accounted for in the Language of Work model.

Next, make a list of the *consequences* that result from your producing your outputs under the prevailing conditions and inputs. Remember that consequences are the positive effects an output has on a person, product, service, or situation. You can easily identify your consequences by asking the following questions: (1) What does your output do for your business and others? (2) How do you feel about what you produce? The answers to both questions are your consequences. For now, list your consequences for each output of your job in the lower right portion of your page or on a separate sheet.

You will also want to identify which outputs help achieve which consequences. For example, every one of the proposal writer's outputs would contribute to customer satisfaction. Make sure your list includes only consequences and not outputs. Also, contrary to what may happen to us in real life when it comes to consequences, they should be stated in positive terms for job models. Job models promote clarity and expectations. Later in this chapter we judge to what extent the consequences are positive or negative. Remember that consequences result from the outputs you have produced. Therefore, do not agree to consequences that you cannot directly influence—otherwise someone may make you accountable when you cannot be.

Proposal writers typically achieve consequences related to client satisfaction, the sense of "winning" new work, and the pleasure of working with others in a team relationship. Whenever you hear individuals complain about their work, you can bet that they are complaining about the lack of positive consequences. By attending to inputs, process, conditions, and feedback, you can change negative experiences to positive consequences. This "attending to" different elements of the proforma to produce positive consequences is but one of the many benefits of knowing and using a commonly applied model of performance such as the Language of Work model.

One final point about consequences. You may be wondering why consequences are not defined with and after outputs. This can be done, but it is better to wait until after outputs, inputs, and conditions have been specified because you need to know the direction (outputs), what resources (inputs) are available, and what controls (conditions) will have an impact on the consequences. When defined with these work elements in mind, the consequences are more realistic and achievable. Consequences are therefore specified immediately following outputs, inputs, and conditions. Process element and feedback are specified after consequences. You won't be held accountable if you do otherwise, but it is a useful procedure.

The fifth element of a job model is its *process elements,* in the form of a series of steps defined for each separate output. The process element is limited to only those things done by that position and does not usually include all the steps of the core process from which it is derived. Many of these steps belong to other jobs. For example, if the core process for constructing oral presentations is a thirteen–step process, and the proposal writer completes three of these steps, then only those three steps would be included in the job model. This is illustrated by the proposal writer completing an overview for the presentation team on the content of the written proposal, answering questions, and reviewing presentation content and visuals against the written proposal. This is in contrast to her process element for the written proposal output itself. In this case, the proposal writer might have almost complete responsibility. Other process elements would have to be included for the other outputs of this job.

The process element for an individual job is composed of a series of mini-deliverables sequenced in linear or branching modes as needed. Each step in the process element begins with an action verb that connotes the deliverable, for example, review, develop, write, critique, and complete a proposal.

Another feature of process elements is that each process is triggered by an input and uses one or more of the various inputs. The trigger for a written proposal is the client's formal request for proposal. During the use of process elements, project managers (as an input) and others may be involved and are defined in the process element. Take any one or more of your own job outputs and write the process element to each.

We have just about finished your job model. The only piece remaining is *feedback.* In one sense, feedback completes the work cycle and in another it is an integral part of the activity—processing, use of inputs, following conditions—that is involved before completing the output. The former sense is a response to outputs that lets us know whether things have been done right, for example, the positive, negative, or neutral reaction from your client when you deliver your output. The other kind of feedback happens while we are processing, using inputs, and attending to conditions. An example of this kind of feedback would be information your manager gives you during processing to improve or adjust for a better output. Some typical examples of feedback from the proposal writer job model needed during processing include responses from the client, the proposal manager, and other team members. Feedback after the proposal is completed would come from clients, a formal review process (that is, debriefing), engineers, and so forth. In the space at the bottom of your job model, or on another page, list the forms of feedback you currently receive and would like to receive.

For individuals, feedback is perhaps the single most neglected of the six elements of work. Nearly everyone says there is not enough feedback.

Feedback can be freely given, not so freely given, sought after, or neglected. When freely given and freely received, it is usually perceived as constructive and helps produce a better output and set of positive consequences. When not so freely given, confusion can abound as to whether the process is being used correctly, whether the output is right, and whether consequences are being reinforced. When feedback is sought, it often indicates that the individual is hungry to be reinforced, even when process elements, output, and consequences are perhaps perfect. To neglect feedback is sheer lack of knowledge about what is and what makes work efficient and effective. Feedback must be planned for and attended to on a continuous basis if it is to produce positive results for individuals and teams.

Now that you have completed this exercise, you should have a first draft of your job map and a better idea of how to define individual work by using the proforma of the Language of Work. Share your job model with someone else to see what he or she thinks. In particular, ask for any points of clarity and incorporate changes where needed. The following section describes additional details on the use and definition of job models.

DEFINING JOBS TO CORE PROCESSES

There is little question that defining jobs in business has been rather random and inconsistent. Generally speaking, business has formed work groups, hired managers, and set them to the task of defining work needs and selecting the people to complete that work. Individuals may have defined their work more than the very business that hired them. The fundamental question is, "Do individuals drive core processes, or do the core processes drive the individuals?" The former is more likely true. The Language of Work model changes this by fully aligning work from business unit, through core processes, by individuals, and into work groups. The lack of work alignment throughout the business is difficult to recognize unless core processes are compared to jobs that should be designed to achieve them. We can, of course, define job models without having defined core processes and use the models for job role clarification, showing relationships between jobs, performance reviews, and the like. This will result in significant performance improvement, but to achieve true alignment to the core processes, the core processes need to be defined first and the jobs based on these definitions.

Figure 5.2 is the sample engineering design process that was used in Chapter 4 to illustrate the business core process level of the business sphere. Three job titles have been specified to the process element to illustrate how one converts core process level definitions of work to job level definitions of work—conversion of the *how* of work to the *by whom* of work.

Because core processes delineate how the business intends in the task (versus the organization) sense to achieve its business outputs, it follows that jobs should be structured to carry out these core processes. If there is no justification for a job within the core processes, the job should not exist.

In looking at a defined core process, there are initially two kinds of jobs that are needed; other jobs will be needed and defined later. The first is technical or professional, and these are the must-have jobs. The second kind of job is also required, but will support the work, rather than directly do it. It is true that second-level jobs do work, but fundamentally they support the first-level jobs. Having made such a distinction, we must avoid any notion that one type of job is somehow superior to any other. Those who like to boast that they are part of the profit center, versus overhead, only serve their own egos to the detriment of others who make their work possible. Any attitude that technical and professional jobs are somehow superior to support jobs is but an example of work noise.

In addition to technical and support jobs, there are other types of jobs best labeled facilitative and executive. These jobs do not manifest themselves directly in core processes, although they are related by function to the core processes. Rather, they are allied to and determined in relation to work group mapping—the subject of Chapter 6. We will deal with these types of jobs there. The four types of jobs are listed below, for easy reference.

- Technical or professional
- Support
- Facilitative
- Executive

For illustrative purposes, three professional/technical jobs are identified at the top of Figure 5.2. These jobs can be described in accordance with specific steps of the process elements in the core process of the model. In the sample engineering design firm's core process, the jobs we identified of a technical or professional nature were:

Figure 5.2. Converting Core Processes to Jobs.

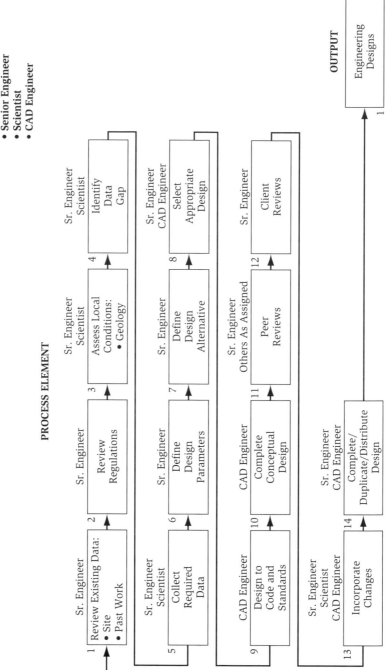

PROCESS ELEMENT

CONVERSION:
Engineering Design Process To:
• **Senior Engineer**
• **Scientist**
• **CAD Engineer**

OUTPUT

Engineering Designs

- Senior engineer
- Scientist
- CAD (computer-aided design) engineer

As a performance consultant who is working with management to define its business, your essential task in converting core processes to jobs is to facilitate how it is best technically to divide up the work. We will assume you and management have an understanding of how much is a reasonable workload; using the proforma will make the task easier by showing the exact steps of the work. For example, as we look at the core process in Figure 5.2, technically the steps can be the overall responsibility of one person, aided by two other jobs that involve specialization. Thus, a senior engineer takes the engineering design from beginning to end, and he or she will be assisted by the technical expertise of scientists (for example, geologists or chemists) and CAD engineers. The process element steps were divided and/or shared in the following way:

Step	Senior Engineer	Scientist	CAD Engineer
1	X		
2	X		
3	X	X	
4	X	X	
5	X	X	
6	X		
7	X		
8	X		X
9			X
10			X
11	X		
12	X		
13	X	X	X
14	X		X

Close inspection of Figure 5.2 will reveal why the particular step has been assigned to each individual job. While some knowledge of engineering design may be necessary to fully understand why particular steps are assigned as they are, in general it is not difficult to see why each position would be responsible for a particular step or share the function with another position.

Using this methodology, how can we build a job model for the senior engineer (or any other position)? In answer, we need to look at all defined core processes and make assignments of the work to named (or to be assigned) positions. Thus, our senior engineer might be assigned outputs from the following core processes of the business:

Assigned Senior Engineer Output	From the Core Process
Engineering Designs	Engineering Design
Scientist Data Reviewed	Scientist
Bid Package Developed	Construction
Associates Developed	Management
Project Planned	Project Management
Cost Estimates & Schedules Developed	Project Management
Peer Reviews	Project Management

In Figure 5.3 you will find the process elements of the job model for a senior engineer in the business case example, along with the inputs and conditions that have been defined for this job. If you compare the core process steps in Figure 5.2 with the job model in Figure 5.3 for the senior engineer, you will see a direct relationship between *job process elements* and the engineering design *core process*. Where the position interacts with another, a coordination (as in Steps 3 and 7 of the senior engineer job) step has been specified. Where one position is an input, the input becomes one of the inputs to the job model, either by job name or information. For the senior engineer, the scientist provides inputs to technology, client need, etc.

Note that the job model for a senior engineer is not exclusively drawn from the engineering design core process. Other outputs—and therefore other process elements—are drawn from other core processes. For example, the process element for the output "bid package" was drawn from the core process of "construction" (not shown). Many jobs derive their definitions from a variety of core processes. Of course, there are jobs that exclusively derive from one fundamental core process. For example, the job model of the CAD engineer would be such a position. All jobs have to be linked to core processes that in turn support (and align to) the business unit.

Once the outputs and their process steps have been drawn from core processes to build technical/professional jobs, their inputs, conditions, consequences, and feedback need to be specified. Each is derived in a similar manner. Let's look at inputs for the senior engineer job.

The inputs from related core processes evolve into inputs for a job. Thus, as you look at the inputs in the senior engineer job, you can see their relationship to the core process inputs. Some of the inputs come from the engineering design core process, and others would come from other core processes not shown. This is one of the fundamental ways we align the work elements of jobs with core processes, or any other work element for that matter. As shown in Figure 5.3c, the specifications for consequences and feedback have been given. These were derived the same as inputs—by aligning them with core processes. Conditions are shown on Figures 5.3a and 5.3b.

One of the key differences between a core process map and a job model is especially important to understand. The level of detail specified in a job model is often deeper than the detail for the core processes from which it is derived. This is generally because the steps of a core process that are assigned to an individual often need to be broken down into more meaningful detail in order to communicate them to those who fill the position. And job models show the exact point at which one job model interacts with another. For example, in Step 4 of the engineering design core process (Figure 5.2), we may want to know what a job holder does to "identify data gap" and how that gap is to be expressed. Thus, we could add substeps to the job model. Measuring current conditions may also involve several steps, whereas projecting future conditions may require only a few steps. We would also have to determine who would collect the information on current conditions (the scientist?) and who would project the future data (the engineer?). Clarification should be included in the models of any impacted jobs and at points at which handoffs occur.

Following identification of technical and professional jobs one then determines the support position(s) required. These second-level jobs come from: (1) the need to have the technical and professional workers devote as much time to their areas of expertise as possible, and (2) the recognition that others are capable of doing some of the tasks that the professional or technical worker can do. It reminds one of the former reluctance of doctors to give paraprofessionals the simple tasks of administering shots and IVs. When one goes beyond the fear of losing control and position, any number of process element steps can be given to others.

Support jobs are basically of two types. The first are those that *directly* support the technical or professional jobs in the accomplishment of the core processes. These used to be greater in number, but with the advent of the computer, many of the outputs of these positions were taken on directly by the technical and professional workers. I once relied heavily on graphics and clerical support jobs as a professional developing and implementing training programs and materials. With the availability of my first computer, I didn't need graphics and secretarial support the way I once did. When I received by second computer, even spell-checking became my function. Especially with downsizing in the 1990s, even more support positions were eliminated. In the sample engineering design core process illustrated here, it was determined that no support jobs of any kind were needed.

Figure 5.3a. As-Is Job Model for Senior Engineer.

As-Is Job Model

JOB TITLE: Sr. Engineer

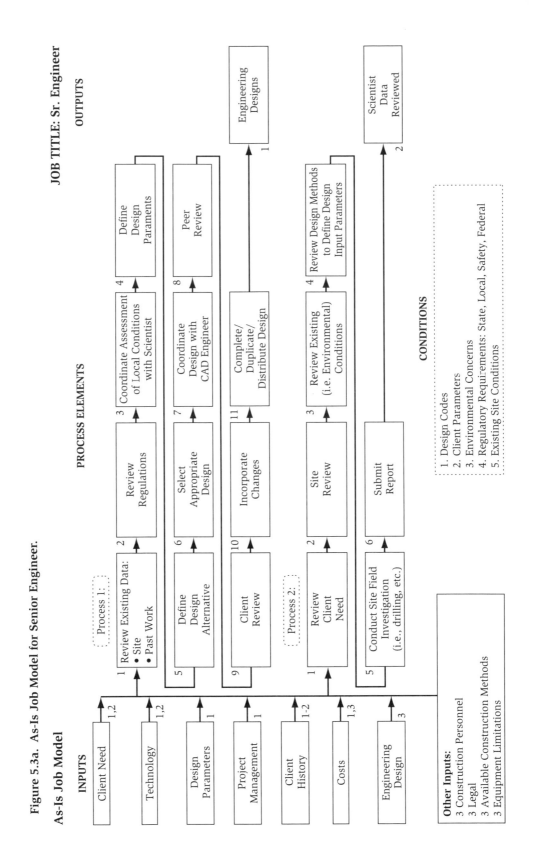

As-Is Job Model

JOB TITLE: Sr. Engineer

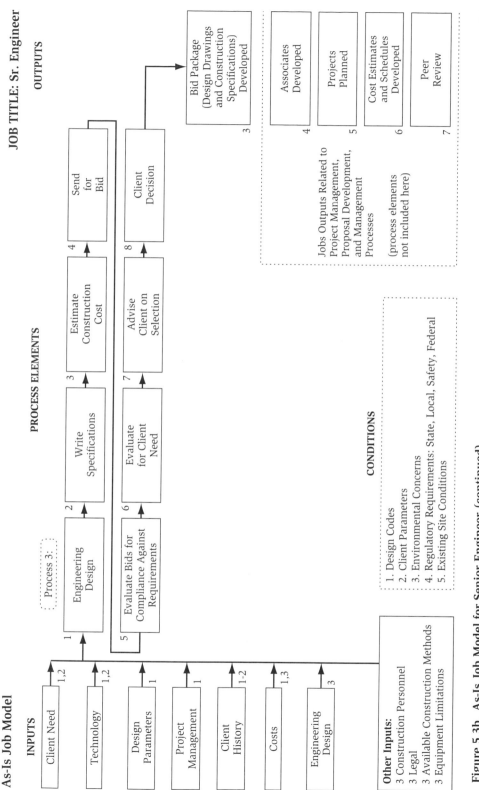

Figure 5.3b. As-Is Job Model for Senior Engineer (continued).

As-Is Job Model   **JOB TITLE: Sr. Engineer**

CONSEQUENCES

1. Cost-effective engineering designs (Outputs 1, 2, 3, 5, 6)
2. Positive community relations (Outputs 1, 2)
3. Customer satisfaction (Outputs 1–7)
4. Safety (Outputs 1, 2, 7)
5. Positive community relation (Outputs 1, 4, 5, 7)
6. Future work (Outputs 1, 4, 5, 6)

FEEDBACK

DURING	AFTER
1. Clients	1. Client satisfaction survey
2. Schedules	2. Repeat business
3. Auditors	3. Employees
4. Employees, i.e., scientists, CAD engineers, etc.	4. Senior management
5. Regulators, i.e., city planners, EPA	5. Project management
6. Peer review	

Figure 5.3c. As-Is Job Model for Senior Engineer (continued).

The second type of support jobs is still quite prevalent and has experienced decline to a lesser degree. These jobs support the business as a whole, rather than being tied to specific core processes. Human resources, financial, legal, and similar work groups contain job positions typical of this kind of support. An internal performance consultant job is one such example of "corporate" support. These jobs are best determined and defined once the core processes and their jobs have been identified and defined. A discussion of these will be included in Chapter 6 on work groups. A discussion of jobs that grow out of work support will be included in Chapter 8.

The third level of jobs is facilitative, a better connotation than "administrative." Facilitative jobs typically include those of supervisors and managers. These are the "heads" of work groups of various sorts, including those arranged around professional or technical jobs, as well as those of various support groups. Engineering design, for instance, might have a manager or director who in turn reports to a vice president of engineering. Other supervisors might be needed as well. For example, project managers are typical supervisory personnel within an engineering function. The head of human resources would have a manager or director.

Finally, there are the executive level jobs. These are the president, chief executive officer, executive vice presidents, and so forth. These level-four positions, like level three, are also best defined in relation to work group mapping (Chapter 6) and relate as well to providing work support (Chapter 8).

THE JOB MODEL AS A JOB DESCRIPTION

The job model described and illustrated thus far has reflected only the six-element proforma. With the proforma as an anchor to modeling a job, other elements of performance can be added to make a more complete "job description." This information can be used in a number of useful ways to communicate and improve individual performance. As a performance consultant, you will find that this goes to the very heart of traditional change issues you have been called to deal with for years.

The job description used here will be far different from those most of us have experienced. Generally, we have found job descriptions of relatively little value. They have principally been used to value work to set salary ranges and meet legal requirements. They have not been of much use in defining work and really letting individuals know what their work is. And they are so static and hard to change that they soon become out-of-date. Most important, they really do not describe performance.

A job description should be capable of communicating and providing useful information:

- To model the individual performance expected in the job
- To identify and structure training and other performance improvement needs
- To know the exact accountabilities and responsibilities one is expected to achieve in support of business needs
- To relate jobs to one another
- To allow periodic review of performance
- To make goals such as "winning behaviors" operational
- To be capable of quick changes to work that reflect rapid changes in the business environment
- To meet other business needs

Job descriptions can be used for a variety of reasons:

- Assessment of skills and knowledge and identification of attributes for evaluating existing incumbents and hiring new personnel
- Reviewing job performance

Work can be modeled through using the proforma. The following are samples of some specific additions that can be attached to the job model to meet specific needs:

- Job narratives
- Job accountabilities
- Skills and knowledge
- Attributes
- Winning behaviors

Job Narrative

As shown in Figure 5.4, a job narrative is simply a way of summarizing a job model in the form of a narrative that links the six elements of the proforma together in a meaningful performance description. From our experience in designing job models for several companies, especially during enterprise-wide changes such as the installation of SAP and ORACLE software, some individuals relate more to work narratives than to graphic models. This is understandable given the way different people perceive and best understand information, as shown by people's preferences for "right" and "left" brain thinking. A narrative often takes care of those who best assimilate information and operate from the right brain.

To build the narrative is a matter of listing or converting from the job model as follows:

1. List the outputs first, as these are the targets of the job.
2. List the inputs that will be used.
3. List the conditions that impact and influence the job position.
4. List the consequences.
5. Rather than listing all the steps of each process element, convert the processes to a sentence that connotes the action of the process in producing the output. Thus, for example, the output engineering design becomes "preparing engineering designs." Convert the action verb using an "-ing." The other outputs in the business case job model are converted as follows:

As-Is Job Model   **JOB TITLE: Sr. Engineer**
Job Narrative

This position is one of the important jobs that is part of Engineering. The principal accountabilities (**outputs**) of this position are:
1. Engineering designs
2. Scientist data reviewed
3. Bid packages developed
4. Associates developed
5. Projects planned
6. Cost estimates and schedules developed
7. Peer reviews

To achieve these outputs, the associate uses key **inputs**, including: client needs, technology, design parameters, project management, client history, costs, engineering design, construction personnel, legal, available construction methods, and equipment limitations.

Certain job conditions impact and influence how the position will function.
The **conditions** include:
1. Design codes
2. Client parameters
3. Environmental concerns
4. Regulatory requirements: State, local, safety, federal
5. Existing site conditions

The position must pay close attention to **consequences** that come through achievement of the outputs, including:
1. Cost-effective engineering designs
2. Positive community relations
3. Customer satisfaction
4. Safety
5. Positive community relations
6. Future work

In order to achieve the outputs and results, given the inputs under certain conditions, the position follows prescribed **processes** that include the following:
1. Developing engineering designs
2. Reviewing scientist data
3. Developing bid packages
4. Developing associates
5. Planning projects
6. Developing cost estimates and schedules
7. Conducting peer reviews

To aid the position, certain **feedback** is necessary. **While processing**, the position benefits from the feedback of clients, schedules, auditors, other employees, regulators, and peer reviews. **After** the **outputs** are completed, the position should seek **feedback** from client satisfaction surveys, repeat business, employees, senior management, and project management.

Figure 5.4. Job Narrative for a Senior Engineer.

Output	*Converted to*
Scientist Data Reviewed	Reviewing Scientist Data
Bid Package Developed	Developing Bid Packages
Associate Developed	Developing Associates
Projects Planned	Planning Projects
Cost Estimate & Schedule Developed	Developing Estimates & Schedules
Peer Review	Reviewing by Peers

> The details of these processes, if needed for use in something like performance appraisal, can be reviewed at any time in their graphic form on the job model.

6. List the feedback while processing, using inputs and following conditions; then give feedback after the outputs are completed.

Job Accountabilities

Job accountabilities or responsibilities, as they are also known, are designed as a shorthand list of the major work or performance targets an individual is to achieve. In traditional job descriptions, they became the primary focal points against which to define the scope of the job. The more in number or sophistication the accountabilities, the "tougher" the job must be and perhaps, the more it would pay. It is not unusual to see accountabilities inflated beyond the realities of the job. However, in job description using the proforma, this is all but impossible because of the source data on which the accountabilities are defined.

A job accountability, in the Language of Work model, is a combination of a job output and the appropriate consequences that it helps achieve. The accountabilities of the senior engineer illustrate the technique.

1. Produce effective engineering designs that meet the desired consequences of your position.

2. Review scientific data to achieve cost-effective engineering designs, produce positive community relations, meet customer satisfaction, and achieve safety standards.

3. Prepare bid packages in response to cost of design and customer satisfaction.

4. Develop associates to achieve customer satisfaction, promote positive community relations, and enhance the acquisition of future work.

5. Prepare project plans that assist in cost-effective engineering designs, customer satisfaction, positive community relations, and future work.

6. Develop cost estimates and schedules for cost-effective engineering

designs and customer satisfaction, and aid in acquisition of future work.

7. Conduct peer reviews that assure customer satisfaction, safety, and future work.

Recall that during job modeling we cross-referenced which outputs produced what consequences. This is the source data for job accountability. By matching consequences to individual output, we can determine accountability. There should be accountability for each job output. Thus, in our sample job, the output "design drawing" is matched to all six consequences of the job because it helps produce all six consequences.

To give other examples, the second accountability is a combination of four consequences (1 through 4) to its output; the third accountability is a combination of two consequences (1 and 3) to its output, and so on. Each of these accountabilities has the consequences listed in their entirety. The list of accountabilities of a position is based on the same formula of output to related consequence(s).

Skills and Knowledge

One of the most far-reaching benefits of using the Language of Work job modeling process is the way in which it helps identify skills and knowledge needed for a job. These accurate and careful listings can be used in a variety of ways. For one, they help identify training and other performance improvement opportunities. It aids job holders in learning what skills and knowledge they possess. From this, it is possible to identify needed skills and knowledge for job enrichment and/or advancement and business changes, such as caused by downsizing, enterprise-wide software installations, etc.

It is usually useful to identify both the skills and knowledge for a job. The differences between skills and knowledge are as follows:

- Skills are the abilities we need to possess and can learn to do a job.
- Knowledge is the background information useful in doing work and is necessary for using job skills.
- If a skill is needed, then there is related knowledge.
- One may need certain knowledge for a job, but not a related skill.

Skills and knowledge should be identified for four of the six elements of a job model: the process element, inputs, conditions, and feedback. We do not need to define skills and knowledge relative to outputs and consequences, as they are the results through use of the other four elements. Stated differently, we need skills and knowledge in process, inputs, conditions, and feedback to achieve the outputs and consequences.

From experience, we have found that the order in which skills and knowledge are identified should take a prescribed path. It is best to define the skills and knowledge for each process element first, prior to identifying those for inputs, conditions, and feedback. Starting with one of the others, especially inputs, tends to result in a "brain dump" wherein everyone in that position adds input—largely negative. They then translate what was said into skills and knowledge that really belong with process elements.

Typically, we define skills and knowledge in a group setting of exemplary job performers (and sometimes others). Then, following this session, the information that is defined is taken back into the work environment for further discussion, refinement, and validation. The skills and knowledge for the first two process elements of the senior engineer position are listed in Figure 5.5.

After identifying the necessary skills and knowledge for process elements, one can identify them for inputs, conditions, and feedback—in that order. The following rules apply to the definition of skills and jobs relative to job models:

1. Define process element skills and knowledge one process at a time.

2. Treat each process element separately, even if this means duplicating skills or knowledge. A complete list for each process is critical for later use in assessments, structuring training and other performance improvement opportunities, performance review, and so forth.

3. You may treat the process element as a whole, or review each step of the process.

4. Avoid listing every possibility for skill and knowledge. There are things that can be assumed to exist, for example, that a person can read.

5. Include for inputs the skills and knowledge needed to identify and deal with client requests or needs and resources.

6. For feedback, include skills and knowledge needed to seek what you are unsure of and to find answers.

Attributes

Attributes represent those strengths or talents that we ascribe to an individual. The person brings these strengths with him or her to the job. Because each job has its own needs, people perform best when matched to a job that requires use of these attributes; we also suffer anguish when our attributes don't match a job. Smart businesses match the right kind of people with the right kind of job when they are hired, or at least help people after they are hired to discover their attributes and help aim them in the right direction for their overall job welfare and the good of the business. Job models are an excellent source for determining attributes.

As-Is Job Model   **JOB TITLE: Sr. Engineer**

PROCESS ELEMENTS

PROCESS for Output 1: Engineering Design

Skills
- Identification of relevant data
- Knowing regulations
- Design alternatives
- Design practices
- Interaction skills with clients
- Construction cost and impact
- Selection of appropriate design

Knowledge
- Scientific knowledge of data
- Regulations
- Design processes
- Scientific theories/facts

PROCESS for Output 2: Scientist Data Reviewed

Skills
- Identification of client needs
- Identification of what is pertinent
- Report writing

Knowledge
- Design processes/methods
- Scientific theories/facts
- Field investigation techniques

Figure 5.5. Skills and Knowledge for Senior Engineer.

There are, quite naturally, a number of possible attributes for each job position. They include things like tolerance for change, detail orientation, sales style, attention to quality, accommodation of others, learning, teaching, and coaching style, adherence to time lines, and on and on. How to attach attributes to job models will be described shortly.

Winning Behaviors

With the emphasis today on maximizing client satisfaction, many businesses have adopted certain common, general behaviors that they would like their workforce to strive to reach. "Winning behaviors" is one way to label them.

These can be included in job descriptions and, to the extent desired, cross-referenced to outputs and consequences that will help actualize them. In this way, the individual knows what behavior in the job will help achieve the desired attribute. Management knows which job attributes contribute to the winning behavior and can encourage, as well as evaluate, employee attainment of them. Figure 5.6 is a sample of winning behaviors that can be attached to a job description.

Other additions to job descriptions can provide clarity and specific business needs. For example, the addition of competency statements, entry-level requirements, and so forth are highly useful.

MEASURING AS-IS JOBS FOR IMPROVEMENT

There are formal and informal ways to improve our own individual performance. We can take advantage of training, for example, or we can take it upon ourselves to find our own ways to improve. The informal way is self-motivating and our personal commitment to excellence. Unfortunately, business does not generally understand performance well enough to know how we could improve our own work. One of the many uses of a proforma is to show us how we can improve our own work. By using the proforma, we are better prepared to know how to define our jobs, measure, and then know where improvements are needed.

One of the realities of work is that workers and managers are generally reluctant to ask others for an evaluation of their performance. Much of this is due, of course, to the privacy with which we surround our work and personal worth. We do not really know what to ask someone else in order to measure our performance. We fear hearing a negative report or feel we can do nothing to change the behavior that caused the criticism. However, with a proforma of our work we have a framework for seeking information to measure our own personal effectiveness and efficiency. Why would we want to do this? The answer is threefold:

1. To know *what* to measure in our work so that we can identify areas needing improvement.

2. To take it upon ourselves to make our own improvements in what we do.

3. To make improvements and adjustments before someone else tells us we have to and uses that information for such things as salary and position changes—up, down, or out.

As-Is Job Model   **JOB TITLE: Sr. Designer**
                WINNING BEHAVIORS

---

1. Customer Satisfaction

Level 1:   Achieve customer satisfaction by exemplary work performance.
           Anticipates customers' needs and seeks ways to provide
              satisfactory solutions.

Level 2:   Viewed by customers as very knowledgeable in your work.
           Consistency in meeting customer needs.
           At times, exceeds customer needs.

Level 3:   Skills and knowledge need development to enhance meeting
              the expectations of customers.

Level 4:   Unacceptable work performance in meeting and resolving
              customer needs.

Figure 5.6. Sample Winning Behaviors.

So, what to measure? Where to begin? We first should look at our outputs (Define Australia first!) and consequences in concert with one another. We should ask our internal and external clients how satisfied (the consequence) they are with our outputs. Ask, for example, what they see as the quality and timeliness of our outputs. If there are problems, we should look for root causes and solutions in the other four work elements that produce output and consequence:

- How well are the inputs being provided?
- How clear are the conditions and how well are we attending to them?
- How good are the process elements and our skill and knowledge in completing the processes?
- How well is feedback being solicited and received?

These are all things we can do as individuals. If we take the time and effort and know what to look for, we can know what to measure. We can take it upon ourselves to make improvements. For example, if we find that an input is late, we open the communication lines with those who provide the input to see what can be done. If the process element is not right, we can suggest how to make it better. We can increase our skills and knowledge to perform better. If the conditions are not clear, we can seek clarification. If feedback is inadequate to motivate us or help in the processing of tasks, we can communicate with our management and seek more and better feedback. And if consequences are not what the client expects and do not give us personal satisfaction, we can work with management (and do certain things ourselves) to look at various work elements for improvement. When we have a proforma in common with others (colleagues and management), we have the means to make effective work communication possible and to seek help. To merely sit back, complain to another worker, or excuse problems as management's responsibility will do nothing except support "business as usual." In these times of quick change, are we prepared to be diligent in job resilience? If not, will we survive in our jobs or be left behind?

Let's look at three formal ways to measure job improvements that will serve basic needs of individuals in the business: job assessment, recognition of attributes, and performance review or appraisal. As a performance consultant or trainer, job assessment will aid you in designing training and other performance improvement opportunities. Recognition of attributes will help you recognize your capacity to do things, and performance review provides management with an ongoing way to facilitate employee development. Together they provide a continuous, ongoing stream of performance data to identify, improve, and maintain training and other performance improvement programs and services.

Job Assessment

A job assessment can easily be developed from a job model. The basis on which the assessment is built is the specification of skills and knowledge. Once the skills and knowledge have been identified, they can be categorized into competency areas, such as the model used in *The Successful Manager's Handbook* (1992), as well as company-developed competencies. The linking of job skills and knowledge to competencies provides a way to identify training needs for jobs. Off-the-shelf courses or development of internal performance improvement programs can fill these needs.

Once the competencies have been paired with the listed skills and knowledge, assessment questions can be generated. In order to provide some coherence to the assessment instrument, questions can be clustered into competency areas, regardless of the source (process element, input, and so on).

Finally, an assessment instrument can be created from the compiled questions and their related competencies. The performance consultant can interview people or distribute the instrument, using whatever anchors and scales are relevant. In this way it can be determined whether skills and knowledge are sufficient for job performance. If skills and knowledge deficiencies are found, then training and other performance improvement interventions can be implemented.

If skills and knowledge are sufficient, but performance is inadequate, then the job model can be used to identify the performance gap and determine what is causing it (for example, motivation, feedback, resource availability, and so on).

Attributes

The question is how to find the attributes required for each job. One of the common methods is to brainstorm what the job would seem to require. This works to a certain degree. We know, for example, that engineers need to be analytical, able to solve problems, plan, see detail, and so forth. But there is an easier way.

There exist some standardized measurement instruments that people can be given to identify attributes. These are usually administered in the hiring process so that those doing the interviewing can better judge whether the individual can do a particular job. Of course, this assumes that the administrator knows what the desired attributes are for a position. How might one know? We recommend that you define a job model, then use these instruments to test a number of exemplary performers in that particular job (model) and include their attributes in the job description. It is about as simple as that. Taken one step further, managers and supervisors of these positions can further validate the results through observation of people exhibiting the attributes in the performance of their work.

Also, rather than just stating a given attribute, attach it to particular work elements of the job. For example, the senior engineer uses "analytical skills [the attribute] in reviewing site data, in identifying data, and in developing design alternatives." This makes the attribute operational to the specific behavior of the job.

Performance Reviews

There is probably no single skill that befuddles a manager more than reviewing a worker's performance. Managers just don't seem to know how to do it and avoid it at all cost. I can personally recall a manager or two who simply announced to me (on the fly), "You're doing a good job!" What kind of performance evaluation is that? And yet, if a worker is ever to grow and to learn on the job, managers have to do adequate performance reviews. The following is an approach to performance review that I have successfully used many times in my role as a facilitator.

First, a good performance review has one basic prerequisite: a full job description or a well-defined job model. As we have seen, a good job description includes a job model, wherein the six elements of work are defined, and an accompanying narrative, a list of skills and knowledge, accountabilities, and perhaps other features. Most jobs have about five to seven major accountabilities.

When it comes time for a performance review, the employee and manager write a description of the extent to which accountabilities of the position have been achieved. Once these descriptions are completed, a detailed discussion follows, centering on the job model for the worker's job. Written descriptions and face-to-face talk between the worker and manager would center on answering these representative measures:

For Outputs. Were the outputs delivered to specifications, on time, and within budget?

For Consequences. Were standards of internal/external client satisfaction achieved from the outputs? When output standards were not achieved, was the client eventually satisfied? How do you feel about what you personally achieved? What would you like me, as your supervisor, to do to assure your continued success and growth?

Then, if there is a need to improve on outputs or consequences, do the following:

For Inputs. What sorts of inputs were provided, or not provided, to do your individual tasks in achieving this accountability?

For Conditions. What conditions changed or were not clear, thus affecting the successful completion of your tasks? Were means provided to compensate for these changes?

For Process Element. What breakdowns, if any, occurred in the process, thus affecting the achievement of outputs? What interrelationships with other departments affected the processing of tasks?

For Feedback. As your facilitator, did I provide progressive stages of feedback that helped you complete your tasks? Did others in the process provide you with the kind of feedback needed to complete your task adequately in terms of quality, cost, and timing?

The manager's part of the dialogue (a little stilted as presented here) might go something like this from Bob's manager, the senior engineer.

Manager: Bob, your performance over the past six months has been quite exemplary. I see that you had opportunity to complete examples of each of your six major outputs, as well as positive results in the consequences of your position. How do you feel about your work in any and all of these outputs and consequences, and are there any you would like to talk about in general?

One of the areas I have some concerns in and in which we might find some improvement is your output of developing bid packages. Did you have any similar concerns? Let's take a look at what went on in terms of bid packages over the past six months. I note that seven bid packages were prepared. Let's go through each of the basic elements of your work and see whether we can identify the problem areas and how to rectify these. Let's begin with inputs.

Were the inputs from the client, engineering design, construction, and others on time? Were the inputs of sufficient quality? If not, in what way were they lacking?

As far as conditions are concerned, were you and others adhering to, or did you see a need to change, any of the prescribed conditions to bid packages?

As far as the process for bid packages, let's look at each step and how well they were executed—and especially look at the involvement of other positions in relation to this process. Where, if anywhere, was there a breakdown in process? Do you feel there are areas in which skill and knowledge could be improved? How might this be done? Anything in the corporate training (or external) training you would like to take advantage of?

Finally, what sort of feedback was used during processing, in regard to inputs and related to conditions, that was good or needed to be improved? What feedback after the package was complete might have been useful to you?

The functionality of this approach to performance review is the structure and clarity it brings to both parties—especially the recipient. It removes a great deal of the anxiety and emotion associated with review and places it in a result, cause, and solution frame of reference. Quite often, performance reviews come across as "problems" the employee has, rather than what employees and circumstances have contributed to not getting things done the right way. Or where can the organization and management do a better job? A couple of examples will help clarify what this means in operation.

By concentrating on the inputs, one can identify what problems exist in the quality, quantity, timeliness, and cost of inputs before the individual receives them. As has been said, "Garbage in, garbage out." How could this be changed? One of the more useful suggestions I have given my employees is an idea derived from the practice known as Kaizen. One of the tenants of Kaizen is that, rather than waiting for inputs to our work, it may be better to go and get the input. This puts us in the position of making sure the input is a quality input before we actually get it. For example, in our case study the senior engineer might talk to vendors about a special piece of equipment needed prior to its use on his project. In that way the vendor will be able to find the most appropriate equipment rather than sending a stock item that is not as good.

A second area of performance review that is enhanced by the proforma is adherence to conditions. Sometimes the rules, regulations, and guidelines we establish for employees limit their performance to the overall good of the business. For example, senior engineers have to contend with design limitations, cost factors, and so forth. During performance review is a good time to explore where, when, and how these "rules" or conditions can be modified to the benefit of the overall project and the client. Is there room to bend a rule—a condition? Is there room for the senior engineer when preparing bid packages to bend the rule regarding certain pricing for certain clients? Performance reviews are good times to learn these rules. There are, of course, similar opportunities when performance reviews address processes and feedback.

When the six elements of the proforma are used for work understanding, the exchange between worker and manager is much more complete in terms of what work is and how it can be achieved. The proforma structure of a performance review gives more opportunity for growth, for learning what went right and what went wrong, and for determining how the job can be done better in the future. The information derived from these meaningful discussions is invaluable for trainers and performance consultants. An ongoing stream of information from management and employees is an excellent source for performance improvement opportunities.

CREATING TO-BE JOBS

As a performance consultant, one of the more significant ways you can help individuals and organizations make the transition to new or revised work is through the active use of job models. Changes in work needs are quite prevalent today because of reengineering, downsizing, and the introduction of enterprise-wide changes, such as new software systems. This section describes how to use the proforma at the individual level to aid in making major transitions of individual work needs.

As distinguished from as-is job models, to-be job models are definitions of individual work as it will be because of some kind of change in the business. The work elements remain the same, but the work information changes in one or more of the outputs and consequences; as a result the related inputs, conditions, process elements, and feedback also change. The importance of to-be job models is that they help us identify the performance gap between current and future jobs. The performance consultant can identify the appropriate interventions to fill this gap and measure to see that it has been filled.

Applications for to-be job models include reengineering, downsizing, and enterprise-wide change.

Reengineering

Reengineering is a business unit's look into what the business will do and how the work will be done. It is an attempt to become more client-centered in its activities. A case study, "Improving Organizational Performance" (1998) details the overall Language of Work approach to reengineering a business.

In reengineering a business, much initial attention focuses on who the clients are and their specific needs. A determination is made on how to better serve the clients. After client and client needs have been identified, a business unit map is developed to show "what" the business will be. Following this, a series of core process maps is delineated to agree on "how" the outputs and consequences will be achieved. Then these core process maps can be converted to job models and job descriptions. These job models are "to-be" jobs of the reengineered business. As performance consultants, we would not only help the business define itself at these various levels, but help each individual in the business understand the exact transition they would have to make. At its most fundamental level, this means helping individuals know their "as-is" job model in the current business and their "to-be" job model in the reengineered business. The difference between these is a performance gap that needs filling, and as performance consultants, it is our job to help fill the gap with the most appropriate and efficient interventions. It can, and often does, mean that jobs are being eliminated or changed significantly. The grey bar case at the end of this chapter is a typical reengineering example from my business partner.

Special Note: Regarding reengineering jobs, it has been our experience that when job modeling is used on jobs that will be completely done away with, two things occur. First, employees affected appreciate the way in which they learn that their jobs are going away. They participate in seeing how and why the job disappeared. Second, individuals learn what their skills and knowledge are in very specific terms. They can use this information to seek other positions within or outside their current organization. Wise companies use the data of as-is job models to help outplaced employees find employment that matches their skills, knowledge, aptitudes, and experience.

Downsizing

Downsizing is the business decision of reducing the workforce because of current or projected economic conditions that will negatively impact the future profit and survival of the business. Downsizing, for all its negative impact on the individual, is a reality due to the rise and fall of economic conditions, changes in consumer needs and wants, the global economy, and so forth. Job modeling can play a significant role in reallocating work.

At the heart of downsizing is the need of a business to decide how it will do output with fewer resources, or how to reallocate the work to do the same output with fewer employees. The problem is that businesses typically undertake downsizing by cutting out work on a percentage basis. We read in the news that XYZ Corporation will reduce its workforce by 15 percent. In the generic sense this speaks to the economics of the total workforce, but it doesn't address the future work itself and how it will be achieved to the benefit of the company. Furthermore, employees are often heard to lament that if management would simply ask them, they could suggest ways to downsize without such drastic cuts. The employee's inability to communicate how this can be done exactly is just as bad as management's inability to figure out how best to downsize. As a performance consultant, you can use the proforma to achieve some sense of how to downsize in a rational manner.

The approach we suggest for downsizing assumes that a company has existing job models or is willing to have them defined in preparation for downsizing. The following sequence is recommended:

1. Decide the number of professional or technical jobs that must be cut to achieve the projected amount of business output and consequences, and decide whether the workload of the current technical or professional jobs can be increased reasonably, thus reducing the number of overall cuts in this category. This involves placing job models side-by-side and deciding whether the current job models can tolerate the addition of one or more outputs from another job model. This increases the workload on as-is jobs.

2. Review the support jobs within the work group that directly aid technical or professional jobs and see whether any of these can be reduced, outsourced, or subsumed by the technical or professional jobs.

3. Review the number of company-wide support jobs and see whether any of these can be reduced or outsourced. (These are the jobs found in work groups other than the technical/professional work groups.)

4. Review the facilitation job models (management positions) and see whether a wider span of facilitation can be tolerated.

5. Review the executive job models and see whether a wider span of executive management can be tolerated.

Note that this form of downsizing is not centered on specific individuals and their functions, but on job models and what load of work they can handle. In each case, the as-is job models should be restructured to to-be job models. This provides clarity to individuals affected both in terms of what the change will be and what their accountability will be. It also reveals what the organization will have to do to make the change to these "new" jobs possible, such as teach new skills, a new orientation to responsibility, new resources, and so forth. No organization should simply announce downsizing in terms of numbers without clear communication as to work expectations and how those expectations can be fulfilled. The performance consultant will play a key role both in the definition of new (to be) work and in the interventions needed to change and become effective and efficient in the new work.

Enterprise-Wide Change

With the increasing infusion of computer technology into business, there has been a change management need nearly as impactful as reengineering and downsizing on organizations. This is the introduction of business-wide—or enterprise-wide—computer application software programs that can be used by a wide range of departments (work groups) to achieve their individual ends as well as the common needs of the business. With new software applications, the business can track and work on projects from beginning to end without switching software applications. It has been common for each department to have its own software application program. Thus, the accounting department had accounting software to do receivables and payables. The inventory people had software to count and track things. The human resources people had salary, wage, and benefit software. The problem has been that these software programs could not speak to one another and data had to reentered at each step. The introduction of enterprise-wide software has meant changes in and loss of jobs. Performance consultants need to use the as-is and to-be job models to approach enterprise-wide change. A general six-stage approach for a performance consultant is provided below, and the grey bar at the end of the chapter gives an example of a recently completed enterprise-wide change for an electrical utility.

1. First, it is very useful to prepare the individuals who will be defining their as-is jobs, through orientation, change campaigns, or having workers analyze their current work intellectually. A change agent might ask employees to describe what they do in a typical work day, identify who they work with as clients and what kinds of challenges they face, and describe how they feel about the impending changes. This kind of activity better prepares people for change in general and greatly aids in preparing to define their as-is job models.

2. The second step is to gather a group of representative workers for each job. We describe these as exemplary, much the same as Gilbert (1996) had in mind. We want to work with those who know the job well and have experience in all aspects of it. A group of about four or five jobholders is ideal.

Sometimes we add a client (if available) and supplier representatives to this group. These people help the job performers keep a proper and honest perspective on the definition of their work. We also add what we call a "core process owner," usually someone who has been working on the actual changes to the procedures—most likely someone from the information technology group.

After introducing this group to what is to be done in a job modeling session for as-is and to-be jobs, we provide a short explanation and illustration of the proforma. As one person facilitates the definition of the job model, another person records the information into job modeling software. Thus, when the "team" leaves the four-hour session, they will have printed as-is and to-be job models for their positions.

3. The facilitator guides the group through defining their as-is job model, including the definition of the skills and knowledge, as described earlier in this chapter (see Figures 5.3, 5.4, and 5.5). The prescribed order described earlier in this chapter is used and takes about two hours to complete.

4. The core process owner gives an overview of the changes that will be brought about by introduction of the new software. The core process owner is either from the information technology group or someone assigned from the line organization to the information technology group that is coordinating the overall changes. Team members can ask clarifying questions.

5. The facilitator guides the group through defining the to-be job model. This involves adding, changing, or deleting key outputs and related changes to consequences, inputs, conditions, process elements, and feedback. In general terms, many of the enterprise software changes occur in the process element steps of the job, although there are also changes in inputs, conditions, consequences, and feedback. A to-be job model generally takes about two hours for a competent facilitator to complete. Necessary skills and knowledge are also added. The definition of the as-is and to-be job models (with skills and knowledge) essentially defines the performance gap. Now the performance consultant takes action to convert these gaps into intervention solutions.

6. The team is encouraged to take the job models back into the organization and talk to a variety of others to bring further clarity, communication, and completeness to the to-be job models. This information can be shared in a follow-up session. All changes are coordinated through a central job change agent—such as the performance consultant working with human resources.

The result of this kind of job analysis is profound. Workers see the direct changes in their work and know what to anticipate and work toward. They are more committed to the change because they were part of its definition. The organization gets the information it needs in order to provide appropriate interventions to make the transitional change to new work. Managers and supervisors see what changes they have to help facilitate in others, as well as how their own job model will change. Even those workers who may have their work eliminated have a clear picture of what their skills and knowledge are as they seek other work inside or outside the business.

One of the activities that makes the definition of to-be jobs more accurate is to create to-be core processes. Thus, for example, if you consider the changes previously defined in the case example of the engineering design core process, you will see corresponding changes necessary in every element of the as-is senior engineer job. These changes and their corresponding effect on the position of senior engineer are summarized as follows:

To-Be Engineer Design (Process Element 1)	Changes to Senior Engineer Job
Inputs	
Project management	Online schedules, data
Client history	Online (if repeat client)
Cost	Design costs online
Conditions	
EW Security	Additional condition
EW Procedures	Additional condition
Process Element	
Review existing data	Past data online
	New data entered in "palm"
	in the field/dump in EWS
Review regulations	All online
Assess local conditions	Online
Consequences	
Online use by internal sources	Additional consequence
Feedback	
EW schedule reports	Online schedules, data

These changes need to be reflected in the to-be senior engineer job model, as shown in Figure 5.7a, Figure 5.7b, and Figure 5.7c. For example, the process element for developing engineering designs reflects the EWS online effect on Steps 1 through 3. Other changes are indicated for inputs, conditions, consequences, and feedback. You will also note the influence that EWS had on Process Element 3. As other outputs of this job are defined from their related core processes for Outputs 4 through 7, the influence of EWS would have to be accounted for as well. Thus, one can see the far-ranging use of the to-be core process in indicating job change. Without such process maps, much of this change process would be a guess at best, and would foresake needed assurances of (re)alignment.

Figure 5.7a. To-Be Job Model for Senior Engineer.

JOB TITLE: Sr. Engineer

To-Be Job Model

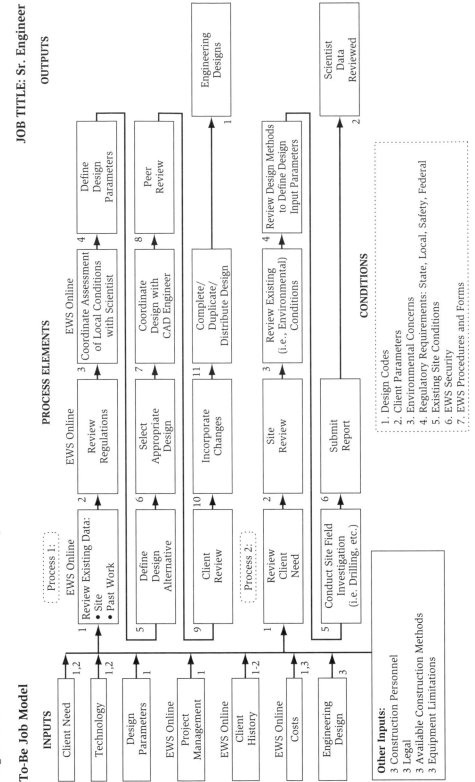

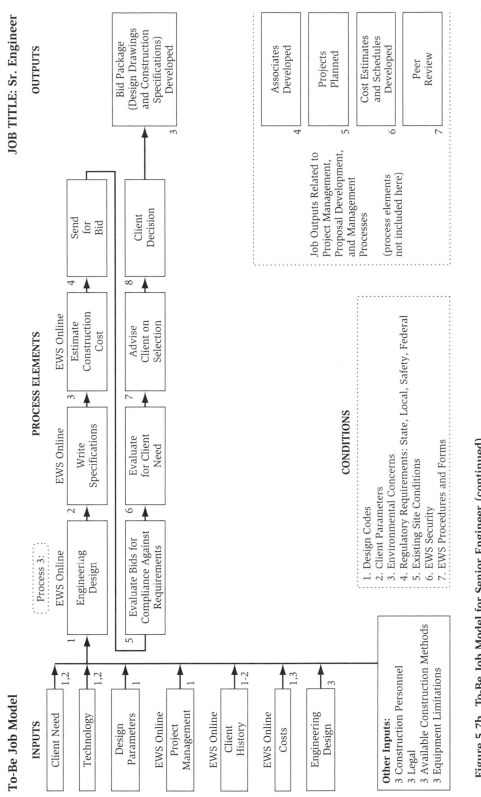

Figure 5.7b. To-Be Job Model for Senior Engineer (continued).

To-Be Job Model   **JOB TITLE: Sr. Engineer**

CONSEQUENCES

1. Cost-effective engineering designs (Outputs 1, 2, 3, 5, 6)
2. Positive community relations (Outputs 1, 2)
3. Customer satisfaction (Outputs 1–7)
4. Safety (Outputs 1, 2, 7)
5. Positive community relations (Outputs 1, 4, 5, 7)
6. Future work (Outputs 1, 4, 5, 6)
7. Online use by other sources (Outputs 1–6)

FEEDBACK

DURING	**AFTER**
1. Client	1. Client satisfaction survey
2. Schedules	2. Repeat business
3. Auditors	3. Employees
4. Employees, i.e., scientists, CAD engineers, etc.	4. Senior management
5. Regulators, i.e., city planners, EPA	5. Project management
6. Peer review	
7. EWS schedule reports	

Figure 5.7c. To-Be Job Model for Senior Engineer (continued).

Although the example illustrates some enhancement of a job brought on by the introduction of business change, many such changes can result in more extensive job changes—even elimination of positions. Several steps of a job process element may be eliminated because that function is to be provided online or by other jobs. For example, a recent job-modeling project we completed at a utility resulted in the elimination of a job where people transported reams of reports to other workers on a daily basis. Because the enterprise-wide software eliminated paper, this job went away. In another case in the same utility, initial entry of client data by others in the chain of work did not have to be re-entered by subsequent workers (on their own software), and thus the job step was eliminated.

Once the to-be job model is defined to reflect the work changes in a job, it is useful to identify corresponding changes in other parts of a job description. Thus, indicating changes in the skills and knowledge of process elements, inputs, conditions, and feedback will provide very useful information for the individual affected, management, and those who will help orient and provide training in the new skills. This is a classical example of performance gap analysis at its most fundamental level—a process greatly aided by the proforma.

Now that you have learned what the jobs will be to carry out the core processes of the business unit, it is time to learn how to use the proforma to define and align work groups.

Grey Bar: Individual Level

Kathleen Whiteside
Partner, Performance International

One particularly useful application of the Language of Work model at the individual level is to create job models during times of great change. In one project of ours, a multi-billion dollar utility was installing enterprise-wide software. Having learned during its due-diligence phase that this particular software had never experienced a technical failure but had failed due to human resistance to change, the company was prepared for a broad change management process. One significant phase of this was the modeling of jobs highly impacted by the software (SAP in this instance) changes.

Highly impacted jobs were identified during a business analysis phase. During this phase, a team comprised of content experts, programmers, and department supervisors defined the business processes in the form of work structure (functional work groups). The titles of jobs impacted were listed and the number of incumbents identified. The department managers were expected to communicate on a general level the changes and the implications to those affected. For example, they might note that with the new software, a certain time-consuming process would be eliminated or that more work would occur because more data would be available to analyze. In this particular case, the Language of Work model was not utilized for process mapping, although it would have illuminated the changes and their impact better. We entered the process after the company's own version of process mapping had been completed. Fortunately, the Language of Work model is flexible and can be blended with other approaches.

Once jobs were identified that were highly impacted, meetings were held with managers and supervisors. The Language of Work model was shared with them, as was a schedule of events for each job modeling session. Incumbents completed a one-page report called "A Day in the Life of [my job]," which helped orient the Language of Work experts to the work as the incumbents saw it. Where activity-based accounting was being introduced, data sheets were also collected that gave current activities and percentage of time devoted to each activity. These were useful, if slightly redundant, because they helped the employees to view their work from above and engaged the group in looking at their work with eyes toward change.

In each job modeling session, we requested the attendance of three to five exemplary performers. However, we did use what the organization deemed necessary. Thus, in some cases, every incumbent attended, so in some cases marginal performers were in attendance. The supervisor of the group usually attended, as did the program manager/change consultant assigned to the project.

The program manager/change consultant was integral to the success of the effort. She appeared to be in charge of the scheduling, but in fact managed the entire front-end process. She arranged initial meetings with supervisors, answered questions, scheduled the job modeling sessions, and coordinated the paperwork (which included editing the resulting document and moving it to final copy). While doing this apparently administrative work, she found multiple opportunities to help the supervisor or manager to understand the changes that were to take place, show how the job model would meet their needs for clarity about the future, and in general do the handholding that major change requires. She allayed fears and identified points of difficulty, suggesting and/or implementing ways to overcome the resistance. Partnering with such an excellent resource aids and supports the effort, making it swift and targeted. It allows the change resistance to be managed under the guise of modeling jobs.

At the appointed hour, the change consultant opened the meeting with introductions and an explanation and agenda for the job modeling session. For this project, it had been decided to do both the as-is and the to-be jobs. One Performance International facilitator then provided an overview of the job modeling process, showing how the Language of Work would be used to create an operational job model. He also explained that he would record the data onto a laptop computer that would allow them to leave the session with a printed copy of their work. Then the session began.

The other facilitator then asked the group warm-up questions about their current jobs, quickly segueing into the first direct question. While posting answers in different colors, the facilitator was internally processing the information as well. Occasionally, the focus would need correcting. It is a delicate art to establishing the deliverables or outputs of a job. Americans tend to think of themselves as having a role or a series of responsibilities, rather than as knowledge workers producing outputs.

This makes getting data on the outputs, which is the first question, difficult. If the group members feel that they are not giving the "correct" answer, they will shut down and be reluctant to work with you. On the other hand, if they develop an undisciplined list, little or no clarity will emerge. The outputs section is often the most time-consuming; the process element was also difficult and time-consuming. Once the as-is job had been posted, the Performance International facilitator obtained what skills and knowledge were needed to perform the processes, inputs, conditions, and feedback of this job.

The next step was to have a person knowledgeable about the way the new software would work explain the changes. Sometimes the participants knew a fair amount; their supervisor had prepared them. Other times the description was completely new. After the overview was completed, the group took another break. This afforded the facilitator an opportunity to make some assessments about how much the new job would change. Depending on the number and complexity of the changes, the facilitator might lead the group through a complete new job modeling process—as if the job were brand new. If much of the job remained the same, then the facilitator would lead a discussion so the group could determine whether each output would remain the same. If so, it was color-coded. If not, the new output was determined, and the remaining five elements were posted. Then the new skills and knowledge needed were posted. Finally, the to-be job was distributed and the change consultant led a discussion of the remaining tasks and deadlines. All of this work was done in four hours or less, although it was physically demanding and intellectually exhausting. (Six hours is probably a better time frame for developing both as-is and to-be jobs, with the skills and knowledge of each identified.)

Feedback from participants was typically very positive. They understood the changes in the organization better, and understood their relationship to the change better. Because the model is so very factual, there was relatively little time spent in arguing, posturing, or trying to influence the outcome. Even when jobs were being eliminated, the fact that outputs would not be needed in the new scheme of things made the conclusions easy to bear. Personal choice was not a part of the decision. The work just was not there. Seeing this fact graphically meant that affected people could get into making alternative plans more quickly. Grieving for the loss of a job was still needed, but less time was devoted to trying to persuade others to obtain a different outcome.

○   ○

CHAPTER 6

The Work Behavior of Work Groups

The Organization of Work

In this chapter we will look closely at how to apply the Language of Work model to work groups. Work groups, as an integral performance level of the Business Sphere, are those divisions of labor and other resources that the business uses to organize and facilitate the accomplishment of its core processes and the workforce. Thus, we move from the *what* (business unit), the *how* (core processes), and *by whom* (individuals) of work to the *organization* (work groups) of work. In this chapter the performance consultant benefits from a clearer understanding of when and how to improve work group performance.

This chapter completes our discussion of the Business Sphere's four levels of performance behavior and develops one of the key areas for instituting changes in performance. The behavior of the four performance levels sets the foundation on which we will establish standards, decide work support, and achieve human consonance in the remainder of the book. As a result, we can align performance in the Business Sphere.

A performance consultant needs to understand the different kinds of work groups, how they should be formed, and the different ways in which they can be improved. This understanding will help in the various kinds of assignments in which a performance consultant might become engaged. Understanding how the work group fits into the Business Sphere and how to align the work group with the individuals, core processes, and business unit will allow the performance consultant to analyze and improve performance within organizations in areas hitherto untouched by the consultant.

Traditionally, work groups have been paid relatively little attention by performance consultants in the design and improvement of performance. They are, after all, the domain of the manager or supervisor. Discussion of work groups also is often relegated to the times when a reorganization is afoot. Either an executive is leaving, causing a shake-up; or a merger, acquisition, or sell-off causes instability; or business is poor, and executives retreat to a reorganization of the work groups as a means of making improvements. Generally, these are exercises in shifting blame and postponing the inevitable, because they are not based on an understanding of the work that must be accomplished to be successful.

The work of work groups is usually summarized in the business's organization chart. While a logical layout of boxes seems to be coherent, as many people know, work groups are often slapped together to give a rising young star—or an aging bureaucrat—some additional prestige. As noted earlier, moving boxes on an organization chart is not the best way to define and organize work or work groups. Organization charts really should be a summary to show what the work groups are by name, who is in them, and their reporting relationships. Examining an organization chart to determine which work groups should exist or to make changes in and among work groups is a futile effort. And moving boxes around on an organization chart is certainly not a systematic way to reorganize the business, even though it is often done this way.

Football as an Illustration of Work Groups

There are different work groups in football, just as there are in any business, designed to accomplish certain functional work. Marketing exists in business to advertise what the business does. Engineering is there to complete designs. Construction exists to build buildings, highways, and dams. In football the offensive team exists to move the football forward in order to score. The defensive team is there to keep the other team from scoring. Special teams take care of the kickoff and other specific performance needs (goal line stance, on-side kicks, and others). Let's see what the defensive team looks like in the Language of Work proforma in Figure 6.1.

The *outputs* of the defensive team include tackles, sacks, recovery of fumbles, interceptions, touchdowns and safeties, and holding or pushing the other team back for negative (lost) yardage. To produce the outputs, the team receives *inputs* from coaches, a set of known and practiced defensive plays, guidance from the defensive coordinator, a playbook, other defensive players, and the defensive team captain.

Figure 6.1. Work Map for Work Group: Defensive Team.

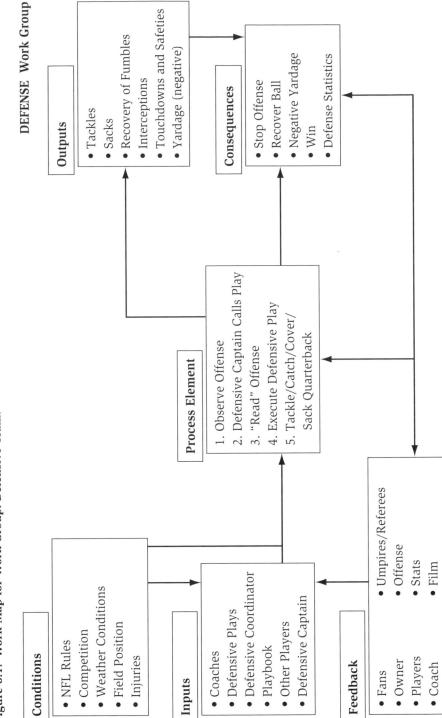

DEFENSE Work Group

Conditions
- NFL Rules
- Competition
- Weather Conditions
- Field Position
- Injuries

Inputs
- Coaches
- Defensive Plays
- Defensive Coordinator
- Playbook
- Other Players
- Defensive Captain

Feedback
- Fans
- Owner
- Players
- Coach
- Umpires/Referees
- Offense
- Stats
- Film

Process Element
1. Observe Offense
2. Defensive Captain Calls Play
3. "Read" Offense
4. Execute Defensive Play
5. Tackle/Catch/Cover/ Sack Quarterback

Outputs
- Tackles
- Sacks
- Recovery of Fumbles
- Interceptions
- Touchdowns and Safeties
- Yardage (negative)

Consequences
- Stop Offense
- Recover Ball
- Negative Yardage
- Win
- Defense Statistics

The rules—or *conditions*—the defensive team follows are pretty much the same as prescribed for all other players, but the team must know those that especially apply when playing defense. You cannot, for example, draw an offensive player offsides to cause a penalty; if you do, you will get penalized. Another specific condition is to know how your position on the field affects what the defense can do and should not do. For example, where do you position yourself when the offensive team of your opponent runs a certain play? Do you position yourself to go inside, outside, or maintain your current position? The *consequences* are to stop the opponent's offensive team from scoring, to recover fumbles, push the other team back for lost yardage, and get the best defensive statistics possible. Of course, one of the consequences is shared with other work groups on the team—winning the game. Other consequences are their own exclusively as a work group—to keep the opposition from scoring and/or to score points as the defensive team.

Finally, *feedback* comes from fans, players, coaches, owners, umpires and referees, the offensive of the team played against, statistics, and watching a game film of the performance. On many teams today, for instance, videos are available on the sideline during the game. This feedback helps your team evaluate current performance and the actions/reactions of the other team to certain plays. The next time the defense sees the same play, known as a formation, they will know better how to react; that is, make them run inside, not outside.

WORK GROUPS: IT DEPENDS ON WHAT THE NEED IS

The description of work groups gets a bit complicated because the definition of work groups, as well as the base of information that ideally forms work groups, depends on where we are in the process of defining work to meet what need. Because of this, we need to be much clearer about the intent of our analysis when discussing work groups than we were at any other level of the Business Sphere. For instance, when we defined the business unit, we determined what the business is or wants to be for its clients. When we defined the core processes, we defined processes against the outputs of the business unit. When we defined the jobs, we defined them relative to the core processes. But, work groups may be defined to meet a number of different circumstances. It is important, therefore, that these needs be well delineated from the outset, for they will determine both the source of information we use to do our analysis and the level of detail required. Let's see what the needs and circumstances are that indicate the kinds of work groups to be defined; then we'll describe ways to define work groups.

Work Groups as Core Processes

Some work groups and core processes are identical. In fact, that's fairly common. This occurs when the work group is exclusively devoted to producing one or more of the business unit's outputs. In our sample business case this is true of at least one major set of outputs, the engineering work group produces both products and engineering designs.

The notion that work groups and core processes may be identical is emphasized here so that when you are working as a performance consultant and it appears that the core process and the work group are identical, you will know that it is possible. However, it is just as likely that you will experience other kinds of work groups that need defining.

Work Groups That Seem to Be Business Units

Some work groups look like business units in that they are composed of several smaller work groups and take on the work definition—but not the size and importance—of business units. For example, the human resources work group of our business case is composed of work groups such as employment, training, compensation, and benefits. This is typical of very large corporations in which there are thousands of employees and many professional/technical work groups need to be serviced. Just the hiring of employees for several work groups is a significant work need. Thus, rather than creating a separate human resources work group for each division, one large work group is formed to serve diverse needs of the business unit(s).

For this kind of work group, the definition of the "process element" of the HR work group would look much the same as a process element for an entire business unit, that is, composed of smaller work groups in relation to each other. Figure 6.2 would be one way to depict such an HR work group's process element. Note how the process element looks similar to the business unit's definition of its process element. The process element in this case is not a single process composed of a number of deliverable steps (like the engineering design core process), nor will it be like a traditional work group definition. Of course, eventually each of the work groups within HR will have to be defined with a proforma showing steps of their process element leading to their deliverables (outputs).

Work Support Work Groups

Two kinds of work groups support work. One provides support to the whole organization; the other provides support needed for a specific core process.

One of four layers of performance has already been identified as support—the subject of Chapter 8. Briefly, work support is the variety of means, identified as interventions, needed by the business to help people, processes, and the business in general behave (or perform) and reach desired standards. These

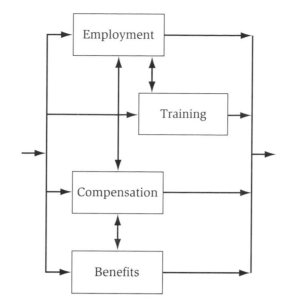

Figure 6.2. Sample HR Work Group Process Element.

include such things as having a mission/vision and strategic plan at the business unit level to the provision of benefits and performance reviews at the individual level. To implement and maintain this support across the entire business, a number of specialized (support) work groups will be required for medium size and large businesses. Human resources is a typical example of one such work support work group. Chapter 8 describes these work groups and provides ways to decide which are needed. They will be defined as work maps in the same manner as other types of work groups described here.

A second kind of performance support work group is the kind that a core process may need to support its needs. You recall that support jobs are defined by core process; thus the work group would be composed of individuals who have these particular kinds of support jobs. Often they need to be organized into work groups. Shortly, we will see illustrations of each of these types of work groups. First, let's see how work groups are mapped using the proforma.

AS-IS WORK GROUP PERFORMANCE ANALYSIS

We begin by assuming that a work group exists and we want to define and improve its work for any of a variety of reasons. The work group may want the performance consultant to help clarify its overall purpose and work; may have the need to clarify its work between and among the workers, and/or other work groups (role relationship); or want to improve the work between the workers and their manager. These situations describe groups that are "out of whack." The other reason for defining a work group may be to conduct some quality improvement effort as part of the company's continuous improvement program. How does the group figure out what it needed and how to make itself better? How can we define a work group so that there is clarity to its being?

In some sense we are back to the beginning of defining our business. You will recall that there were several work groups that made up the engineering business case illustrated throughout the book, beginning in Chapter 3. For illustrative purposes, we will define training, one of the boxes shown in Figure 6.2, as a work group within the human resources group. We are not defining a work group as part of a new business or when reengineering a business, but rather simply defining a work group prior to making any effort to improve it.

As with any other performance level of business, the work group must first determine what it is supposed to produce. It needs to "Define Australia first!" Naturally, these are the *outputs* of the work group. To do this, we typically look at who their clients or customers are and the products and services delivered to them. This would vary from company to company as to what it wants from training, but we will suppose the following is representative.

○

Step 1: Orientation

Introduce the proforma in ten minutes.

A sample map may also be useful, but is not necessary, and may present some problems in copying what others have done rather than thinking through the issue.

Provide an orientation to the task of defining a work group. Introduce team members and their expected roles. Overview the data sources available. Orient the work group to the proforma.

Step 2: Define Outputs

Use the proforma job aid. "Define Australia first!" You have to agree on the targets (outputs) of the work group first. Sources for outputs:

Individual jobs to be part of work group

Core processes

Work support matrix

We will limit the outputs of our training group to two: training programs developed and classes scheduled. These are listed in Figure 6.3a and b, along with other work elements of the training work group.

Step 3: Define Inputs

The key questions to be answered are

- What triggers the work of the work group?
- What are the primary resources used in the work group?

To produce the outputs, triggering and resource inputs are needed. They are best determined by reviewing each output separately to see what inputs are required. When the same input is used by more than one output, list the number of each output. For example, several inputs, such as client request, needs assessment, and performance reviews apply only to one output. Training facilities applies to Output 2 only. Still others, such as managers and workers, apply to both outputs. Inputs for work groups come from either the core processes and/or the jobs members of the work group perform.

Work groups typically derive their primary inputs from client needs, as business units do. These inputs may stem directly from the needs of workers around which the work group was formed, but they can come from other sources. In the case of training, needs are also determined by managers in various work groups. For instance, a manager may determine that specific numbers and kinds of workers will need to receive training from

Figure 6.3a. As-Is Work Group Map of the Training Group.

As-Is Work Group Map

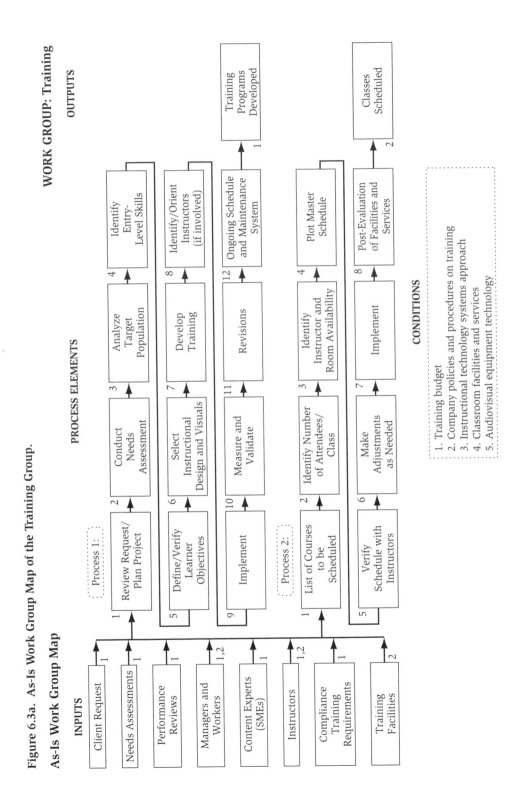

WORK GROUP: Training

OUTPUTS

PROCESS ELEMENTS

INPUTS

CONDITIONS

1. Training budget
2. Company policies and procedures on training
3. Instructional technology systems approach
4. Classroom facilities and services
5. Audiovisual equipment technology

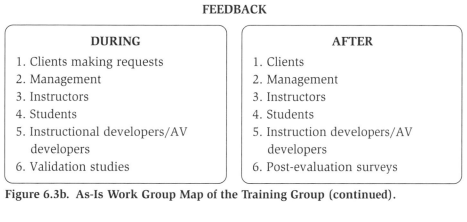

As-Is Work Group Map   **WORK GROUP: Training**

CONSEQUENCES

1. Effective and efficient training programs that meet individual and company needs (Outputs 1–2)
2. Instructor satisfaction (Outputs 1–2)
3. Meeting clients requests, especially from managers and executives (Outputs 1–2)
4. Classroom scheduling that meets instructor and student needs (Output 2)

FEEDBACK

DURING	**AFTER**
1. Clients making requests	1. Clients
2. Management	2. Management
3. Instructors	3. Instructors
4. Students	4. Students
5. Instructional developers/AV developers	5. Instruction developers/AV developers
6. Validation studies	6. Post-evaluation surveys

Figure 6.3b. As-Is Work Group Map of the Training Group (continued).

our sample. The manager may determine this based on the need to execute his or her own group processes in a better way. Although these needs generally originate with managers, today, with the increased emphasis on work teams determining their own needs, the origin of need may shift to the work team. In the case of the training group, relying solely on managers in various groups to identify client need is not consistently effective. For the training work group, needs assessment studies and integration with performance review are more systematic ways to identify client need on a continuous and reliable basis. For instance, doing performance reviews based on job models—the same work paradigm thus being used to identify as well as validate needs—is an excellent source of needs.

Other work groups can be an important source of inputs for work groups. Outputs from other work groups that become the input to the work group being defined are critical areas where things can go wrong. This kind of "white space" (much the same as process white spaces à la Rummler and Brache) is critical because one group may unknowingly, partially or wholly, ignore the needs of another—particularly when it comes to work issues around time. I am reminded, for example, of how the service repair workers in one group regularly ignore the need to give the marketing support work group information on products needing repair. The support group had no idea that problems existed because the service people didn't think it important to pass on the information. The repair group saw itself as being in the repair business—which it is. As long as their outside client was satisfied, why worry about anyone else—especially someone in their own company? "Repair," in this instance, did not see themselves in the problem prevention mode. The point is, problems like these cannot be identified in organizations if the source—an input—is not defined as part of the map of the work group that will take care of it. Sounds like a no-brainer, but it is often overlooked.

Another input typical of many work groups is their need to respond to internal project needs. In the engineering business, the project needs of construction, engineering, and project management may require training. By business recognizing that training should be part of other groups' work, we ensure that training is part of the on-going business. If not, then the support groups become mere appendages that are used whenever someone thinks about them or gets into some kind of trouble. If this integration can be done directly between work groups for profit, then all the better. For example, how can engineering sell the services of training to their own clients as part of their on-going activities? One business did this on a continuous basis and was quite successful, thereby providing a variety of activities for the training group. It will not happen, however, if it is not planned. If engineering doesn't plan to sell testing services in our sample business case, testing services will not be sold.

Step 4: Define Conditions

Ask

- What external rules and regulations are to be followed?
- What internal policies and procedures apply?
- What are the conditions for the use of inputs, process element, and feedback?

Do not include judgments of why things do not work, such as "not enough time" or "multiple platforms." These will come later.

The conditions of the training work group include their budget, company policies and procedures related to training, a systematic system of developing training, the facilities, and training-related technologies.

Conditions for work groups should be derived and related directly to those of the business unit, core processes, and individuals. If the business has established policies and procedures, then these need to be "owned" by the work groups affected. If they are not part of the definition of the work group's work, they will not be known and may not be followed. This may sound familiar. It is not surprising, for example, to find that work groups are far more aware of the rules that come from outside their business than they are with those from inside their business.

When we analyze for work group conditions, it is imperative to make sure the conditions are identified for the process element, inputs, and feedback. There is a tendency to think of conditions only for the process element. For inputs, look for conditions that impact costs, facilities, compliance, and people—and especially for those that impact identifying client needs completely. For feedback, look for information needs, client feedback, and ways to reinforce others' work.

Step 5: Define Consequences

Look for consequences for clients, the business, and the workforce. There should be at least one or more consequence per output; they should be stated in positive terms only; and the consequences significant to those outside the work group must be included.

Consequences for the training work group are listed in Figure 6.3b and include those things that are the desired results for each output the group produces. As shown, significant consequences are the completion of training programs and the class schedule.

Work group consequences relate to the completion of work done in common. With individual work, the consequences are the individual's own, even when many individuals have the same consequence. In the work group, the individuals work together toward common consequences.

In defining work group consequences, each output should be evaluated for the consequences that it will help achieve. These should be in concert with those consequences established for the business unit as a whole. Once defined, key each consequence to output(s) that produce it.

Step 6: Define the Process Element

Define steps to produce each work group output.

Use action verbs to begin each process step.

The process element of a work group includes the steps that produce each output. The typical process element of the training work group is shown in Figure 6.3a.

The steps of the process element are the mini-deliverables used by the group to produce or service its output. Action verbs are the common way to specify steps. They should be defined only to the level of detail required to communicate meaning.

The process elements of a work group should be derived from defined core processes, if they exist. In the case of training, this would not be the case because it is a support to the core processes in the sample business case. Because there is no core process in the example, it would have to be developed, perhaps as an instructional technology process. This systematic process would be tailored to the business environment in which it is to be used.

Step 7: Define Feedback

Ask how the work group will decide whether clients are satisfied and how it will decide whether the workforce is satisfied.

As with other levels of work, there are two kinds of feedback for work groups. One kind occurs after the output is completed, the other while processing in relation to the process element, inputs, and conditions. Our training work group receives feedback from a wide range of sources, as it typically interacts with many others in the business and receives specific feedback from clients, management, instructors, students, and others. Feedback that aids communication with other work groups and management is particularly crucial.

Step 8: Reach Consensus/Achieve Commitment

In light of the input from others, keep the definition of the map at a high level. Too much detail will defeat the purpose. Such detail comes later. Drill down until clarity, communication, and consensus are reached.

Share the initial draft of the work group map with others in the work group, other work groups that have a relationship to yours, and customers and suppliers for their input. Reassemble the definition team and hold a discussion to arrive at final consensus of the work group map.

MEASURING WORK GROUPS

Except for some special features, measuring work group performance involves exactly the same technique and order as those for measuring the business unit, core processes, and individuals.

In general, measurement ought to be a cascading procedure that starts at the business unit level, then moves through core processes and individuals to work groups. Only when a problem is revealed at one of these levels should there be further measurement at a subsequent level. This avoids duplication of effort and unnecessary measurement that can only waste time and resources. Of course, if the prior performance levels have not been measured, measurement of work groups should be undertaken on its own. Measurement can be undertaken to isolate a particular problem that needs fixing.

The guiding principle of measurement in the proforma is to first measure outputs and consequences for effect. Find any problems with the outputs and their related consequences in a work group. In the case of the training work group this means measuring training programs and the class schedule, which are fairly easy outputs to measure—determining how effective and efficient each training course is and whether the class schedule works for those utilizing the course offerings are also straightforward. If there are problems—and only then—measure for root cause.

Root cause calls for measuring the inputs, conditions, process element, and feedback. For example, in relation to training programs as an output we need to return to our work group map and devise measurements such as the following:

Inputs:	Are client needs accurately defined?
	Is needs assessment valid?
	How well do performance reviews identify training needs?
Conditions:	Does the training budget allow for optimal training methods and resources?
	Does company policy support training opportunities?
Process Element:	Has the target population been accurately identified?
	Are competencies reflecting job skills and knowledge?
Feedback:	Is student feedback incorporated to improve training programs?
	Are the post-evaluation surveys valid indicators of training program effectiveness and efficiency?

MEASURING RELATIONSHIPS
WITHIN AND BETWEEN WORK GROUPS

One of the more important measurements is between the various work groups of a business. Work group relationships are formed in two fundamental ways: (1) by sharing processes, and (2) by one group's output becoming the next group's input. Both must be measured.

Relationships, of course, can also occur *within* a work group. Handoffs, for example, occur within a human resources group when a new employee (from the employment group) enters an orientation program (to the training group). This could be as simple as knowing when the employee will be available for orientation to the more complex knowing specific information about the employee to structure the orientation to meet special needs. More complex relationships occur in our business case when engineering and construction work groups have to interrelate over the content of designs during development, as well as the use of designs during construction due to client changes. Whatever the relationship, it should be defined and measured. The easiest way to do this is to build work maps to see where these relationships exist and then measure them. These relationships are of the following kinds:

- When one output becomes the input of another
- When the steps of a process intersect
- When conditions are shared
- When feedback is desirable or needed to proceed

We know that the four groups of human resources have a relationship to one another, depicted in Figure 6.2. But we have to define each of these group's work group maps to see the precise relationship. The same may be said of any work groups in the business. We have, in our own practice as performance consultants, on occasion simply taken two groups that were having some unidentified relationship concerns and facilitated separately as each defined its own work group map. Then, we brought the two groups together to discuss their relationship. Or, as an alternative, we sometimes map each group in the presence of the other so each can provide input to the other from their work perspective. This use of the proforma typically results in the groups' seeing where their problems are on their own. As a result they become more committed to the solutions because they identified the problems. This methodology is also excellent for determining when measurements need to be done between work groups and for verifying or further identifying other problems between the work groups.

Another useful way to depict relationships and thus measure them is shown in Figure 6.4. Unlike work maps that show all the elements of work and where groups may relate, this method focuses on the outputs of the work groups in the form of performance questions. The performance questions used to measure each output of each work group have been defined in the figure for the four work groups in human resources from the case example—in this instance at a very high level without detail. Note that the performance questions have been linked by lines to show the various relationships. The questions will often be more useful than work group maps because they show links in more detail. This technique is one alternative to work group maps in facilitating work group relationships.

Two types of relationships are shown in Figure 6.4, plus a reference to other work group relationships outside of human resources that will need to be attended to. Let's look at the two primary types of relationships within the HR work group first.

The first type of relationship, shown on the left side of Figure 6.4, is labeled "interwork" group relationships. Lines are used to link these relationships. For example, the first performance question under "employment" is linked to several other work group outputs, including the four outputs in "training." Note that at the bottom of the relationship map a representative performance question has been defined to measure the relationship between "skilled employees hired," as a part of employment, and "skills training programs" as a part of training. This question is identified as the link between performance question E1 (Employment Question 1) and T1 (Training Question 1). The question measures the relationship that should exist between the two specific outputs shared by employment and training. Other questions would be defined and used for measuring other relationships, shown by the linkage between lines. *Note:* We are identifying only things to measure. The details of measurement are not addressed nor illustrated here—only the needs.

The second type of relationship occurs within work groups and is labeled "intrawork" group relationships. Lines are also used to link these relationships. For example, within compensation you see a relationship between Outputs 1 and 2. Wage surveys are related to wage adjustments. A performance question illustrating this relationship is shown at the bottom of the map, designated by C1–C2 (Compensation 1 and 2).

The four groups in human resources may also have relationships with other work groups in the business. For instance, some of the four have working relationships with project management, legal, and so forth. For example, in hiring practices, employment may interact with legal over issues regarding fair employment. We could not possibly show all the details of all the relationships involving HR. We do, however, reference various work groups on the right side of the figure. These relationships between major work groups are called "linkage group relationships." For example, Output 1 of employment has a relationship with project management that needs to be mapped and measured. This relationship needs to be specified on another work relationship map (which can be number-coordinated for ease of reference). As appropriate, next

Intrawork/Interwork Group Relationships	Linkage Group Relationships
Employment (E)	
1. Are skilled employees hired?	Proj. Mgmt.
2. Are recruitment programs successful and cost-effective?	
3. Are in-house resumes available/updated?	
Training (T)	
1. Are skills training programs available to meet employee needs as shown in performance reviews and career development plans?	All Managers
2. Are new employee orientations provided?	Mgmt.
3. Are evaluations conducted for work elements?	
4. Are effective performance improvement programs developed and implemented for business work-element needs?	Mgmt.
Benefits (B)	
1. Are employees enrolled in company programs?	Payroll
2. Are benefit programs administered to workforce satisfaction?	TQM Adm.
3. Are conflicts resolved?	Legal
4. Are cost-saving strategies proposed?	Exec. Mgmt.
Compensation (C)	
1. Are wage surveys conducted?	Exec. Mgmt.
2. Are wage adjustment proposals formulated?	
3. Are jobs graded?	
4. Are employees given performance reviews and career development plans?	Mgmt.
5. Are job descriptions written and kept up-to-date?	Proj. Mgmt.
6. Are wage discrepancies resolved?	
7. Are employees paid appropriate to the market?	Exec. Mgmt.

Examples of Typical Relationship Measurements
Intrawork Group
E1 - T1 What skill deficiencies need to be filled between entry-level skills and on-the-job training?
Interwork Group
C1 - C2 Are wage adjustments formulated against timely wage surveys?

Figure 6.4. An Alternate to Work Group Maps for Showing Relationships Among Work Groups.

to each work group output for human resources are listed other work groups to which each output would flow and become an input. Making these linkages visible is a more powerful tool for identifying, measuring, and improving the business than would be possible by showing an organization chart, individual core processes, or isolated work groups.

DECIDING WHAT THE WORK GROUPS WILL BE

If we were defining a new business or needed to reengineer or reorganize an existing business, then we would either not know what the work groups were or would not be predisposed to redefining work groups. How would we go about defining these work groups?

It is imperative to begin by not having to name a work group from the outset. This may seem a bit odd, but the reason is that by naming something we tend to let the very name drive our thinking. When people said the world was flat, it wasn't surprising that most people thought it was, made maps to reflect it, and traveled (or did not travel) accordingly. If I told you we were going to form a "training" department you might begin to tell me what it should be doing, how (as process elements), and who it should employ. These projections would be based on your experience and prejudices with training departments. The same would be true if I said we were going to form an engineering, human resources, research, or other work group. This is to emphasize that we should not begin by naming a work group. Call it "X" to begin with, or give it an action title, "The Design Makers." Put together what is needed that serves good business work reasons, and then give it a name. So how do we decide what the work group should be?

When we "organize" work, it follows that we should know first and foremost what the work would be. Again, it is a case of "Define Australia first!" In Language of Work terms, this means knowing the business unit, core processes, and jobs. It means having the work maps and models of those three performance levels, as they contain the details of what, how, and by whom. Of course, certain other things need to be known in forming work groups, but for our purposes these three are the most critical. For instance, it is important to know who the clients or customers are, where they are located, and how they are best served, what the cost controls will be, and so forth. Will we centralize or decentralize work groups and how will they best serve the customer? Or if we regionalize the nature of the work product or service (that is, product sale and repair), will this better serve a particular client base? How will cost enter into the grouping of people and processes? These need to be considered, but only show up in work maps if you have done your up-front planning analysis around client need, delivery systems, and so on. As a general rule, decide the work groups using the Language of Work model, then consider other things that would strengthen or limit the best organization of the work. In this way, you can adjust to the optimal desired performance, rather than building up from minimal possibilities. As we said, here we will consider only the influence that business unit, core processes, and individuals have on the formation and need for work groups.

Recall that in the use of core processes to create jobs we create professional and technical jobs first, followed in order by support, facilitation, and executive jobs. The formation of work groups follows a similar pattern, but utilizes a wider base of accumulated, desired business knowledge. This base of knowledge includes the definitions of the business unit, core processes, and jobs. By forming work groups by following this order, the work groups practically reveal themselves because of the great clarity about the work these various analyses make from one performance level to the next. Thus, the definition and discussion of work as we cascade from business unit to core processes, then processes to jobs provide greater and greater detail as to what the business should be, and therefore how it is best organized. This is particularly true of defining jobs from core processes, where the jobs almost leap out at you. It is no less so in defining work groups from a knowledge of business unit maps, core process maps, and job models.

There are four kinds of work groups; each has its best sources for when and how they are defined. These groups include professional and technical, support, facilitation, and executive work groups. For two of these we will add managers as facilitators.

Forming Professional or Technical Work Groups

Professional or technical workers are those who implement, along with certain kinds of support workers, the core processes of a business. These workers, by the nature of their work, often need to be grouped together. This allows them to share their expertise in producing their collectively shared outputs. We are not referring to *how* the work will be done, such as in self-directed teams, matrix management, or just individuals in common. These arrangements can be formed within and between work groups. Rather, we are discussing *what* the work group should be and what jobs will be a part of it. There are three sources of information for making this decision: the business unit map, core processes, and individual jobs.

Deciding the formation of work groups of the professional or technical workforce requires some content knowledge. However, a performance consultant versed in the proforma can easily facilitate the formation of a work group with a group of engineers and others whose processes and jobs have already been defined. Essentially, it is a three-step facilitation process:

First, the reengineering team or business development team conducts a review of the major *outputs* of the business by reviewing the business unit map. The outputs of our sample business case are shown in Figure 6.5.

OUTPUTS   **WORK GROUP**

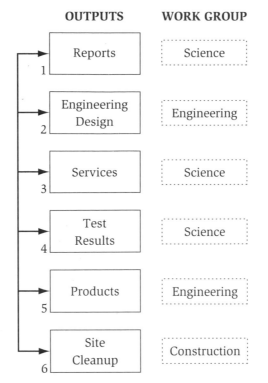

Figure 6.5. Assigning Outputs to Work Groups.

These outputs could be grouped further based on their similarity relative to those core processes and individuals who produce each output. Thus, if engineers produce Outputs 2 and 5, engineering designs and products, respectively, then it follows that they should be grouped. If there are compelling reasons to keep these two outputs separate, then that would dictate their being kept separate. The factors that influence this kind of decision generally include work group design criteria such as manpower availability and utilization; cost; facilities availability and utilization; technology availability and utilization; manpower jobs, skills, and knowledge; and marketplace location.

Because our focus here is on desired work behavior, we will leave the description of many of these factors to others. As you can see, however, the knowledge we have gained through the job models provides us the information for the fifth criteria, jobs, skills, and knowledge. The business unit map and related core processes also provide relevant information for technology availability and utilization.

Let us assume that an analysis of the sample business case outputs and related criteria has resulted in the following combination of outputs to be delivered by the work groups. (We have named them, but this was not really necessary at this time.)

Work Group	*Business Unit Outputs*
Engineering	Engineering Design
	Products
Science	Reports
	Services
	Test Results
Construction	Site Cleanup

Having identified the outputs for these work groups and placed them in work group maps as the outputs, we must define the other five work elements. One complete work group map is shown in Figure 6.6a, Figure 6.6b, and Figure 6.6c. In the case of the business unit outputs, the work groups have already been defined. We have already developed, as in the case of engineering design, the process map used to produce the engineering designs. We need merely transfer this process (with its jobs, senior engineer, and CAD engineer) to the work group map we are forming. To complete the engineering work group map, we would also transfer the core process for the products output (and its related jobs) to the work group we are forming.

In the third step, the work group is refined and changed by taking into account the other work group design criteria indicated previously. For example, we might decide, because of the highly technical nature of the work, that the work group could benefit from having its own proposal development people; this group would be included in the work group map. We would label this group by a functionally descriptive name, reflecting its business intent. Perhaps rather than merely engineering, it becomes engineering products and design.

This method of grouping business unit outputs, then transferring core processes and job and applying work group criteria, can be done to form the science and construction work groups for our sample business case, as it would for any business being reengineered or reorganized. For professional or technical work groups, the task of forming work groups is rather straightforward and well-defined.

Forming Support Work Groups

Support jobs and their work groups were previously identified as coming from two sources. First are those directly related to core processes (as described in Chapter 5), including support jobs like clerical, legal, proposal writing, computer

Figure 6.6a. To-Be Work Group Map for Engineering.

To-Be Work Group Map

WORK GROUP: Engineering

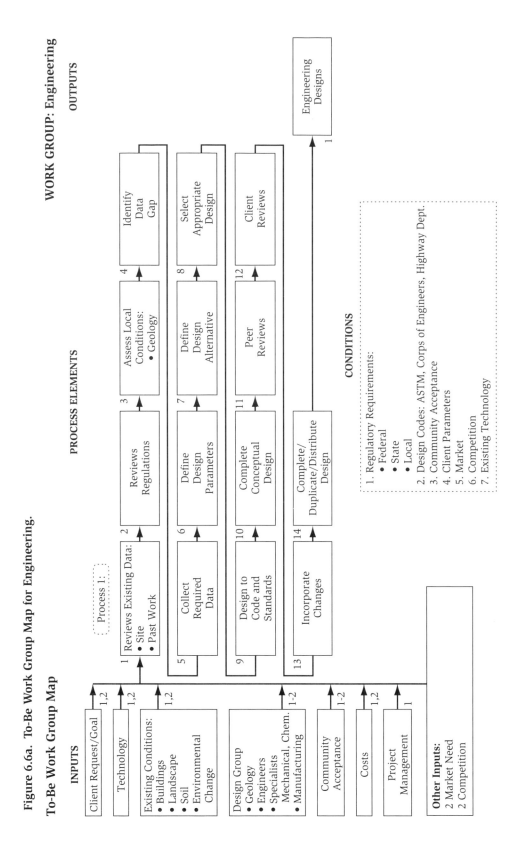

INPUTS   PROCESS ELEMENTS   OUTPUTS

179

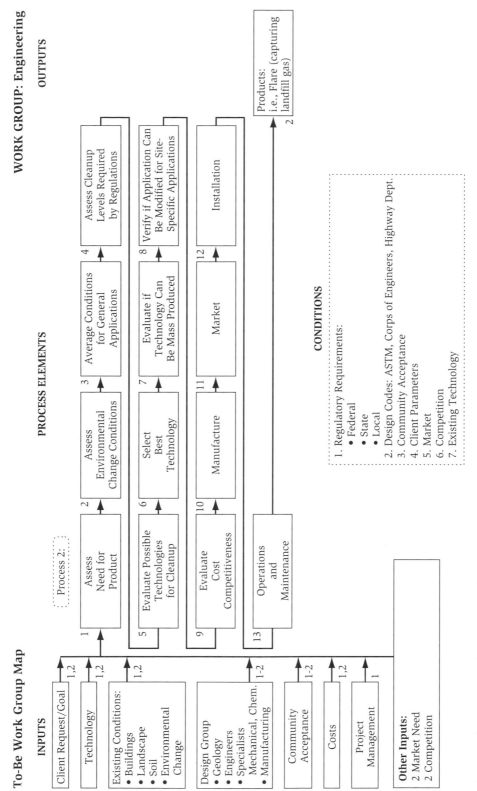

Figure 6.6b. To-Be Work Group Map for Engineering (continued).

To-Be Work Group Map   **WORK GROUP: Engineering**

CONSEQUENCES

- Cost-effective engineering designs and products (Outputs 1–2)
- Safety (Outputs 1–2)
- Designs and products within compliance (Outputs 1–2)
- Community acceptance (Outputs 1–2)
- Ease of manufacture (Outputs 1–2)
- Customer satisfaction (Outputs 1–2)
- Achieve environmental goal in most cost-effective way (Output 2)
- Meet regulations (Outputs 1–2)
- Cost effectiveness and profit (Outputs 1–2)
- Adaptability to existing technology (Outputs 1–2)

FEEDBACK

DURING	AFTER
1. Permits	1. Client need is met
2. Client: Conceptual stage	2. Regulatory compliance
3. Project team	3. Construction personnel
4. Regulatory agencies	4. Professional engineer signoff
5. Project manager	
6. Engineers, manufacturing, materials	
7. Architects, construction, landscape	
8. Client: Stages of design	
9. Community	

Figure 6.6c. To-Be Work Group Map for Engineering (continued).

support, and other support related directly to the professional or technical needs. The engineering design core process requires such support.

The second kind of support is the work support the business in general needs. This typically includes support in the way of training, employment, benefits, compensation, quality assurance, equipment, continuous improvement, and even performance consultants. These kinds of support also support the technical or professional work, but are deemed necessary for the business and workforce as a whole. This kind of support is the subject of Chapter 8.

The criteria for determining whether a support group needs to be formed to support a core process include group size, specialization, cost, legal requirements, and efficiency and effectiveness of shared resources.

For example, if our engineering design work group was of sufficient size to warrant several support positions in, say, technical computer support, it might be wise to form a support work group within engineering. Thus, we take the jobs that have been defined related to computer support and determine how best to structure the work group, using work mapping to define the group. If there were insufficient numbers of support jobs, or any of the other criteria could not be met, a support work group should not be formed. Rather, positions should be attached directly to specific professional or technical positions in the engineering work group.

Forming Facilitative Work Groups

The "management" of a business typically takes the form of a series of managers, directors, and supervisors who serve, in varying degrees of direct authority, as the administrative heads of various work groups. The numbers have recently declined somewhat due to "downsizing" and the so-called "flattening" of the organizational hierarchy so that there are fewer layers of management between the workers and the customers they serve.

Of course, management is typically not a work group in itself, but a series of work group heads. The more supervisors or managers who report to a person, typically the more highly ranked an individual is. Such higher rank often brings special privileges. It is generally also true that the more highly ranked an individual is, the greater his or her influence. This makes sense when using a military model for an organizational scheme. However, if one uses a rational, alignment-based model for determining work groups, then one needs to reconsider the functional needs served and the job needs of executives and managers.

When work is determined by core processes and individual contributions to core processes, then an important role for the manager or supervisor immediately emerges—to facilitate or make easier the flow of work from one group to another and/or one process to another. Rather than serving as a "commander," this new leader serves to ensure that the needs of the work group are met. For instance, do inputs arrive in a timely way? If not, then it would be the facilitator's role to work with the source of the input to solve the problem so that the work can be accomplished in a more timely way. This is just one example of the work of the facilitator. Imagine the facilitation possibilities within and between the other work elements of conditions, process element, feedback, and consequences.

We know that a number of problems exist in business between work groups. What happens if one or the other does not cooperate with the other? Indeed, these relations, or "handoffs" as they are commonly called, share the same fundamental problems at any level of the business sphere. There is a lack of coordination and alignment. By defining all the core processes and work group maps as well as the job models in a business, we can more easily identify and improve the handoffs. Simple awareness through using a proforma is quite powerful. Still, it takes the attention of individuals to ensure excellent handoffs, because the workforce is quite prone to do its individual or collective work within the group while neglecting the interfaces with other groups and individuals. Managing these handoffs is a useful role for managers.

Given the need to do one's own tasks, it is quite common for individuals to ignore the needs of the ones who receive their outputs. For example, a secretary may complain about a boss who gives them work late in the day, making it very stressful to meet delivery service deadlines. This is a process element consideration. This is also true for other work element interfaces. Inputs are not high quality, one group ignores conditions they should not ignore, desired consequences are not shared, or feedback is not sought or given. Therefore, it is appropriate for management to be responsible for ensuring that the process proceeds well. A key role should be removing obstacles to performance within their own groups, as well as with other groups. Their output should be "removed obstacles."

Barriers between work groups should not exist just because a manager belongs to one group and not the other. The right kind of business unit condition can encourage greater facilitation. Having said this, what are the outputs and related work elements that could be defined for a group of facilitators sharing a common work need? Here are some suggestions:

"White space" problem identification and resolution

Work schedules developed or facilitated

Quality improvement point resolutions

Budgets developed and monitored, and

Work planned and coordinated

A group of facilitators (managers) with these outputs could meet on a regular basis and interact continuously in order to be an effective alignment tool in business. These facilitators would be aided in this daunting task by core processes and work group maps, and by job models that have been defined and used. Determining the need for and the required numbers of this critical work group is easier with this kind of information. For example, in our business case one group of facilitators might be formed that includes the engineering, construction, science, and proposal development work groups, and another within the human resource work groups composed of employment, training, benefits, and compensation. Training, as can be the case, would then be rarely left out of the loop. One needs to review the work groups in the process element of a business unit map to see where facilitation work groups are needed and then detail the kinds of work relationships by reviewing their related core processes and job models.

Forming an Executive Work Group

An executive work group is probably most open to interpretation and hardest to influence. After all, because they "run the place" they get to do what they want, although it may not be the best for overall work performance.

A typical executive work group is a combination of senior executives who should work in harmony and model facilitation behavior to the rest of the business workforce. We find in this work group the president, CEO, senior level executives, and sometimes highly placed support functions, such as legal, civil affairs, a chief information officer, and so on.

In forming an executive work group, the question is two-fold: (1) "Who should be part of the executive work group?" and (2) "How should the work group be defined?" The larger question is, "What does this group have to do with the work of the Business Sphere?" The broad answer is that executives should represent work in the same manner as anyone else.

Obviously, the key professional or technical work groups need to be represented in executive management. Unfortunately, many businesses stop here and guess which others should be involved, partly from the failure to recognize that work is dependent on support as much as it is on the professional or technical outputs that go directly to clients. For example, to suggest in our case business that legal or finance should be represented, but not human resources, proposal development, and sales and marketing does not make sense. The question is often answered by power and influence, rather than by what makes sense for accomplishing work. This phenomenon will change only as executives develop a greater understanding of work or performance. Understanding work, in this instance, means forming work groups based on what they can best accomplish, including the executive work group.

The criteria for selecting executives and creating a work group should include

- The linkage between the business and its investors and other stakeholders

- The linkage between the overall management of the business and its workforce

- The determination of how the business will plan and execute for the present and the future

- The necessity of traditional executive level positions in today's business from the standpoint of doing the work and achieving customer satisfaction

- The determination of how many levels of administration will be tolerated between the client and the execution of work on their behalf

One other key data source for executive management should be their individual job models and the need for work support in the organization. Unfortunately, many executives don't have job models that describe expected performance. For example, the output of an executive's job model should generally include making strategic and business plans, establishing policies (internal conditions for the organization), tending to external relations, and overseeing profitability through business unit performance.

There are two significant cautions in determining who should and who should not be a member of the executive team. In the same way that we noted that executives create the conditions the rest of the organization must follow, we recognize that executives can cause noise by their own personalities. This is best viewed in light of work consonance, which will be covered in Chapter 9. Noise in this instance relates to the overbearing personality of some executives that can get in the way of work, that changes direction away from paths already set, and that sets bad examples. Executives need to see the negative effects their personalities can have on the whole organization and take steps to ensure against these effects. One CEO we know does not personally like to deal with conflict, so he waits as long as possible before making decisions about issues that may cause conflict among staff. Unfortunately, this aspect of his personality gets in the way of work being accomplished. Another vice president we met did not have the patience needed to wait for results from his programs, so he would change programs almost monthly. The 1,200 people reporting to him soon tired of these changes; they felt like they were at the tail end of a long whip. Executives who use the privilege of their office to indulge in inappropriate sexual or social behavior are also contributing to the noise of the organization.

The second caution in forming the executive work group is the degree to which some executives have assumed power and influence beyond their positions in the company. One example is the chief financial officer who interferes with operations or the marketing vice president who tries to determine how products will be made. Each of these executives has an area of expertise and can contribute well to the overall direction of the company, but in areas in which they have no real expertise, they should remain silent. Another similar example is legal officers whose real contribution should be on legal matters, yet they have been known to prevent managers from accomplishing their work by imposing fears of litigation. Staff work should remain staff work; it should be advisory in nature and based on true expertise relative to the work being planned or executed. Other opinions can be proffered, but should be labeled as such.

In conclusion, executives present special challenges to work and performance improvement, but using the proforma gently makes explicit what has been implicit for these positions and their work as a group for the business. Clarity about what is happening can build in discipline at all levels of the organization, causing even executives to improve their own performance and help achieve successful performance alignment.

CLOSING THE LOOP: CHANGING THE BUSINESS UNIT PROCESS ELEMENT

You may have noticed that some changes were made in the composition of work groups for the sample engineering business case in Figure 6.8, where new work groups, science and construction, were added. The types of work group changes revealed by using the Language of Work model to reengineer or reorganize a business afford the opportunity to demonstrate how changes in a business (or establishing a new business) result in change in the process element of a business unit. This is a key concept.

Recall that the process element of a business unit is composed of the work groups and their relationships. When we are defining a new business or reengineering an old one, we don't have, in the first instance, and should not be influenced by, in the case of reengineering, an existing process element for the business unit. Recall that the process element of an existing unit is composed of the work groups and their relationships. For example, Figure 6.7 is the process element of the existing business case used throughout this book.

When using the Language of Work model to define a new business, we would not know what the work groups are when the business unit is being defined because we are defining the "what" of business first and the organization of work though work group definition will come as the fourth major level of definition. Similarly, as a business is being reengineered we would not want to define the business unit process element (the work groups) from the outset, because we are taking a new look at the business. We don't want to be influenced by what the current business unit process element is, so we have to wait (with as much patience as that may take) until we have defined the business unit and defined the core processes and job models. Then we can define the work groups, as we learned to do in this chapter. The resulting work groups would then be arranged to form a process element for the business unit. This, in a sense, completes the "loop" of work behavior definition. The work groups become the business unit process element. A sample of such a definition of a process element is shown in our reengineered business case in Figure 6.8. Here we see that science and construction have been added as work groups. Furthermore, the role of project management is actually clearer in relation to the other groups, and legal reports directly through project management. To executives who are used to defining

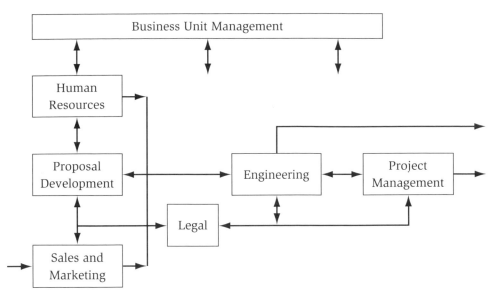

Figure 6.7. As-Is Process Element for Business Unit.

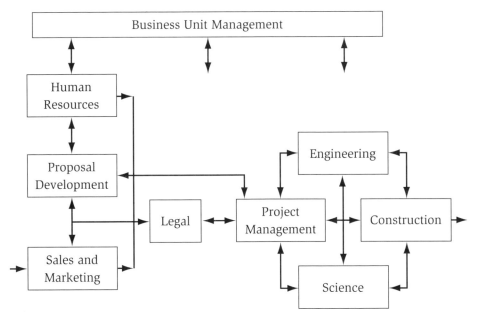

Figure 6.8. To-Be Process Element for Business Unit.

(or reorganizing) work groups at the start of a change activity, the order rec-ommended here will seem alien. However, it is the best approach for defining and improving a business. It may take some time to teach an old dog new tricks, but it can be done! When we had the opportunity to do this with enlightened executives, they enjoyed the methodology very much because they truly learned what their business was and saw it change to something much better. A case study illustrating this can be seen in an article by Phillips (1998).

Thus far, we have learned how to define, measure, and improve the behavior of business units, core processes, individuals, and work groups. Next we will consider work standards, work support, and human consonance to work behavior, which will lead us to performance alignment.

Grey Bar: Work Group Level

Kathleen Whiteside
Partner, Performance International

As noted elsewhere in this chapter, there are a number of reasons that work groups get "out of whack." Three short cases are cited below, each demonstrating one of the major reasons.

One reason groups are not aligned is that a major change has occurred, but the work group is still operating in its original way. For example, at a major weapons installation, the Nuclear Energy Commission created a safety and health watchdog group to ensure that violations were stopped. When first formed, this group needed to establish its seriousness of purpose and chose to do so with a certain no-nonsense approach to all meetings, whatever the purpose. However, having achieved their objectives (a very safe plant) they continued in their fierce approach toward all colleagues, even though it was no longer functional. They were now "out of whack" with their purpose, so they defined their work group and refocused their outputs and consequences.

A second reason that work groups get "out of whack" is reorganization. In management's attempt to be cost-conscious, they will often reorganize without thinking through the goal and purpose to be served. This results in apparently common groups being blended together; once together they find themselves at cross-purposes and in competition with themselves. An excellent example of this occurred in a major health care center where the human resources group, once centralized, was decentralized. The small group remaining at the corporate headquarters had a charter to provide design of corporate-wide programs and audit the training function in the divisions. The divisions were responsible for all implementation and the design of division-specific programs. Both groups

188 ALIGNING PERFORMANCE

joined together to go through a work group alignment process. They determined the outputs first, then mapped their outputs, inputs and processes, consequences, conditions, and feedback. What became startlingly clear was that processes, consequences, and conditions were identical for both the corporate and division groups. Although the outputs had similar names, outputs were different because the input was different. The input triggers were generally federal and state law changes and corporate strategy needs and new programs. The input that triggered division programs was generated at the local site and had no corporate-wide implications. Once the group had clarity about the similarities and differences between their two work groups, all the sniping and complaining, as well as the political posturing subsided. People got down to work.

A third reason a work group might need to be aligned is the influx of new personnel. For example, when a work group has a new boss, the work group alignment process can be used to orient him or her very quickly. The reason for this is simple: In talking about their work, a common language is used between manager and the work team. This provides the level of detail needed, while helping the emotional issues to come out in light of work needs and how best to resolve them. Without a common work language, the methodology for getting work done is often obscured, leaving the new boss with insufficient data. When people know something very well, they are often incapable of describing a whole system. Instead, they leave out significant points, assuming the other party is working from the same data points as they are. This leads to confusion, at best, and erroneous opinions at worst. There is no basis for generating good questions and systematically understanding the work. However, by taking a Language of Work approach to this problem, a great deal of shared understanding can be built in a few hours.

CHAPTER 7

Work Standards

The Excellence of Work

O nce it is known what behavior is needed in the business at the four performance levels, it is necessary that everyone understand the standard that
behavior should reach. In other words, "How well should the work be performed?" A systematic way to establish them ensures that all necessary standards are set, while avoiding over-definition. The system of setting standards
described here builds on the proforma of defining behavior. We will refer to this
as "layering" the standards, as we will later refer to layering work support and
work consonance.

Standards are the level of excellence to which we want work behavior to rise
so that it is acceptable to business, professional, and/or personal needs and
growth. If a fish's behavior is represented by its swimming, then the height it
is to jump and the speed it is to swim are some of the standards it should meet.
The question before us is, "How fast do you want the work groups, individuals, core processes, and business units to swim?"

In the Language of Work model, standards is one of the four major *layers* of
work, along with behavior, support, and human consonance. Standards must
be set after the work behavior has been defined and normally before work support is established. Sometimes standards may need minor adjustment due to

the kind of support the business is able to provide. In the same way that work support may be inadequate to achieve optimum work behavior, so too can standards suffer from lack of work support. This takes many forms, only one of which is the setting of unrealistic standards.

In the Language of Work model, standards are not considered part of work behavior. This is because one certainly can behave on the job and yet give little attention to standards. It is like watching a football team perform badly. You know they are playing football by the behavior you see, but the team is not meeting the standard of play desired.

In this chapter you will learn how to set standards in a systematic way consistent with the defined work behavior in a proforma. Not to set standards systematically against well-defined behavior is at best a guessing game. At worst not setting standards means that the possibility of excellence may be ignored—and therefore not achieved. It may mean also that critical standards are missed altogether. One need only be served in a retail store with no customer service standards to see numerous painful examples of nonexistent standards. Even when standards are well set, they require constant attention to be well understood and reinforced and improved on by everyone.

Every business has some standard for work it wants achieved—be it written and well-understood or implied in the very nature of the work. The proposal writer in our business case is supposed to produce a well-written document that wins a new contract for the company. The engineering department is supposed to produce well-conceived designs that conform to client needs and are cost-effective. The human resources department is supposed to select the right people to match the jobs, work groups, and core processes. It is obvious that many businesses simply do a poor job of setting standards, probably from a fundamental lack of understanding of what work is and therefore how to set consistent standards. If you cannot define the work behavior, it's likely you cannot accurately set the standards!

The business settings the author has worked full-time for have primarily been the construction, engineering, design, ship-building, and environmental industries. These businesses had stringent standards related to safety, as do many companies. The standards were well attended to, given company support, and produced positive consequences. Most of these companies supported the standards through hours of required training, results tracking, and full-time personnel in quality assurance and safety specifically assigned to the effort. Their desire to meet standards was driven by regulatory requirements, the wish to promote general welfare, avoidance of litigation, and expressions of genuine concern for a safe work environment.

In other businesses, such as the insurance industry, automotive, oil, electrical distribution, high-tech, or wholesale there are relatively few existing, stated standards. For the average worker the standards seem to be unwritten: "Do your job right!" and "Don't make waves."

For most businesses, a disparate level of standards exist and there seems to be no systematic way of setting them. They may assign some department or individual to the task, who then searches for areas of need based on function, rather than well-defined work behavior. They might ask, "Where are there danger points and what standards are needed?" "What quality program can we devise?" "How do we imbue the standards into our culture?" "Where is there a lack of productivity that would improve with standards?" All of these are good faith efforts, but those asking the questions do not recognize the four performance levels (business unit, core processes, individual jobs, and work groups) in any business that require standards. Not only does each level need to be analyzed for standards, but there should be an alignment of these standards across the four levels. Otherwise there is a standards vacuum and breakdown. For example, if the business unit has standards for identifying customers and maintaining contacts, they must have support at the individual level to achieve the business end.

WHY WE SET STANDARDS

The question is really why we set standards, not whether they should be set. Think for a moment of why you or the business you work for would set standards for your own job or work group. Also, consider standards that ought to be set that currently are not. There are four reasons for having standards:

1. They are required.
2. They would help the business reach its goals.
3. They motivate the individual or group to a higher level of personal work behavior than they might achieve without them.
4. Standards can reinforce behavior.

Standards That Are Required

Usually the government sets standards that protect the general welfare of workers and certain businesses as a whole. Standards might also be designed to promote the performance consistency of members of a profession (such as medicine or accounting). Regulated standards are primarily in the areas of health, safety, and employment, familiarly known in the United States as OSHA, EEO, and fair labor laws. Standards for weights and measures impact some businesses; still others affect workplace conditions, litigation, fines, record keeping, and so forth. Most of these standards are rather explicit and relate to specific behavior.

Standards That Help Businesses Reach Their Goals

Some standards are set by the business in order to achieve specific ends. These types of standards include production goals, service life, lead time, cost of materials, budget variances, amount of waste, loss time, cycle time, due dates, return on investment, and many others. These standards make clear for individuals, groups, core processes, and the business unit as a whole what is acceptable as cost, quantity, quality, or timeliness of behavior.

It is assumed that when everyone attends to standards, the standards will be achieved. Of course, merely directing attention (through policy manuals, orientations, or pep talks) is insufficient. People may forget, not be motivated, or lack the skill and knowledge to obtain and then attain the standards. Therefore, the business must provide appropriate interventions to encourage the attainment and subsequent reinforcement for business standards. A major subject of performance consulting, the interventions for attaining standards is one of the topics under work support in Chapter 8.

Standards That Motivate People to Higher Levels of Work Behavior

Motivational standards are much like business standards, but rather than being formal attributes the business desires, they are set by individuals or work teams to assure higher performance (and recognition thereof). Self-directed work teams, for example, set standards on the number, quality, timeliness, and/or cost of their production. They look for ways to improve their work in order to improve their standards and provide rewards to their team members and group. They may even "benchmark" their standard of achievement against others inside and outside the business. Self-motivating standards are some of the strongest for achieving excellence of work behavior. They impact work group and individual levels because they are driven by the human element. They should be tied to core process and business unit level standards set by the business; otherwise there can be gaps in achieving overall standards. Be this as it may, individuals and groups have the same difficulty that the business in general has in knowing how to systematically set standards.

Standards That Assure Reinforcement

One of the universal facts of business behavior is that individuals, teams, and work groups receive far less feedback than is needed to ensure acceptable levels of efficient and effective performance. Employees complain their managers don't tell them enough while they are processing or don't praise them enough when things go right—only when it goes wrong! Managers complain that their executives are the same way. And, it doesn't make much difference whether it is feedback to a team or work group—there isn't enough feedback—and when there is, it is often not of the right kind. Setting standards to schedules of reinforcement can help lead to more satisfactory levels of feedback. This means specifying what type of reinforcement will be given, when, how much, and by whom. Work maps are especially useful in helping identify where to set standards related to reinforcement; look in the feedback element in particular.

WHAT TO SET STANDARDS AGAINST

Standards must be set for work behaviors on the four performance levels of work as defined in the Business Sphere. Within each of these levels, set standards for each of the six elements of the proforma. This means analyzing each level and its proforma for standards, but standards will not be needed for everything. It is not necessary, for example, to have a specified standard for things that can be assumed to be performed to a given level of excellence. To specify too many standards is like over-defining work behavior. There is an acceptable level that communicates intent and achieves desired results. It is relatively easy to know what standards to set, but knowing when you have enough requires some guidelines and some experience. Some examples for each performance level of a business and its proforma are provided as guidelines for setting standards. Later, these will be put into a matrix for specific, systematic ways to establish standards where and when needed.

At the Business Unit Level

Inputs	Accurate identification of client needs
	Number of clients to be identified
	Standards of inputs the business expects of its vendors and suppliers
Conditions	Attention to regulations
	Attention to business policies and procedures
Process Elements	Individual work group goals and production standards
Outputs	Models of desired outputs
Consequences	Level of customer satisfaction
	Profit goals
Feedback	Timely reports and records

At the Process Level

Inputs	Equipment specifications
Conditions	Professional ethics
Process Elements	Production standards
Outputs	Models of outputs
Consequences	Efficiency
Feedback	Quality standards

At the Individual Level

Inputs	Does the individual seek out input?
Conditions	Do managers adhere to EEO standards?
Process Elements	Cycle time
Outputs	Number of outputs expected in a time frame
Consequences	Client satisfaction level
Feedback	Rating by client

At the Work Group Level

Inputs	Attention to individual contribution of new ideas
Conditions	Group adherence to team rules
Process Elements	Number of rejects
Outputs	Timeliness of outputs to other work groups
Consequences	Satisfaction of other work groups
Feedback	Consistent use of suggested improvements

This was quite a formidable list in and of itself. But it is not the complete picture of standards! Imagine the entire range of standards that is possible in any given business. How can we possibly identify all the standards that a business needs? How can we limit it to those that are really needed? We will deal with the how, then a way to limit standards to those that are really needed.

HOW TO SET STANDARDS CONSISTENTLY

Figure 7.1 provides a Work Standards Matrix (WSM) as a method to capture the standards of a business and analyze work behavior to set standards where needed. Remember that standards are not needed for every behavior. Many standards are and should be implied. We can assume, for example, that you can find many of your resource *inputs* and use them appropriately. This assumption may also be valid for some *conditions, process elements,* and *feedback.* We can assume, for example, that you know to get the football to play football. We don't have to say, get the football 95 percent of the time. It can also be assumed that you will have the usual tools for your job, whatever they may be. Standards need to be identified and evaluated in terms of their need throughout the business. Then the way that the business will use the standards to support, achieve, encourage, and reinforce adherence to them must be developed.

The Work Standards Matrix has the proforma on the horizontal axis and four general categories of standards recognized in business (quantity, quality, timeliness, and cost) on the vertical axis. Quantity and cost are perhaps the most commonly used standards.

Quantity simply says that the individual, work group, core process, or business unit will strive to achieve a certain number and will be evaluated against the number on a periodic basis. Total sales, number of jobs won, and number of returns are a few examples of quantity measures. Various examples of quantity have been listed on the matrix for inputs, conditions, process elements, outputs, consequences, and feedback. All of these will have to be given a numeric value.

Quality of late has taken on new meaning as competition has grown. The Malcolm Baldrige awards are given nationally to encourage quality. Quality was a critical part of work in the days of craftspeople. The Industrial Revolution, for all its merits, was a strong contributing factor to driving quality from individual and group accountability to core processes that became efficient in terms of time, but sloppy in quality. Business units now often strive for numbers and profit at the expense of quality (as measured by repeat business). Quality is the measure of the effect of work on customers and clients, either internal or external. Quality is especially problematic if the client is external and there is no possibility for correcting problems. The customer simply does not return and the business never asks why. When quality is promoted and standards are set, then there is no need to worry whether customers will return.

Timeliness is the degree to which delivery, response, conformance, schedules, and other time parameters set by the client, organization, individuals, or others are agreed on and met. A measure of time is needed to assure that others will have our product or service when they need it, that we have complied with conditions, and that feedback (such as reporting, communication) is received. To the extent these agreed on times are not met, work schedules suffer, information is not available when needed, compliance is not achieved, delivery is not on time, budgets are exceeded, profits diminish, and customers become unhappy.

Figure 7.1. The Work Standards Matrix.

The Work Standards Matrix

	Input	Conditions	Process Elements	Output	Consequences	Feedback
QUANTITY	Client Needs Identified RFPs Responded to Leads Provided Ideas Submitted Documents Available Orders Taken	Litigations Settled Fines Imposed	Breakdowns Steps Hands Touching Revisions Amount of Scrap Milestones Met	Total Sales Total Work Delivered Amount of Service Changes Billable Hours	Work Won ROI Expectations Met Marketshare	Returns QIPs Service Calls Changes
QUALITY	Client Needs Identified Usability for Processing Servicelife Measure of Other's Output as My Input	Stability Lemon Laws EEO Guidelines Injuries Compliance	Amount of Waste Rejects Loss Time Record	Rework Delivery Condition	Recalls Repairs Reject Rate Error-free	Complaints Kinds of QIPs Claims Level of Communication
TIMELINESS	Lead Time Just-In-Time Schedule Cycle Time	Conformance Regulation Reports Schedule	Hours Expended Overtime Hours Down-Time Response Time Schedule Cycle Time Delays Due Dates	Delivery Time	Lag Time On-Time	Response Time Schedule Cycle Time
COST	Raw Materials Cost Vendor/Supplier Cost	Cost of Regulation Budget Variance Budget Hours	Funds Committed Project Cost Labor Cost	Cost/unit	Profitability Cost/Benefits Ratio Value	Sales Figures Cost Per Sale

One of the more interesting aspects of timeliness is that we may guard our own time, to the detriment of someone else's time (and work). Timeliness is a *shared standard* throughout the business, not just an individual issue. Perhaps the fact that timeliness is a shared event is not emphasized enough. It is an instance in which attention to the "white space" is vital.

Cost standards represent the dollars and cents we attach to work. The most important standard for business is profit, unless the business is motivated by service or welfare of others. Other cost standards besides profit include cost per unit, cost of materials, budget variances, labor costs, and sales figures, to mention a few.

USING THE WORK STANDARDS MATRIX

To use the WSM to set standards in your business, you will first have to tailor the list to the business and make it complete. The model presented here is a skeleton to get you started and to serve as a general reference point. Tailor the WSM to your own environment. Add to and clarify the matrix with each use. Other standards will tend to come to bear during subsequent uses as the team sets standards at various performance levels of the business.

The second thing you will have to do is determine appropriate metrics for each standard. Metrics are the measurements in terms of numbers, dollars, percentage, time, and so forth. Thus, a standard such as fines (under conditions) could be measured in terms of the total number, kinds, dollar amount, and so forth. The business will first decide whether the standard is appropriate for a given work behavior, then set the metrics and level that is desired. For example, say that total sales are to be $2M within six months—both a number and a time metric. Some other examples in Figure 7.1 may help make this clear:

- As an input, client needs identified require an indication of how many needs.
- As a condition, litigations settled will need a number of cases and/or dollar amount.
- As a process element, revisions will need to be minimal in number and reflect dollars spent.
- As an output, rework will need an amount.
- As a consequence, work won will need to reach certain numbers and dollar amounts.
- As feedback, complaints will need standards of how many and length of time to respond.

Standards vary according to the element of work they are applied to. Let's use cost standards to illustrate this variance by work element. Viewing the WSM, you can see how cost relates to each element.

Input. Cost standards for input have to do with such things as raw materials and vendor or supplier costs. These costs must meet standards in order to assure low overall costs relative to producing output and achieving consequences. In order to assure adherence to input standards, businesses have more recently shifted the burden to suppliers to guarantee their costs or pay a penalty, rather than the business doing so. Thus, standards set by one business drive the standards of another.

Conditions. Condition cost standards have to do with meeting needs such as regulations, budgets, and the like. Businesses that have failed to comply with regulations pay the price of additional cost later for rework. For example, in the waste cleanup business it is difficult to predict underground conditions, contamination is difficult to control, and cleanup costs to recover and dispose of waste while doing the work are expensive. In the construction industry, failure to attend to condition costs specified in contracts results in litigation and total project overruns in the millions of dollars. The most common example of lack of attention to cost condition standards is the failure of an individual to attend to a budget, such as for a project.

Process Elements. Cost standards for process elements typically have to do with labor, project materials, and other funds committed to the process, for example, wages paid for producing or servicing goods. These standards relate directly to the work people do and the materials used. Businesses typically achieve cost standards through such things as labor agreements, technology, automation, efficiency of processing, or moving an operation to a cheaper location.

Outputs. Standards for output in general relate to the roll-up of the other standards and overall work for a unit cost per service or product. Although we set standards for output, it is really dependent on what goes on in the other work elements of the proforma and achieving standards for inputs, conditions, process elements, and feedback.

Consequences. Consequence cost standards are also dependent on other cost standards, specifically of outputs—which in turn depend on the other four elements. The prime example is profitability. Other typical cost measures include cost/benefit ratios and value per dollar. The link between quality, quantity, and timeliness standards that produce cost-effective outputs and then result in positive cost consequences cannot be ignored. It is one of those fine subtleties that executives and managers must learn—especially how their own actions and planning adversely affect cost. Profit, for example, cannot be produced directly as an output. It is the result of quality, quantity, timely, and cost-effective work in all performance layers and levels of work.

Feedback. Cost feedback standards relate to what happens to products and services once they leave a business and to those internal cost standards that relate to feedback while processing. Sales figures give us feedback on the acceptability of our product relative to the competition and returns give us feedback on the quality of the product. Labor cost overruns also give feedback during processing.

WORK LAYERING

Work layering is a technique unique to the Language of Work in which one layer of work (such as standards) can be used in concert with other layers (work behavior, support, and human consonance) to systematically determine how one layer aids or supports the others. It is one of the key methods of achieving performance alignment. Setting standards with the Work Standards Matrix is one example of layering. In a similar way you can use other matrices to layer work support and human consonance. In its generic form, the idea of work layering is illustrated in Figure 7.2.

In Figure 7.2, we see that work behavior must first be defined for each level of the Business Sphere. Work behavior is the bottom layer. Recall from the discussion in Chapters 3, 4, 5, and 6 that work behavior represents *what* (business unit), *how* (core processes), *by whom* (individuals), and *organization of work* (work groups). It is the anchor or foundation on which we then overlay other *layers* of work. For now, imagine that the work behavior represented in the figure is the engineering design core process of our business case.

The next layer is work standards, which represent how high we want the work to rise in its level of excellence. You would use the WSM to layer standards to work behavior. We will shortly provide an example of using the WSM to layer on standards to the engineering design core process.

The next layer is work support, a healthy environment in which the work behavior and standards can best be achieved. Chapter 8 contains an example of using the matrix and layering for the engineering design core process.

Finally, we layer in the human consonance to identify what human relationships are critical to achieving work group and individuals performance, systems (core processes), and organizational (business unit) performance needs. This will be described and illustrated in Chapter 9.

Figure 7.2. Work Layering.

Work Layering

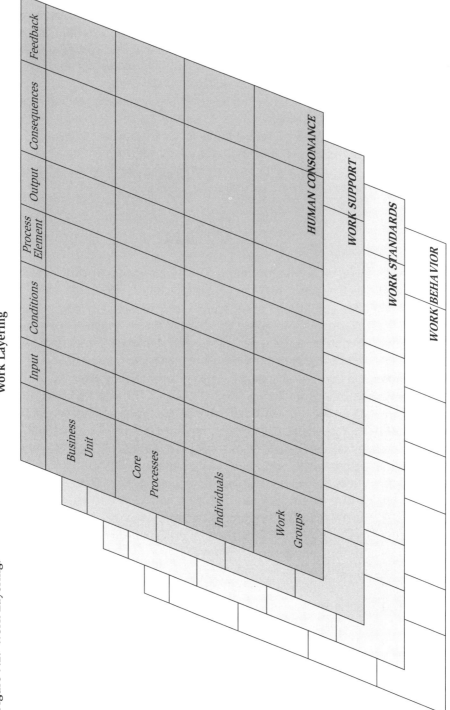

You will note that each layer involves the use of a matrix. The matrices are versions of job aids that performance consultants and others can use in doing work layering. With the exception of the Work Standards Matrix, each of these matrices has the same structure. Each is a combination of the four performance levels of business on the vertical axis and the proforma on the horizontal axis. The matrix is layered separately over each of the four levels of a business. In this chapter, we will give an example of layering work standards with work behavior in the case of the engineering design core process. The WSM can be used in the same way with any other levels of work.

USING THE WORK STANDARDS MATRIX TO SET STANDARDS

An example of layering work standards to one layer of work behavior should easily illustrate this methodology. Let's take the previously defined engineering design process level (Figure 4.7a, b) of our case business and layer in the work standards. Figure 7.3 is a listing of some of the work elements from Figure 4.7a, b, converted to a matrix. The matrix also includes the four categories of standards from the WSM. An abbreviated listing of the work elements for this core process is shown. In actual application, the entire core process would be listed and reviewed for places where standards would be desired. Review Figure 7.3 for a moment to familiarize yourself with it.

Essentially, what you see is that the environmental business has established the standards it wants and needs for the (abbreviated) engineering design core process. These standards were determined in the following way.

First, with the assistance of a performance consultant and experts in engineering, the business development team that defined the four levels of our case business has reviewed the Work Standards Matrix (Figure 7.1) and tailored it to their business environment, as shown in Figure 7.4. The custom version of the WSM was developed by asking general questions, such as

- What kinds of standards are expected of the business by regulatory requirements?
- What should we expect of our vendors in the way of standards?
- What kinds of standards does the business need for processing?
- What standards promote individual initiative?
- What standards should overall consequences achieve?
- What should be the standards of feedback on work?

Tailoring the WSM (or any other work matrix) involves looking at each of the boxes in the generic WSM and crossing out, or filling in new standards that are appropriate for the business. The selection criteria include those previously

	Quantity	Quality	Timelines	Cost
Inputs				
Client Request/Goal	RFP Identified /Responded	All Clients	Schedule	Cost of Proposal
Technology	X	Best Technology	X	X
Project Management	Leads Provided	Best Technology	Timeliness to Process	Cost of Proposal
Conditions				
Regulatory Requirements	Litigation Fines Changes Violations	Stability EEO # Injuries Compliance	Conformance Regulation Reports	Cost of Regulations
Design Code	Litigation Fines Changes Violations	Compliance	Conformance	X
Community Acceptance	Litigation Violations	Lemon Laws Compliance	X	X
Process Element				
1. Review Existing Data	# Changes Milestones Met	X	Hour Expended Response Time Schedule Delays Due Date	Material Cost Labor Cost
2. Review Regulations	X	Reports	Schedule Due Dates	X
3. Assess Local Conditions	Changes	X	Benchmark	Due Date
Outputs				
Engineering Designs	Billable Hours Total Sales	Delivery Condition	Delivery Time Schedule Adherence	Cost/Unit
Consequences				
Cost Effective Engineering Designs, Services, etc.	# Jobs Won ROI Marketshare Total Revenue	# Recalls Reject Rate % Error-Free	On-Time	Profitability Cost/Benefit Ratio $Value
Feedback				
Schedules	# Change Orders # Returns # Service Calls # Changes # Rejects	# Complaints # Claims	Response Time	Competitiveness

Figure 7.3. Sample Standards for the Engineering Design Core Process.

Work Standards Matrix for Case Business

	Input	Conditions	Process Elements	Output	Consequences	Feedback
QUANTITY	# RFPs Identified to # RFPs Responded to # Leads Provided # Orders Labor Available	Litigation Fines Regulatory Changes Violations	# Equipment # Breakdowns # Steps # Revisions # Changes Milestones Met	Total Sales Total Work Delivered Amount of Service # Changes # Billable Hours	Work Won ROI Expectations Met Market Share Workforce Retention # Employees Total Revenue	Returns QIPs Service Calls Changes Rejects Change Orders
QUALITY	All of Client Need Identified Best Technology Win/Loss Ratio Measure of Other's Output as My Input	Stability of Regs. Lemon Laws EEO Guidelines Number of Injuries Compliance	Reports Review Cycles Rejects Loss Time Record	Amount of Rework Delivery Condition	Recalls Repairs Reject Rate Error-free Test Accuracy	Complaints Kinds of QIPs Claims
TIMELINESS	Lead Time Timeliness to Process	Conformance Regulation Reports Schedule	Hours Expended Overtime Hours Down-Time Response Time Schedule Benchmark Delays Due Dates	Delivery Time Schedule Adherence Overruns	Lag Time On-Time	Response Time
COST	Raw Materials Cost Vendor/Supplier Cost Cost of Proposal	Cost of Regulation Budget Variance Budget Hours Competition	Funds Committed Equipment Cost Material Cost Overhead Cost Labor Cost	Cost/Unit Actual to Bid Cost Ratio	Profitability Cost/Benefits Ratio $ Value $ Fines	Sales Figures Cost Per Sale Overhead Competitiveness Cost/$ Revenue

Figure 7.4. Work Standards Matrix for Case Business.

noted related to business goals, motivation of individuals, regulatory requirements, and reinforcement needs. The results of the business tailoring to the
WSM is a set of standards like those illustrated in Figure 7.4. This WSM is a
convenient job aid that can be used in setting standards for already defined
work maps, such as the engineering design core process. Let's see how this is
done and what the results would look like.

Using the custom-tailored engineering business WSM, the business development team reviews each work element of the engineering design process listed
on the left in Figure 7.3. In the example you see a representative sample listed
for the core process proforma. By reviewing each element one at a time, one
can determine its needed standard with the aid of the standards listed in the
WSM. For example, "client request/goal" as an input in the engineering design
core process would benefit from the following standards:

Work Element		Standards		
Input	Quantity	Quality	Timeliness	Cost
Client Request	RFP Identified/ Responded to	All Clients	Schedule	Cost of Proposal

This example illustrates that a quality standard is being set to make sure that
requests for proposals (RFP) are clearly identified and responded to in all cases.
This may not seem important, but often a careful study of what the client says
he or she wants is not undertaken. This happens because the engineer sets off
to design what he *thinks* the client needs, rather than what the client specified.
It will come back to haunt the company later through rework. The standard is
there to help the company head off problems and be more proactive. In this
instance, a quality standard is set for all clients, timeliness is defined according
to a predetermined schedule, and the cost is estimated according to a proposal
document.

Specific metrics must be established for each standard, for example, "respond
to all clients within fourteen days," "respond to clients in terms of all needs
specified in RFP," and so forth. There must be a systematic setting of standards
for each element of defined and agreed work behavior.

In cases in which no standard is needed, or may be assumed to exist by common understanding, an "X" has been entered in Figure 7.3. Remember that
there is no need to over-specify standards or over-detail work behavior.

Let's look at one more example so that the method of identifying standards
is clear. Again, we tailor the WSM to the business. We will set the standards for
one of the steps in the process element of the engineering design core process.
In Figure 7.3, we see that the first step in the engineering design process is
"review existing data." Figure 7.5 illustrates how the WSM was used to derive
the standards for this step.

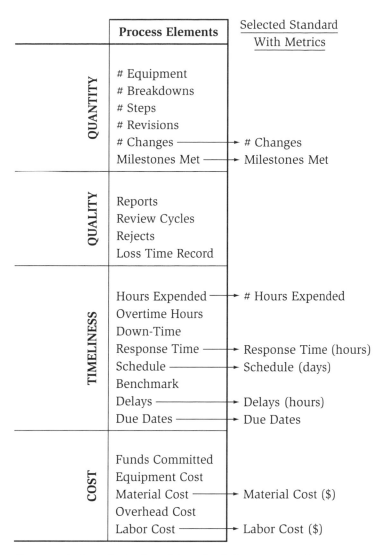

	Process Elements	Selected Standard With Metrics
QUANTITY	# Equipment # Breakdowns # Steps # Revisions # Changes ⎯⎯⎯⎯➤ Milestones Met ⎯⎯➤	 # Changes Milestones Met
QUALITY	Reports Review Cycles Rejects Loss Time Record	
TIMELINESS	Hours Expended ⎯⎯➤ Overtime Hours Down-Time Response Time ⎯⎯➤ Schedule ⎯⎯⎯⎯⎯➤ Benchmark Delays ⎯⎯⎯⎯⎯➤ Due Dates ⎯⎯⎯⎯➤	# Hours Expended Response Time (hours) Schedule (days) Delays (hours) Due Dates
COST	Funds Committed Equipment Cost Material Cost ⎯⎯⎯➤ Overhead Cost Labor Cost ⎯⎯⎯⎯➤	 Material Cost ($) Labor Cost ($)

Figure 7.5. Sample Assigned Standards for Process Element.

By working our way through the process element standards in the tailored WSM, we can identify the ones that are appropriate to each work element. Thus, among the six standards for quantity related to the process element, two (number of changes and milestones met) were selected. Other standards shown in Figure 7.5 were derived by using the same method.

Determining standards to this degree of detail can be an arduous task. Consider setting standards at a more generic level when possible. For example, one can take all the existing inputs for the engineering design process and match them to the appropriate standards from the WSM. Whether to be highly specific or more generic is up to you. However, the following recommendations are especially helpful for determining the number of standards to have in a business.

WHAT STANDARDS NEED TO BE RETAINED AND ATTENDED TO?

We can truly have too many standards in business. It's like over-specifying work behavior and not getting the results that communicate and achieve what we want. So, too, the purpose of layering standards should not be to have so many standards that those trying to follow them are overwhelmed. Even if we set a number of standards, how do we decide on an ongoing basis which are most critical, retain these, and attend to them? Those that are required by law and are critical to business survival are a must. How do we identify and limit the others?

One of the ways is to use a classic *performance gap analysis approach.* With this approach, we can measure the extent to which any standard is being followed (achieved) and devote more attention to it if necessary. If the standard is being achieved, we would not emphasize it and drop it from our specifications for standards. For example, if client requests are not being responded to in a timely way against a seven-day standard, we would attend to it. If, however, engineers attend to all client requests in terms of quantity by reviewing the RFP, why put this standard at the forefront of the engineer's attention? A periodic review of work standards would be an excellent activity (output) for the management facilitation work group described in Chapter 6. This could take the form of a continuous improvement process at the operational level of the business.

The second method for deciding which standards to attend to is for the executive management work group to *review standards in various categories on a regular basis* looking for strategically important standards that would have long-term impact on the business. This method is often used in businesses with safety standards if accidents are increasing and standards are being missed. Other standards would be treated the same way. That is, the executive management team would develop strategic initiatives for important identified standards that were not being achieved. Thus, if the executive team reviewed the business and noted that shipment delays were negatively affecting the business, then the executives would focus attention on this issue. The actual standard itself should be set by those who are close to the work. Therefore, the facilitator's work group—one level below the executive team—would meet together to determine what is causing the deliveries to be delayed. Problems would be analyzed by senior management. Solutions would be part of strategic analysis and planning around standards. Then the individual work groups would participate in setting standards around delivery time. These activities would result in a presentation to the executive team, which could approve the standard and measures or urge a more aggressive standard, and the team would start over.

Now that you know how to set and pay attention to standards, we move to the next layer of work—work support. If we have the work behavior well-defined and know what standards it should rise to, the next step is to determine whether the business can provide the kind of support that makes the performance levels of work achievable.

CHAPTER 8

Work Support

The Health of Business

The third layer of work is work support. If the fish swimming is behavior and the height the fish jumps is a standard, then the water provided for the fish to swim in is the support needed. Pristine clean water allows optimum behavior and standards to be achieved. Dirty, oxygen-deprived water doesn't support the optimal behavior of the fish. As performance consultants we have a great deal of work to do in helping to establish work support throughout the business. Work support is the very health of the business.

A performance consultant could spend a lifetime facilitating nothing but building and improving work support. Indeed many specialists in the performance field have done just that. Some of these are called trainers, while others go by names such as organizational development specialists, work simplification engineers, HR specialists, managers, and many others. Their job has been to apply one or more specific interventions that support the work in the business. These specialists are there to improve the health of the organization so that work can take place in an atmosphere that promotes efficiency, effectiveness, and growth. They are vital to the business. This chapter will bring a new and systematic way to look at this support; it will broaden your professional scope to that of performance consultant who operates throughout the business. As a performance consultant dealing in all available interventions you will be able to make your business more effective and efficient. This is true whether you are a full-time performance consultant or a manager who is trying to facilitate his workforce in doing its best. Improving the health of the business will enhance the performance of the business unit, core processes, the individuals, and work groups.

Being a performance consultant requires becoming more of a facilitator than a developer or implementer of interventions. As noted, if you want to spend your professional career just doing work support, it is possible. However, a complete performance consultant facilitates development of all four layers of performance, not just the work support. This phenomenon recognizes that work is a multilevel and a multilayer set of dependent relationships aimed at achieving alignment. Concentrating on one layer of work or a single intervention cannot solve the wide range of work needs. An excellent intervention or combination of interventions cannot overcome poorly designed work behavior or meaningless or ineffective standards. We ideally don't want one side of the performance boat rising, while the other side is sinking. Therefore, a superb performance consultant will understand work and facilitate at all levels and at all four layers. A great performance consultant will be able to identify the need for support, but will not be fooled into thinking that he or she is providing superb service if he or she stops at work support.

You will find as a performance consultant that executive management and other facilitators often place work support into the business in an inconsistent, programmatic manner. For instance, an executive (because he read an article in the *Harvard Business Review*) will decide that the business needs a particular intervention, one which worked well at XYZ Company. For instance, remember the time before the proliferation of mission and vision statements? Once one executive said it worked, the others acted like lemmings, demanding those statements in every organization. Such initiatives are often actualized through a special project team, perhaps aided by an external consultant. The next thing you know, mission and vision statements are emblazoned in plaques and banners all over every McDonald's, public library, and convenience store. The problem with this approach is that these interventions cannot be operationalized within themselves. There is little way for the vision and mission statements to affect work behavior or standards directly. There is no question that the mission and vision are good work support, but when they are not aligned to the other layers of work needed to operationalize and give them meaning, they can be insignificant.

Business is replete with examples of establishing work support in less than an optimal manner. Even mandated initiatives, such as a performance review program, can suffer the same fate. All are good ideas for work support, but they are rarely well-integrated into the work they purport to support. This chapter will show you ways to achieve alignment and integration.

WHY WORK SUPPORT IS NEEDED

Work support, again using our fish analogy, is the water quality the fish needs to swim (behave) in and reach the desired standards of performance. Murky waters simply mean that the business unit, core processes, individual, and work group behavior cannot reach their potential.

Whenever you hear someone in the organization saying things like the following, you know that work support is inadequate or missing:

- "If something goes wrong, it's hard to know who to turn to."
- "There isn't enough equipment to go around to get our work done!"
- "If I only had that kind of software I could get this project done so much faster and with greater reliability."
- "There is no communication between our department and theirs!"
- "If you have a good idea, there is nowhere to present it, and if there were, no one would do anything about it!"
- "How do they ever identify client needs around here?"
- "Customer satisfaction? What about my job satisfaction?"
- "Too many meetings. All we do around here is have meetings!"
- "The number of e-mails is driving me crazy!"
- "We need a different culture around here."

To know where work support is marginal, just listen for the word "communication" to pop up. Poor communication is a sweeping term often used by both management and the workforce to indicate that things just are not right. This is a way of saying that the mechanisms for getting things done—one aspect of support—are weak and need some attention. So, the management calls in a consultant and says communication needs improving. Unfortunately, they often follow this statement with, "Give us a training program." But training is not *the* answer. If the need for "communication" indicates a need for work support, there are five primary reasons for providing it.

First, *work can't be done as effectively and efficiently without support.* It's one thing to say, "Use this equipment, pay attention to this rule, follow this process element, and measure this." It is quite another thing to provide the means and mechanisms that make these things accessible. For example, in one organization we worked in, the secretaries often asked the executive team members (their bosses) the rules regarding time off, hiring, and firing. If one secretary gave an answer someone did not like, the person would call another secretary until an answer he or she liked was given. The rules existed in a policy manual that only executives had access to. Rather than reading the policies to determine the answers, secretaries would answer based on what they thought was right or on what they knew the boss had "ruled" in another case. Thus, supervisors and department heads were dependent on low-level interpretations instead of having the actual manuals themselves. This was rectified by placing policy manuals in every supervisor's hands. Policies were re-written so that exceptions could be requested and granted, according to policy, not the whim of secretaries or executives.

Second, *support aids communication.* Some sample communication channels include establishing a way to get a work assignment, learning what your benefits are, knowing where to take a grievance, or knowing where suggestions can be made and who will follow through. These communication channels support getting the work done. For example, the rest of the support provided in the organization described above was a course for supervisors in how to look up, read, understand, and apply policies to a variety of situations that were likely to occur. The training was in a learner-controlled delivery system, which allowed the trainee to respond to simulated questions that employees might ask. Supervisors were able to be trained this way because systems had been built to meet every communication need. Systems were built for getting work assignments, submitting grievances, making suggestions, determining benefits, and completing claims. Then policies were written. Once the policies were approved, employees received two forms of communication: An article in the house organ summarizing the policy changes and an update to their employee handbook. This was an organization that took communication and employee support seriously. By the way, the abundance of support was a strategic decision, not just the belief of well-intentioned executives. Trained employees were in short supply and readily recruited to other organizations if they did not feel well taken care of.

A third reason for having work support is that *it focuses the business on its drivers* and reminds the business to attend to these drivers, lest it fail. For example, having mechanisms in place to identify customers needs, to do strategic and business planning, and to identify and monitor changing regulations are proactive ways for a business to stay in business. These are some of the support mechanisms that continue the link between external business alignment and internal performance alignment described in Chapter 1. Businesses fail for many reasons. An analysis of failures will show that not having a system in place that forces the business to analyze drivers can be a significant predictor of failure. Therefore, annual retreats, required publication dates for strategic plans, and systems that force the organization to keep abreast of new technologies and see how client needs are changing, all support staying in business. A performance consultant can have significant impact by ensuring that such systems are in place and facilitating their effectiveness.

As is the case with standards, some of work support is mandated. The business must have safety programs, follow equal employment opportunity guidelines, do safety training, and so forth. For example, within the human resources department, someone keeps track of employee selection so that the business is not in violation of equal employment opportunity rules. Others ensure that payment is in keeping with the Fair Labor Standards Act. The important thing is to ensure that employees know about and follow mandated work support.

Finally, a fifth reason for work support is that *it focuses our attention on customers and clients so that we don't take them for granted.* Thus, we provide work support in the way of installing customer satisfaction surveys, promoting our reputation, enhancing public relations, and establishing our measures of success. These factors ensure that the business remains viable and that our customers are retained. Without an atmosphere that makes customers return, no other work support mechanisms will be necessary.

With these five reasons in mind, a systematic way to look at and identify work support in the organization will aid us in ensuring total work support. As a performance consultant you will need to help your business identify the various work support factors that are key to achieving its desired work behavior and meeting standards. Although there are some aspects of support no business can do without, there are others that are only needed at a certain size, maturity level, or even industry. Of course, having carefully defined the work behavior and aligned it with standards will help in any case, because the work support should be anchored to that foundation.

WHERE TO PROVIDE WORK SUPPORT

It will come as no surprise to readers that every level of a business needs support: business unit, core processes, individuals, and work groups. The nature and scope of this support varies; some of it is directly related from one level to another. Other support stands on its very own within a particular level. Others are so dependent that without adequate alignment, one can seriously diminish the overall effectiveness of a given support merely by neglecting other levels. Goal setting, for example, needs to be consistent from one level of business to another. So, support is needed at all four levels and needs to be identified, provided, monitored, and continuously attended to achieve an important layer of performance alignment.

SUPPORT NEEDED AT EACH LEVEL

As with the determination of work behavior and standards, work support should begin at the business unit level and cascade its way through core processes, individuals, and work groups. This is true whenever support at one level drives and should be accounted for at the other levels. For instance, when goals are supported at the business unit level, we should find concomitance with individual assignments at the individual level and project assignment at work group levels. This need was identified a few years ago as "line of sight" goal setting, and now has (as with other support) a place within the general work support system throughout the business.

We will first provide an overview of each work level in terms of its need for and the value of work support. Following this, we will look at a systematic method for determining necessary support in the business and layering it to the behavior. We will also identify support for the related standards. We will be looking at the specific support the business must provide to ensure a healthy environment for work to occur at all the performance levels.

Business Unit Support

The business unit level has a unique support need that is designed to achieve two purposes. The first use provides the "drivers" to determine what the business will be; the second use provides the same support to the overall business unit as is needed for the other three levels. Thus, the business unit has a unique duality to work support. Let's look at the first set of "drivers" to the business that should be considered during initial organization, reengineering, or reorganizing a business and should be reassessed on a periodic basis.

Any business first should consider the several factors that make it a business doing what it does (the behavior). It should then determine how it would differentiate itself from other businesses and, similarly, what it must do to maintain a level of competitiveness that ensures its survival. This awareness of differentiation and competitiveness is needed so that the business can remain profitable. These "driving" considerations are commonly known by the overall title of "strategy and business planning." In the Language of Work model, they are inputs to the business unit. They include considerations related to knowing customers' needs, the competitive advantage the business will seek to achieve, its driving force, its mission/vision, and strategic plan. Other inputs can, of course, be added as desired depending on the nature of the business, its marketplace, and competition. For a performance consultant, some knowledge of and awareness of strategic issues is important. However, diagnosing the need is more critical than being able to meet it.

A second general category of "drivers," affecting what the business will be and how it strategically approaches the marketplace, are the controls or limits that exist on what it can be. It's one thing to have a desire, but quite another to be realistic about that desire. External controls, rules, and realities can significantly affect ones ability to survive in certain businesses. For example, wanting to be a toxic waste disposal company is a fine goal. But knowing whether toxic waste can be deposited in your state is a critical factor. These conditions may be labeled the "culture/controls," and would include, among others, budget/funds, competition, decision authority, organizational units, regulations, desired culture, and methods of change.

The "culture" of the organization is a factor at the business unit level. In a company that is highly regulated, the culture will reflect that fact. On the other hand, a highly entrepreneurial company, a start-up business, or one that is highly leveraged will show a very different culture. The culture is the way the rules and expectations are imbedded in the organization. It is the thought patterns that cause people to see opportunities and threats in similar ways. As a performance consultant, you will often be asked to help change the culture or to help manage the change from one culture to another. Whole books have been written on this topic, so we won't diminish that thinking by summarizing it here. As a performance consultant, you may well contract with experts in this arena. The important thing to know is where the culture and control issues reside at the business unit level. They are support issues within the conditions. Remember that conditions are difficult to change and influence other elements of work, and so enter into the fray with caution.

Note that the *input* and *condition* drivers of a business are also part of the ongoing support to the business unit. This is because ignoring any one of these could lead to a degradation of business unit work performance; this could also be a cause of failure or degradation of other support input or conditions on other levels. Recall that some support depends on the business unit level support—especially those established and maintained by executive management. For instance, if the "method of change" as a condition is not attended to, quality processes (core process level), individual continuous improvement initiatives (individual level), and self-managed teams (work group level) might not do what they need to support continuous change. Visit any quality initiative that does not have ongoing senior level management participation and you will see the breakdown of the initiative from lack of business unit support.

The *process element* of a business unit requires a number of "administrative systems" to support the business unit level. These affect the degree of centralization or decentralization, and cover organizational hierarchy, flexibility, consistency of operations, and others. The business unit process element is, after all, the combination of work groups that comprise the business and need administrative support. For example, we know that in highly decentralized organizations getting business unit support for a favored new business activity can be very time-consuming. This is traded off against a highly centralized authority in which too much control also prevents getting things done. The central question in the process element at the business unit level is, "What administrative support is needed in order for the business to achieve its work behavior?"

One could argue that work support for business unit *outputs,* as with other levels of output support, is not a consideration. However, we have seen too often companies that do not clearly know their output at the business unit level.

This confusion in deliverables comes from not looking strategically enough at the company or a combination of other causes, such as these:

- When companies have just grown, without doing the hard thinking needed to be clear about who they are and what they do
- When merger mania has been the corporate modus operandi, or
- When the core processes have been ignored, and many ancillary functions have been added to the company

What is needed in the way of support is a mechanism that regularly looks at products and services and rationally reviews their contribution to the company. Naturally, there is a connection to the inputs and the consequences. The task of the work support is to ensure the connection.

Work support for business unit *consequences* relate to "business results." What will the desired market share or the dominance strategy be? What will the measures of success, customer satisfaction, and stakeholder satisfaction be? Support to business unit consequences is primarily support that sets the goals to be achieved—mainly in terms of market and various levels of satisfaction. These goals can be monitored to measure overall satisfaction with the business.

Finally, business unit *feedback* support encompasses the "business measurement and evaluation." What specific measures will monitor the business unit so that the information can be fed back to reward, make adjustments, and see that the drivers and behavior are working? These measures might include such means as return on investment, reputation indices, reactions or requests from stakeholders or clients, and so on.

As a performance consultant, there are a number of ways you can ensure that support exists at the business unit level. The ideas above show you a way to impose some order on the confusion. Because performance consultants do not always have a business degree, and because we specialize in the human side of the business, we may not have as much expertise as is needed to credibly lend support. But understanding where the elements for support belong can go a long way toward being able to advise clients in the need for support at the business unit level. Our ally can be the experts in such matters, who in turn need our expertise in performance to identify and achieve it. We are the facilitators of performance and not the experts in content—but we must at least have some level of business acumen.

Core Process Support

In examining the need that core processes have for support, we see that there are fewer human issues, but there are other performance issues nonetheless. Core process level support answers the question, "What will the resources, regulations, technologies, quality, and measurement support be for core processes? And, if these are not in place, how can they be put there?"

In terms of *inputs,* core processes require support in terms of various "process resources." These generally include the right kind of equipment, raw materials, and intellectual knowledge that will be used during processing. We have all seen the failure of a business to provide adequate equipment and the effect this can have on productivity. Inadequate or untimely knowledge can be just as negative. As performance consultants, we may be the ones to identify these inadequacies. People cannot do their work—the fish cannot swim when the water is inadequate.

Conditions at the core process level are the "regulations and policies" that govern processes. Many of these come from external sources such as the government. Others are internal policies established by the business to govern process implementation. Still others include professional ethics and standards. How will the business know what these are and see that they are supported and by whom?

Perhaps the largest and most expensive forms of core process support are the "technologies" for the *process elements.* In our fast-paced, ever-changing, global economy, the computers required to provide the hardware and software technologies to support business processes are very expensive, labor intensive, and ever-changing with updates. Most businesses have to support knowledge transfer in the computer arena to a tremendous extent. Whole information technology support organizations have arisen as the way for businesses to gain support. Without these kinds of support, many industries are at a competitive disadvantage. Thus, millions of dollars are devoted to process element support of processes—perhaps at times to the detriment of other support needs.

The core processes are supported in terms of *consequences* through creating the mechanisms that will measure and monitor processes. Consequences for core processes or "process results" generally are supported by delineating the means and ways for cost, delivery times, quality, and quantity metrics the organization needs.

Finally, *feedback* support takes the forms of programs for continuous improvement, management reinforcement, quality checks, schedule monitoring, and many other forms. Without these, core processes can atrophy and not recognize the need to change or improvement, or simply not stay on schedule.

Individual Level Support

Surprisingly, the average business provides far less support at the individual level than at any other level. This is surprising because this is the key level where work is done. It may be understandable in that the individual is the most complex of entities. The business unit and core processes can be affected without complaint, but give an individual or work group something or take something away and see what happens. Even when it is a desirable form of support, such as a quality improvement program, some individuals will complain. Many people do not like change; therefore, to them any form of work support that brings about change can't be all that good! From a manager's or performance technologist's point of view, it's damned if you do, and damned if you don't. It can cause even the bravest and most innovative of executives and managers to get a little "gun-shy" trying to institute other kinds of work level support. Who wants to invite resistance? Unfortunately, if you want to achieve that ultimate culture with a positive support system, struggle and change management will be required. As my trusted graduate advisor, Dr. John Rufi, once said, "Change brings conflict, but change isn't all that bad, so get used to it!"

Fundamentally, if we want a healthy business, we have to provide a variety of kinds of support at the individual level and suffer some unavoidable agony while getting people to where they need to be. It has been retold often that when Xerox decided to pursue the quality initiative, at least one executive left the company believing such a support strategy was wrong-headed and bad for business. Often new managers, prepared to provide an ailing department or division with the appropriate support measures, experiences turnover or grousing among the veterans who liked it the way it was. For example, a manager we knew installed a system to give feedback monthly. Resistance sprang high, but the manager persevered, and before long, all the individual performance improved. One of your allies is time and knowing when and how to introduce several interventions. It can take several years to establish a healthy organization, depending on the starting point.

Readiness is another issue to take into account. Achieving the types of support suggested in this chapter, and recognizing what support exists and what is lacking, means the performance consultant can always provide a valuable addition to the support of the organization. The proforma view of individual work support needed to make a business operate effectively and efficiently includes the following.

Individual *input* support relates to "client needs and resources." There is no question that individuals need clear work assignments, good equipment, goals and objectives, a functional job description, and ways to identify client needs— just to mention a few kinds of input support. Some may think of identifying client needs as skill or knowledge, but I believe that the organization needs ways and permission for the individual to seek out clarity around these needs. In working with individuals who have been my primary clients as an internal consultant, I did not often find business support for me as a trainer to do careful client assessments. For example, a manager would tell me he needed a training program to solve a particular communication problem he was having. When I suggested we undertake an analysis to see what the exact performance problem was, he told me to forget that and give him the training. In short, there was virtually no support in the organization to suggest, "Hey, wait a minute. That ain't right. I am an expert in performance analysis!" What that manager (and others like him) doesn't understand about work is how his lack of support affects my work behavior. By not allowing me to do the analysis, I can't produce the best solution, and he doesn't get the best solution to his need. Such questioning of support at an input level is necessary, and there are ways for organizations to make sure it becomes part of the culture. Healthy cultures in businesses like Hewlett-Packard and others foster (support) inquiry. Managers who do not allow analysis keep us from providing the best possible solution. Every business can benefit from supporting people's need to expand questioning, inquiry, and open communication.

Individual *condition* support is "work influences." What conditions impact your own work and what does your company do to make those conditions known, adhered to, and efficient for doing your work? What kinds of benefits and pay does it provide, and do you consider these sufficient for doing the kind of work you do? Are the ergonomics desirable, ranging from a comfortable chair to adequate lighting. Is there a handout or access to a computer program that outlines what your benefits are, how to process a claim, and so on? What is your workload and how does it impact your getting work done—especially if your business has been recently downsized? Would you judge this work support adequate, or does it have a somewhat negative impact on your work?

Individual *process element* support generally has to do with "work methods." Are you provided training and other forms of performance enhancement to update and refresh skills and knowledge? One of the more interesting observations to be made of individual process support is when, in the throes of downsizing, the business forgoes individual support of work (training). Over time you see the skill of the workforce no longer keeping pace with production and the progress of other businesses like it. One support mechanism that the author has personally seen taken away at a time the business needed it the most was a continuous improvement program. If there were ever a way to help the business during distressed times, it was this particular support effort. Yet management often finds training, continuous improvement, and others convenient "programs" to eliminate until times are "better."

Support for individual *consequences,* as at the core process level, is mostly tied to customer satisfaction, although other important consequences, including personal and job satisfaction, should be supported as well. It has always been an enigma that a business may give quite a bit of attention to supporting customer satisfaction, but much less attention to the job and personal satisfaction that have so much to do with helping achieve customer satisfaction. What does the organization do to promote pride in one's job? What is done to make the quality of personal satisfaction reflected in that person's opinion expressed to others about the company? These "individual results" are the key support needed for achieving overall individual consequences.

Finally, work support for *feedback* includes the "confirmation and self-adjustment" means and modes for improving one's work. Performance appraisal or review, rewards and recognition, adequate compensation, and such are prime examples of work support for individual feedback. One sure sign that this support is inadequate is high turnover in the workforce. What support is lacking to keep the workforce in place? Is it merely compensation, or are there other things?

Work Group Support

As you might suspect, work group support to some degree parallels support for individuals—naturally with some difference to account for group versus individual work requirements. Many of these represent not only support for the group itself, but also relations with other groups. It is often the transition of outputs from one group to another as input that can be a source of work problems if not supported appropriately.

Input support for work groups represents "client needs and resources." This is consistent with the definition of inputs as triggers and other resources. Thus, project and business needs are typical supports to trigger inputs. Surprisingly few resources are in need of support at the work group level, mainly because these are accounted for at the individual level, except in the case of team resources. Certain scheduling of inputs would be in order. For example, scheduling classrooms is certainly a support to instructors doing training.

Condition support for work groups is represented as the "values and practices" of the group. This title doesn't particularly suggest it, but conditions would also include budget allocation support. The values and practices include things like conflict resolution mechanisms, decision authority, ethics, management and leadership practices and expectations, and other group practices. With the knowledge of other group practices, for example, each group is left to its own autonomy without any regard for another group that they share work processing with. These relationships cannot be left without any support at all.

Process element support for work groups is much like that for individual support. Some questions to ask include: What is the management system? How will personnel be selected into the group? How will skills be maintained? and How is work flow developed? As with conditions, process elements also need special support emphasis around "interface relationships." Support in the way of partnership agreements and work group ties is important.

The *consequences* support for work groups relate to work group results. Client retention mechanisms, how to support the company's reputation, and teamwork are important. Accounting for consequences with other work groups means attention to goal consistency across all units.

Finally, *feedback* support for work groups is both management and team information systems. Continuous improvement methods, measurements, and information systems are key. Some questions include: How will meetings be structured? How will the group work be facilitated?

In summary, we have described a great number of support interventions. Performance consultants must be able to understand and apply these in a systematic way and, when they are not present or weak, justify the need for improvement to management.

HOW TO IDENTIFY THE SUPPORT NEEDED IN A SYSTEMATIC WAY

Figure 8.1 shows the Work Support Matrix of the Language of Work model, with the proforma on the horizontal axis and the four performance levels of the business sphere on the vertical axis. The matrix shows support interventions required for each work element and associated performance level. Under each heading the various kinds of work support are listed. Each has been shown in numerous business situations to be required for a business to be healthy. The matrix is organized in such a way that, at the business unit level, we find a title that expresses the kind of support for each element of work. Thus, inputs at the business unit level have the intent of "strategy and business plans." Business unit conditions have the intent of "culture and controls." And so on with titles of intention for each work element in each performance level.

It is not intended that a complete list be provided on the matrix, although it is fairly exhaustive. It is intended both to show the range of interventions needed in an organization and to serve as a guideline for others that may need to be identified in your own unique organization. As with the standards matrix and other aids provided in this book, the performance consultant, with the assistance of others, will have to tailor this support matrix to each business, in terms of support interventions and the titles by which they are best known in the organization.

The Work Support Matrix may be used to identify and assess work support needs in two ways. The first is commonly referred to in performance consulting as an "organizational scan." It grew out of the early work of Dr. Donald Tosti (Dean, 1997) in the field of performance technology in the mid-1970s. His work, and subsequent work of others such as Bob Carlton of the Vector Group, closely influenced the development of the Language of Work model as related to work support. The organizational scan is one useful performance analysis method for the performance consultant.

The second way to use the Work Support Matrix is a version of work layering, a method we used in the identification of standards in Chapter 7 and will use in Chapter 9 for identifying human consonance. Layering is unique to the Language of Work model. Let's look at organizational scanning first.

Work Support Matrix

	Input	Conditions	Process Elements	Output	Consequences	Feedback
BUSINESS UNIT	*STRATEGY and BUSINESS PLANS* Competitive advantage Customer needs Driving force Mission/vision Strategic plan	*CULTURE/ CONTROLS* Regulations Budget Competition Decision authority Desired culture Methods of change Organizational units/ functions	*ADMINISTRATIVE SYSTEMS* Consistency of operation Degree of centralization/ decentralization Flexibility Linkages/interactions Organizational hierarchy	*BUSINESS DELIVERABLES* Business Plan • Knowledge • Products • Services	*BUSINESS RESULTS* Market share Measures of success Satisfaction of customers Satisfaction of stakeholders Public relations	*BUSINESS MEASUREM./EVALUAT.* Measures of success Reaction/requests of stakeholders/clients Reputation ROI
CORE PROCESSES	*PROCESS RESOURCES* Individual and Work Group Needs: • Equipment • Raw materials • Intellectual knowledge	*REGULATIONS/ POLICIES* External regulations Internal policies Professional ethics Professional standards	*TECHNOLOGIES (SOFT and HARD)* Hardware technologies Knowledge transfer mechanisms Software Systems approach Schedule Management facilitation	*PROCESS DELIVERABLES* Process: • Knowledge • Products • Services	*PROCESS RESULTS* Product or Service: • Cost • Delivery • Quality • Quantity	*CONFIRMATIONS and CORRECTIONS* Continuous improvements Management reinforcement Measurements Quality checks Schedules
INDIVIDUALS	*CLIENT NEEDS and RESOURCES* Assignments Boss/organization Equipment Goals and objectives Identified client needs Job description	*WORK INFLUENCES* Benefits/pay Budget Ergonomics Ethics Employee handbook Policies Safety Workload	*WORK METHODS* Documentation Job aids Skill maint./devel. Skill update/enhance-ments Work flow Work tools	*JOB DELIVERABLES* Individual unit: • Knowledge • Products • Services	*INDIVIDUAL RESULTS* Customer satisfaction Job satisfaction Personal satisfaction Tie to work group	*CONFIRMATIONS and SELF ADJUSTMENTS* Adequate compensation Career development plan Dialogue Internal client evaluations Performance appraisal Rewards and recognition Turnover
WORK GROUPS	*CLIENT NEEDS and RESOURCES* Projects Business needs Knowledge Orientation	*VALUES and PRACTICES* Budget/Funds Conflict resolution Culture Decision authority Ethics Mgmt/leadership practices and expect. Other group practices	*INTERFACE/ RELATIONSHIPS* Management system Partnerships Personnel selection Skill main./ devel. workflow Work group ties	*WORK GROUP DELIVERABLES* Plans: • Knowledge • Products • Services	*WORK GROUP RESULTS* Client retention Goal consistency across units Repeat business Reputation Teamwork	*MANAGEMENT/TEAM INFORMATION SYSTEM* Continuous improvements Facilitation methods Information systems Measurements Meetings

Figure 8.1. Work Support Matrix.

Organizational Scan

An organizational scan is used as an independent instrument in situations in which knowledge about the work behavior and standards has not been defined well. It may be used in any existing business organization to assess the current level of work support (or organizational health, as it is also known). It is a very useful systematic approach to work support analysis, although it is more generic and less detailed than work layering. For conducting an as-is analysis for work support, organizational scanning has been utilized quite successfully in a number of business applications. For instance, Whiteside (1997) has written and presented on the topic and applied the technique quite successfully in several organizations.

Essentially, an organizational scan involves interviewing, observing, and assessing an organization to find which of the interventions on the Work Support Matrix are in place and which are lacking. One can highlight on the matrix where the support exists and whether it needs improvement. When sufficient data has been collected so that every piece of work support has been identified as (1) present, (2) present but needing improvement, or (3) not present, then a report can be compiled (usually for senior management) of the state of work support (health) in the business. For example, in one of the companies analyzed by Whiteside, this scan revealed that the organization was strong in input and output support, but had almost none in process element, consequences, and feedback. Not surprisingly, this was true at each level: business unit, core processes, work group, and individual level. It was a young, aggressive, and growing company that was "trying to get the work done." Naturally, they asked for some communication help and needed a great deal of work support help.

If support is lacking at one level, you can almost surely assume that it is missing at other levels. Or you may find it strong at one level, but weak at another; or it might be present, but weak at all levels. This type of missing work alignment will be further described in Chapter 10.

Organizational scanning will identify areas needing performance improvement; strategic efforts can be launched over a period of time to make these improvements. Further resources on organizational scanning are in the references section at the end of the book.

Work Layering

Work layering was defined earlier as a technique in which one layer of work can be used in concert with other layers to define how each aids the others. At this time we are looking at how to layer work support onto the already defined set of work behaviors and standards. The result will be a detailed and specific list of needed interventions.

The layering work we did previously involved using the Work Standards Matrix for each separately defined work level. Standards for quantity, quality, time, and cost were applied at each of the four levels of a business. The Work Support Matrix identifies work support interventions at each of the four levels of work. Some interventions will be common from level to level, but within each level are those that are deemed necessary for most organizations. Figure 8.1 shows that each of the four levels generally has its own unique support interventions.

During work support layering, these interventions will be applied to *each* business unit, core processes, individual job model, and work group map (up to a point) to determine what support is needed for the work behavior. After all the work support that is required has been determined in the Business Sphere, the information collected can be rolled up into an overall matrix that represents what is or will be provided as work support across the entire business. Thus, work layering is a very systematic method for identifying all work support. It is quite necessary and useful. It is a way to examine our matrix (business), to update it if work changes, and specifically to make sure that each and every level of work behavior has the support (health) it needs to be the best it can be.

Work layering is applied to work maps, job models, and related standards. We will demonstrate this using the engineering design core process map and the standards for this process identified in Chapter 7. We will be layering in the information provided in the core processes row of the Work Support Matrix in Figure 8.1. We assume that this has already been tailored by the engineering business to its own business environment. Led by a performance consultant facilitator, experts in the engineering design core process, as well as members from a business development team, review the core process for needed support.

The inputs in the engineering design processes include (from the core process map) client/request goal, technology, existing conditions, project management, design group, community acceptance, cost, client history, and proposal.

The review team will be asking, "What work support will be needed for the specified process inputs?" They are aided by the Work Support Matrix and can ask questions relative to each item in the matrix, equipment, raw materials, and intellectual knowledge. Thus, for example, "What kinds of work support are needed for equipment related to input in the processes?" As shown in Figure 8.2 this would include computers.

Questions would then be asked about support for raw materials and intellectual knowledge. Note that there are far more support needs for intellectual knowledge, such as technology updates, files of various kinds, a project tracking system, and means for staying abreast of community awareness needs. None was deemed needed for raw materials, as there are no raw materials involved in the engineering design process. One should note as well that not all inputs (for example, existing conditions) necessarily require work support.

The level of detail specified here is directly related to the core process input needs. This provides management and the workforce with specific information

---

What equipment is needed?

Computers

What raw materials are needed?

Does not apply

What intellectual knowledge is needed?

Technology updates, i.e., newsletters, associations
Cost history records
Proposal files
Client history files
Community awareness meetings, bulletin board
Project tracking system

Figure 8.2. Results of Work Support Analysis for Inputs.

on what support will need to be put into place to maximize work behavior. Any less support means some form of negative impact on behavior—that is, efficiency or effectiveness. Let us look at one more example, this time on the human side at the individual level. This is the support required under consequences for a senior engineer drawn from the job map in Figure 5.3c.

1. Cost-effective engineering designs
2. Positive community relations
3. Customer satisfaction
4. Safety
5. Positive community relations
6. Future work

The review of the work support matrix at the individual level for these consequences reveals the results shown in Figure 8.3.

Not surprising, when it comes to the human side of work support there are often many more support interventions needed. We find in Figure 8.3 that customer satisfaction is attended to in the way of work support through various surveys, programs, and measurements. Similarly, there are specific interventions for job satisfaction and personal satisfaction. Finally, the tie between individual and group is supported through job models and work group maps.

Work layering is an excellent way to identify systematically the details of needed work support. When such analyses are done on enough individuals,

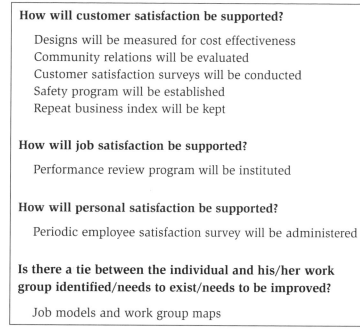

> **How will customer satisfaction be supported?**
>
> Designs will be measured for cost effectiveness
> Community relations will be evaluated
> Customer satisfaction surveys will be conducted
> Safety program will be established
> Repeat business index will be kept
>
> **How will job satisfaction be supported?**
>
> Performance review program will be instituted
>
> **How will personal satisfaction be supported?**
>
> Periodic employee satisfaction survey will be administered
>
> **Is there a tie between the individual and his/her work group identified/needs to exist/needs to be improved?**
>
> Job models and work group maps

Figure 8.3. Results of Work Support Analysis for Consequences.

work groups, core processes, and the business unit as a whole, the findings can be rolled up into a picture of the total work support needed in the business. The new, tailored Work Support Matrix can be used to identify and periodically review what needs to be improved and what is missing and needs to be developed. This is the essence of ensuring the required work support in a business.

The work support for related standards could be identified in much the same way. There is no matrix to use, but the identification builds on the methodology. One will find that the support needed is less because much of the support has already been identified for work behavior. There is, after all, a direct relationship between work behavior and standards.

However, there are some unique support needs for standards, which fall into three major categories. The first is a kind of management support that comes in a variety of classical ways such as facilitation, feedback, reinforcement, and information. This is largely because people, core processes, and business units can run into "unexpected" problems and need management's help and encouragement.

The second class of support to standards is data. This is to be expected because standards are about data. Quantity, quality, cost, and timeliness as standards are data points. To know what standard is acceptable requires comparative data, for example, when benchmarking is a data point, what is the exact benchmark and is it a moving target?

The third source of work support related to standards comes from that which is mandated, such as safety programs that must be put into place. Generally, these are identified and covered by the existing generic or tailored Work Support Matrix.

Let's see what this means in relation to identifying work support for standards in our business case engineering design core process. In Figure 8.4 are some of the standards (from Figure 7.3) for the engineering design processes. The figure shows some of the support that might be needed.

We can see from Figure 8.4 that data is the primary work support requirement. We must determine what data and where it will be found. For example, data is needed on number of changes, billable hours, total sales, delivery times, and so on. How will the business provide this information, and how does one gain access to it while working? One can also surmise that some typical management support will be required as well in such a technical area as engineering design. Who and when?

Now, given all the support that is identified through work layering, we need to evaluate whether the support is doing its job and where to fix it.

Justifying Work Support in Business

Perhaps the single most disheartening aspect of work support is that, even after the needs have been identified, the need for support can be easily ignored by others in the process of improving or establishing it. Someone comes along with a need to provide greater support for job satisfaction, but is ignored or rejected by some manager who has no time to deal with that. Or one work group needs a simple orientation from another group to support its understanding of the other group and they are ignored.

There are many instances of work support simply not being attended to or ignored. The problem with this, of course, is that it makes it harder to do the work and to reach the desired standards. From experience, the author believes that many of these problems could be overcome by having a behaviorally linked model that explains how the lack of or incomplete provision for support affects desired behavior and standards. Many times workers and managers simply don't see the cause and effect relationship—not that they are malicious. By using a common model of performance to define the business, they can talk with one another using the same terminology and understanding. Furthermore, a common model usually provides a way around the emotional baggage that gets in the way of constructive discussions. A couple of examples will help illustrate how you can justify the need for support against behavior or standards.

One nonprofit organization we worked with had tremendous rivalry and animosity between its two "arms"—one was a research and education-based group

	Quantity	Quality	Timeliness	Cost
Process Element				
1. Review Existing Data	# Changes Milestones Met	X	Hour Expended Response Time Schedule Delays Due Date	Material Cost Labor Cost
2. Review Regulations	X	Reports	Schedule Due Dates	X
3. Assess Local Conditions	Changes	X	Benchmark	Due Date
Outputs				
Engineering Designs	Billable Hours Total Sales	Delivery Cond.	Delivery Time Schedule Adherence	Cost/Unit

Figure 8.4. Required Process Elements and Output Support for the Business Engineering Case.

and the other provided the delivery of services. Although a great deal of history contributed to the rift, the fact that the business unit had not established the processes it needed, including administrative systems that would provide consistency of operation, linkages, and interactions, was a key problem. Undertaking a project to establish an organizational hierarchy and to determine the degree of centralization that made sense allowed the organization to thrive. The introduction of a paradigm that showed the relationship of research's output as input to the service delivery arm made sense to both groups. The rifts and differences of opinion were fewer once attention was paid to understanding the relationship in terms of the Language of Work model.

This same issue of establishing a common language can be critical in resolving tensions between a sales organization and the rest of the company. Traditionally, sales has been isolated from the rest of a business, partly because the needs of the sales force are very different from those who develop products. When the product is knowledge, the division is often even greater, because the product developers think they know everything about how to sell a product. In one consulting firm we have worked with, providing work groups with a common language to discuss issues has contributed significantly to increased sales. Sales understand that its output is contracts and that the consequences are clients and revenues. Product design understands that it needs input from sales to create and develop products. Customer service needs input from sales in order to set up a client relationship and service it accurately. All of these are part of the interface and relationships support at the work group level. They have become a part of the processes of this firm, contributing to growth of sales and new products.

DECIDING ON SUPPORT WORK GROUPS
BY USING THE MATRIX

A topic first introduced in Chapter 6 was how work groups are formed. At that time it was intimated that some work groups are determined because of the work support that is needed. While some support work groups, such as the clerical, legal, proposal, and computer work groups in our business case, are determined as a result of support for others' professional/technical processes and job needs, other support work groups result from business-wide needs. For example, the engineering business case, through use of the WSM in Figure 8.1, might form support work groups such as training, employment, benefits, compensation, quality assurance, equipment, and so on.

Essentially, these support work groups would be identified by analyzing the Work Support Matrix once the support in general has been layered in a business. Certain work groups would emerge from this analysis. For example, a strategic planning work group might be needed for many of the work support needs embedded in business unit inputs that include competitive advantage, customer needs, driving force, and the strategic plan itself. The work groups for various kinds of human resource needs are self-evident: employment, benefits, and so on. Depending on the nature and size of the business, other work support needs might even be suggested for ergonomics, continuous improvement, and performance consulting. Whether work groups are identified from needed support to core processes or in general from the Work Support Matrix, they have a foundation in supporting work behavior and standards—not some arbitrary want or constraint.

Having decided the work support needed for our work behavior and standards, we are left to see how human consonance is critical to achieving these three layers of work. We specifically need to identify and minimize the work "noise" that might interfere with all our good efforts at achieving efficient and effective work in the business. We can then see whether all the work is aligned, as it should be.

CHAPTER 9

Human Consonance

Reducing the Interference of the Human Element

A s we come to closure on the Language of Work model, the human element and its influence on work must be addressed for a complete picture of performance. Human consonance is the fourth and final layer of performance. There is no question that the human element has both positive and negative effects on the work behavior, work standards, and work support in business. The performance consultant will not only have to know how to identify human element needs and problems, but be able to tie it specifically to its impact on work behavior, standards, and support—otherwise there is little likelihood of human change in a positive direction.

If the fish swimming is behavior, the height the fish jumps is a standard, and the health of the water the fish swims in is work support, then the interference caused by humans fishing in the water is the "noise" that can cause problems in behavior, reaching standards, and realizing work support. The term "work noise" will be used here to represent the problems caused by human behavior in the business. "Human consonance"—the harmony or agreement among humans—is the antithesis of noise. We seek human consonance in the way we treat one another at work. Work noise will be referred to many times in this chapter, but the goal will always be human consonance— the positive human relations we want to occur in work. By taking a systematic approach to identifying it and its effect on other layers of work, we can see that human consonance will bring forth the best in the work environment from and for everyone.

Human beings are the biggest problem for any business. As the old saying goes, "If it were not for the people, we really could get things done around here." Of course, it really isn't true. Still, it makes a poignant statement about the human element at work.

WHAT WORK NOISE IS

We all come to the work environment with personal "baggage." We have an attitude; we have likes and dislikes. It is also very possible that we don't like or are not well prepared to do the work we are doing. Add to this a business culture in which little attention is given to promoting and supporting people to be the best they can be, and you have a potential powder keg of problems. These problems, if not rectified, radiate throughout an organization as dissatisfaction sets in. The effect on clients and customers can be profound.

Have you ever walked into a business and felt the tension and the grudging feeling of service? Then, you know that noise is palpable. Ever sit in your car, building up the courage to go face your boss and co-workers? Then, you know how tangible noise is.

Noise is so pervasive and comes in so many forms that knowing what to do about it is a key struggle in every business. We need to have some basic understanding of what it is and some systematic ways to identify and deal with it. Otherwise, there really isn't much point in talking about it. We could simply let everyone complain and continue with business as usual, treating noise as an expected part of every work environment.

Although this is not a book on human behavior, we do want to get a handle on dealing with human behavior at work because noise affects the totality of work behavior, standards, and support. The rest of the chapter is devoted to understanding why we have noise and the context that determines what we can and cannot do about the noise to achieve a more positive human consonance. Certain kinds of noise are simply much more difficult to do something about in a business and are best left to the specialists—psychologists and psychiatrists. Most of the other kinds of noise are within the domain of the performance consultant. The goal of this chapter is to know why the noise exists, to learn what we as performance consultants can realistically do about it, and to develop a systematic way to go about reducing that noise.

Noise exists in business (and life in general) in five broad categories: prejudices, addictions, attributes, values, and life experiences. Each is discussed next.

Prejudices

It is well-established that prejudice is a learned behavior. Not liking someone or a group because of race, sexual orientation, age, sex, or any other characteristic comes about because someone modeled that negative behavior and passed it on. It could also come from observing someone and developing a prejudice out of jealousy or misconception. When a prejudice is brought into the work environment (or public domain), it manifests itself in very ugly and very, very subtle ways and it affects work. Some people may not be promoted because of prejudice. The prejudice often masquerades as rational thought: "I can't consider her for promotion because, with two small children, she would never want to relocate. Why ask her and put that agonizing decision on her shoulders?" Others are outplaced because they are too old. The thought process goes like this: "At 45, I pay him so much. I could get the same expertise more cheaply and a lot more work out of someone who is 29." (For other examples, see the January 1999 issue of *Fortune* magazine.)

Some people don't receive special assignments or jobs because of prejudice. Still others are simply talked about and are not approached for input, feedback, or processing. Behavior may be so subtle that it cannot be easily seen and something done about it.

Perhaps the noise problem of prejudice has been most public in the U.S. military. Not that the military is any worse than many of our major businesses. It is just more public and easier to expose than in privately held organizations. The military provides us a convenient example of the problem of noise and its relation to work performance. The military has done an outstanding job of defining work behavior, attaining standards, and providing work support. This is not to say that they could not still improve many of the specific elements with these layers, or that they, like most businesses, could not do a better job of more accurately and completely defining performance. Still, they have defined work behavior, standards, and support pretty well. Their results show in the achievement of their prime mission. So, when a major kind of work noise like prejudice emerges, why is it not easily removed? Immediate denial by management that prejudice even exists is one pervasive response. Legislating the noise of prejudice is another. Admitting to prejudice would lead to lawsuits and expensive judgments, but not doing anything deters good performance for the organization. It is easy to recognize this kind of noise, but it will take some real effort to reduce it—certainly more than legislation, judicial orders, and so on. The up side is that prejudice can be reduced, if not eliminated. The down side is that it takes a long time and does require constant attention and action. Performance consultants need to be well-versed in the role of prejudice in organizations; one of the interventions that can make a difference is called "Leveraging Diversity" from Langdon, Whiteside, and McKenna (1999).

Addictions

An area of noise that cannot be treated at any length here, but must be mentioned, is the noise created by addictions such as to alcohol and drugs (prescription as well as street drugs). For rank-and-file employees, there usually are policies and procedures for dealing with the aberrant behavior caused by substance abuse. There is less in place for managers and executives who contribute to the noise because of their use of the same substances. As a performance consultant, you may find yourself working in an organization that is detrimentally affected by someone with this problem. This is a delicate situation that requires wisdom and support to handle. Partner with the human resources department in order to determine the best route: Employee Assistance Program (EAP), medical help, intervention, or counseling.

Attributes

Attributes are the things we come with at birth. In the same way we are born with a certain hair color, body build, face shape, and gender, so too are we born with certain traits that affect how we live our lives, many of the choices we make, how we interact with our communities, and how we organize our spaces. A great deal of research has gone into finding the correlation between these traits or attributes and success at work. Prevailing theory now says that certain jobs require people with certain attributes in order to achieve successful performance. By placing people who possess the particular attributes required into certain jobs, the likelihood of successful performance is enhanced. The logic of this is simple and proven easily in real life. Place a person who needs quiet in order to think in a busy, noisy office as a receptionist, and the person is unlikely to be able to be friendly and warm to callers and visitors.

One typical list of attributes drawn from a general list developed as part of the Kolbe Index (1999) includes the following:

- Tolerance for change
- Willingness to take risks
- Intuitiveness
- Attention to quality
- Sales style
- Ability to see the design, system, or steps in a process, operation, or procedure
- Need for information
- Adherence to time lines
- Detail orientation
- Need for closure

- Method of analyzing data
- Management/leadership style
- Willingness to follow procedures
- Learning, teaching, training, mentoring, or coaching style
- Preferred method of communicating

This list demonstrates that a range of personalities, perceptions, attention spans, analytical approaches, and leadership styles reside simultaneously in the workplace. It isn't hard to imagine the noise, cacophony in fact, that is possible because attributes differ among employees and between employees and their supervisors. If we are matched with others, especially managers, who are very different from us, problems are going to arise. It doesn't mean we have to work for someone exactly like us. Rather, performance consultants help employees and managers work within the different attributes and achieve a desired mix that realizes diversity of ideas, opinions, and approaches. Given that we are born with these attributes, we have to figure out what to do to reduce the noise.

The answer to work noise is not always to eliminate it, but to learn how to reduce it. No one would argue that the workplace should be filled with clones of the managers. The answer lies in large part with education and the recognition of differences—education on how differences can complement one another and on the increased strength achieved by bringing disparate parts together. Another solution is to select people who have attributes that match job needs. Some progress in noise reduction has been realized through the use of such instruments as the Meyers-Briggs Type Indicator® (see Hirsch & Kummerow, 1989) and change style preference indicators (Langdon, Whiteside, & McKenna, 1999). Further progress is needed and represents fertile ground for performance consultant activity. Various assessments can be used to increase self-understanding and awareness and provide a language to help people understand their differences.

Life and Work Experiences

Prejudice is a life experience so vile that it was addressed separately. Other life experiences we have also influence the noise we create and the experience of business, so they need to be recognized and dealt with as well. Many of these can be improved or extinguished more readily in business.

It is not our intent to produce a complete list of life experiences. Here we will focus on experiences that might have begun when people were children, but which affect people in their daily business lives. Recognition of the role these life experiences can play will go a long way in reducing noise in business. A partial list includes

- What it's like to give someone a suggestion
- What we expect in the way of feedback when we work with others
- Who we feel we can trust (in management, for example)
- What might happen if we come up with a new idea and present it
- Whether it is worth speaking up in meetings
- Whether executives say hello to us
- Whether our time at work is respected
- How people get along in our work group
- Whether we are encouraged to speak to clients and customers
- Whether we can really talk to our supervisor
- If it's alright to talk about Bill or Nancy behind his or her back

As a performance consultant, it is hoped that your reaction to this list is two-fold: (1) That you recognize most of these experiences as potentially creating noise and (2) that you know that many of these can be resolved if the organization or specific people would simply pay attention to them. This is a major arena in which we can identify and reduce work noise. Again, education and awareness create an immediate effect, but long-term culture building interventions are also needed.

Values

The reason for identifying values as a separate source of noise is that values take on a very personal connotation. We all have values that shape our behavior. In any situation our values, such as honesty, ethics, ambition, and the like, will shape our decisions. Values can be taught, easily identified, and involve a conscious decision on our part to be in, out, or a little gray in our application of a value. Thus, when it comes to ethical issues regarding what relationship to have with a client, what degree we are honest with our colleagues and those we manage, and how our own ambition affects work with others, we can personally choose to act in keeping with our values or not. We need to determine whether we can truly "live" with the results of our actions.

In terms of the five different categories of work noise presented here, values affect what the individual can personally do more than what the business can do. There is a relationship between what the individual does and what the business does, but the individual cannot and should not expect the business to be totally responsible for all value decisions. Good businesses promote good values, but they are different from individual values. Individuals bring their own values to the workplace and thrive in businesses that allow good values to thrive.

As performance consultants, it is important to understand the role that values play in the performance of individuals, work groups, and business units. When identifying performance gaps, it is important to recognize that a difference in the values between the employees and the organization can cause a problem. In one situation we'll use as an example, an employee seemed to have "looser" values than the manager and the manager had difficulty receiving information from the employee and believed the employee was often lying. The intervention used by the performance consultant in this case was to initiate a discussion in the monthly staff meetings on values. Once the employee heard his new boss articulate a set of values different from those other bosses had coached him on, he adapted to the stricter set of values.

HUMAN CONSONANCE

As noted, human consonance is a term I have devised to capture the way business and individuals should act as humans to help achieve work behavior, attain work standards, and not interfere with work support. Consonance, by definition, means "harmony or agreement among components." Thus, it seems appropriate to see how it is possible to have humans behave in harmony and in alignment with the other three layers of work.

Human consonance is the opposite of work noise. We can choose to describe and act on human relations in either the positive or the negative sense. It is easier to identify the problem of work noise when we think of the negative things that humans cause to happen by their actions, attitudes, and attributes. We will use a method designed to identify work noise in an ongoing business. However, *the goal is not to concentrate on noise, but to promote consonance.* Given this, how can we systematically view human consonance as our business goal in the positive sense? Then, how can we use work noise to identify the negative elements in a business and at least minimize the noise in order to achieve human consonance? Here too, it is possible to define the ideal (to-be) of human consonance, and where things are presently (as-is) through work noise. We will look at the goal first.

Figure 9.1 shows the Human Consonance Matrix that is part of the Language of Work model. As with other matrices in this model, it must be tailored by each business to its environment. This can be done by group representatives from each level of performance and hierarchy in the business. Working together, they would determine what human consonance would mean operationally (rather than merely as a goal) in the business.

The horizontal axis of the Human Consonance Matrix is the proforma and the vertical axis is the four performance levels of work as depicted in the Business Sphere. The matrix suggests that human consonance needs to exist at all

Figure 9.1. Human Consonance Matrix.

Human Consonance Matrix

	Input	Conditions	Process Elements	Output	Consequences	Feedback
BUSINESS UNIT	*STRATEGY and BUS. PLANS* • New Business Ideas Encouraged • Customer/Client Input Requested • Communications Sought • Realistic Strategic Plans	*CULTURE/CONTROLS* • Positive Culture • Equal Opportunity • Friendly • Personal Compliance with Guidelines • Adherence to Contracts • Equitable Application of Compensation • Career Development • Advancement Equity	*MARKET SYSTEMS* • Responsive processes • Cooperation Encouraged	*BUSINESS DELIVERABLES* • Quality Work Encouraged in Products and Services	*BUSINESS RESULTS* • Positive Reputation • Repeat Business • Customer Is Right	*BUSINESS MEASUREM./EVALUAT.* • Positive Client Reaction • Bottom-up Information Flow • Management Listens & Responds
CORE PROCESSES	*RESOURCES* • Positive/Constructive Worker/Manager Input • Resources Provided	*REGULATIONS/ POLICIES* • Compliance Sought • Rules/Regulations Followed • Ethics Required	*TECHNOLOGIES (SOFT and HARD)* • Process Followed • Changes are Possible • Time is Important • Innovation is Okay • Value is Added • Sabotage is Not Okay	*PRODUCTS and SERVICES* • Outputs are Supported/Important	*PROCESS RESULTS* • Quality of Work Encouraged • No Delays	*CONFIRMATIONS and CORRECTS* • Feedback Encouraged • Suggestions Made • Feedback Sought
INDIVIDUALS	*CLIENT NEEDS and RESOURCES* • Selection by Skill & Experience • Client Attended to • Resources Available • Mgmt. Information Available • Clear Expectations	*WORK INFLUENCES* • Clear Productivity Expectations • Positive Environment • Policies Followed • Pay Equity • Ethics • Job Growth	*WORK METHODS* • Processes Followed • Quality Expectations • Continuous Learning • Defined Processes • Assignment by Skill & Ability • Personal Productivity • Ideas Encouraged • "Not Blaming Others"	*PRODUCTS AND SERVICES* • Quality Outputs • Valuing Others' Output and Input	*INDIVIDUAL RESULTS* • Client Valued/Right • Individual Valued • Product/Service Valued • Individual Rewarded	*CONFIRMATIONS and SELF-ADJUSTMENT* • Information Encouraged • Reinforcement Given • Useful Performance Review • Questions Asked/ Answers Given • Productivity • Information Provided
WORK GROUPS	*CLIENT NEEDS and RESOURCES* • Team Input Sought • Client Attended To • Resources Used • Group Needs/ Requests Sought	*VALUES and PRACTICES* • Clear Productivity Expectations • Positive Environment Supported • Policies Followed • Ethics Required	*INTERFACE/ RELATIONSHIPS* • Teamwork Used • Processes Followed • Quality Work Sought • Defined Processes Followed • Productivity Achieved • Continuous Learning Expected	*PRODUCTS and SERVICES* • Collaborative Output • Quality Products/ Services Produced	*GROUP RESULTS* • Group Rewarded • Client Valued/Right • Individual Valued • Group Satisfaction Encouraged	*MANAGEMENT/TEAM INFORMATION SYSTEM* • Positive Client Reaction • Information Shared • Individuals Get Along • Information Flows • Questions Asked/ Answers Given

levels of a business in various ways—and in some instances must be aligned with consonance at other levels. For example, achieving freedom of employee input is important at the business unit level and is in alignment at the core processes, individual, and work group levels. To help you understand each level, a brief description of the nature and scope of human consonance throughout the Business Sphere is provided on the following pages.

Human Consonance at the Business Unit Level

A business unit should encourage new ideas from within, as well as from its clients. Stagnation of ideas leads to stagnation of business, if not its demise. For example, IBM Corporation's decision to stick with mainframe computers with networked work stations led in part to Apple's moving into and dominating the personal computer market for years. One wonders how much the corporation valued personal and client input. The critical question around human consonance in the business unit is, "What does the business unit want to promote in the way of basic input to the business in what it does?" If the answer is nothing, then the business unit will receive nothing.

One of the more positive things a successful business would want is widespread *input* to the strategic plan. In one business we know, the plan is routinely circulated for employee input at virtually every level of the business. Good ideas are incorporated, and the ideas are manifested in later action. In another company, the strategic plan is held "close to the vest" and not shared at all below the executive level. The plan appears as a cookie-cutter every year, and everybody knows it. The plan is almost meaningless and the results are not that great either. In this case, the company protects its competitive information, but shows a lack of trust of employees. If people were allowed to give input, it could have a profound effect on understanding and commitment to the strategic plan.

In many respects, business unit *conditions* are the official source for what a business seeks in human consonance. Written and unwritten policies, attitudes of executives, and adherence to mandated regulations are found here. If these are not defined and attended to, what does it mean about an organization's concern for human consonance?

The business unit *process element* demands responsiveness and cooperation. You recall that the process element of a business unit is composed of the various work groups, the flow of work between the groups, and their relationships. Are these relationships encouraged to be responsive and cooperative? Or can groups simply dictate to one another when the output will move from one group to another. Do they respond to one another's requests and questions?

Business unit *outputs* are produced from the work elements of input, conditions, process element, and feedback. Thus, there is relatively little human consonance to be concerned with except in the broad sense that insisting on and exemplifying quality work and products or services is critical.

Business unit *consequences* are critical because they represent the results we desire from output through inputs, conditions, process elements, and feedback. We want to promote a positive reputation, repeat business, and the idea that the customer is valued. By not tending to the customer's needs, the business creates an impression across all levels that people don't need to be concerned with customers. People see the goal as simply providing a product or service, and that's the end of it. How many times have you decided not to go back to a business because there was no genuine concern for your needs? "The customer is right" doesn't mean that they get everything exactly the way they want it, but rather that there is common ground to satisfy the customer and the business needs at the same time.

Finally, business unit *feedback* promotes positive reactions, information from the bottom up, and management that listens and responds. There are other means for promoting feedback that encourages communication, reinforces positive actions, and corrects what needs correcting in a positive, rather than negative manner.

Human Consonance at the Core Process Level

Human consonance at the core process level involves human relations related to seeing that the primary outputs of the company are produced through processes that are efficient and effective. The human element can also interfere with these core processes.

Because core processes present special problems in terms of achieving work behavior and standards, it is vital for those dependent on the core process be served in such a way that they can contribute constructively. The processes are there, after all, to service their needs. This means that workers, managers, and especially clients should be allowed continuous *input*. This should occur at the very outset of a process, as well as during the process. The business, for example, may be well into a process producing an output, but the client (or others) should feel free to give continued input to help achieve the desired results. This is not necessarily the way work happens. Some adopt an attitude of, "Well, you told us what you wanted, so now get out of our way." A balance should exist between getting the work done and seeing that the client gets his or her say. This holds as well for others who have input, such as workers, managers, vendors, or suppliers. We would not want a supplier to hold back information vital to the success of an output just because he thought we would not be receptive!

Human consonance regarding the *conditions* of core processes has to do with things like compliance, rules, and ethics. Here we need to make sure rules are being justly applied, that compliance issues are not being buried, and that ethics don't count, because they really do.

The *process element* of a core process requires human consonance related to such things as assuring that the process is followed and that changes are possible, recognizing that time is important and that innovation is okay, and so forth. The problem faced in this regard is not just that people resist any of these needs, but rather that business doesn't necessarily provide the basis of information to know what to do and how. Because business rarely defines core processes on which it then defines jobs, it is to be expected that the human element would not know what was expected. Rather, people attend to what they believe their individual level responsibilities are and what their manager says. This is especially the case in the process element of a core process because there are usually many, many steps involved that also require relationships to many others in the business.

The general human consonance for core process *output* is that it be supported and valued as being important. This, as in all other cases of output, is derived from the other elements of the core process proforma.

The *consequences* of a core process require us to value quality of output, avoid delays, and so on. These are long-range goals and, when focused on and emphasized, more readily assure that the inputs, conditions, process element, and feedback will be present to reach these goals.

Finally, the human consonance of core process *feedback* relates to encouraging feedback, making suggestions, seeking feedback, and the like. The notion that a core process is something the business "owns" and it is therefore sacrosanct is foolish. If a business is to be effective and efficient, how better than to encourage humans who use the core processes to speak freely on how they can be improved? This does not mean something has to be done about every suggestion, but that every one has to be encouraged to contribute as much as possible. We don't need feedback only from customers whom we value, but also from employees, the people who follow the core process to assure that those customers' needs are fulfilled.

Human Consonance at the Individual Level

As we move from the organizational (business unit) and systems (core processes) levels of human consonance to the remaining two work levels, we enter into the very essence of personal interaction. That is, we must know what we are personally responsible for ourselves (in our job) and also what we are responsible for in relation to others (in our work groups). It is one thing for the business to identify and support what it desires for the business unit and core processes, and quite another to get individuals to do their part. It helps a great deal if the business can explicitly define what it wants individuals (and work groups) to do in terms of human consonance. If individuals are unsure as to expectations of desired work behavior—which they commonly are—you can be sure they do not know what human relations are expected. A definition of explicit human consonance tied to the job models and work group maps will go a long way in improving human relations. To this end we will see what aspects of human consonance are critical to the individual level, beginning with outputs.

Individuals should first know the expected view of desired human relations to their job *outputs*. There are two fundamental aspects of output. First, each person should know what quality means for *his or her own work*. Second, each person should value *others' output as his or her own input*. In essence we have an obligation to produce the best output we can because it should be valued by others. In turn, we value other's outputs because they will become our own inputs.

Individual quality sounds easy to define, but often is not. For example, how do I know when I've written a good book? To answer this I can, with the help of my publisher, define quality for this output—sentence structure, organization of material, number of examples, and so on. So knowing and achieving personal quality output is the beginning point. The second point is somewhat more difficult to understand: valuing others' output as one's own input.

Earlier in this book, I alluded to the Kaizen principle. It perhaps best captures the very essence of valuing others' output as our input. This principle says that the individual worker should *seek the outputs of others (as his or her input) rather than waiting for them* to come to him or her. The implicit meaning of this for business is that we would seek outputs of others that

- Are delivered on time, as we need to use them in a particular time frame for completing our work
- Meet our quality standards, because our use of them will determine the quality of our own output
- Are of sufficient quantity to complete all the work we have to complete

Waiting for output from others may mean receiving something that meets few of these criteria, which would, in turn, mean that our own work is less likely to be high quality or on time, and so on. A proactive stance in expecting quality work from others is far superior to waiting and then complaining after the fact.

The results or *consequences* of our jobs relate, of course, to the outputs we produce. Our human consonance should relate to valuing client satisfaction and their being right. We should also value our individual contributions in regard to products or services. This speaks as much to the issue of assuring that people are in the right kind of job relative to their attributes, skills, and interests as it speaks to how to keep jobs interesting. Assuring individual consonance in inputs, conditions, process element, and feedback goes a long way in helping to assure interest in one's job.

On the *input* side of individual work, as managers and workers we need to be concerned with factors such as selecting individuals for their skill and experience, attending to client input, making resources available, establishing clear expectations, and assuring that management information is available. All of these are important, but the first and last especially illustrate the human consonance requirements implicit in job level input.

One can wonder to what degree people are selected for work based on skill and experience. While most managers would certainly say they are, the lack of understanding often seen around what skills and experience are needed for a job lead one to believe otherwise. If the work of a job has not been concisely and accurately defined, such as in job models, and skills, knowledge, attributes, experience, and so forth have not been defined, then the interview process cannot be used to find the requisite skill and experience. The interviewer must fall back on a general impression of the individual. Good job models help manager and worker alike.

Assuring management information as an input to human consonance is a "sticky wicket," as the English like to say. One doesn't quite know what the problem is, but it is likely one of perception. On the one hand, managers don't feel the need to spend time on providing information, and workers, for their part, might not really know what to do with the information if they had more of it. Perhaps the problem is the form in which the information is given. If there is no common language of work, people cannot understand as well. Managers and workers can plan their work using the proforma. It can then be used to plan work, resolve conflicts, solve knowledge problems, review performance, and so on. The proforma has great value for addressing the effectiveness and efficiency of management information. Other models and interventions can also be used, of course, such as objectives, bulletin boards, touch-base meetings, and so on.

Human consonance for *conditions* that apply at the individual level are numerous. Conditions address to a large degree the culture (required and desired) we want work to take place within. Of course, culture is more than conditions, but a large measure of culture is governed by the right kind of conditions implicit in the policies and procedures of a business.

For individuals, this means conditions that promote clear expectations of productivity and a positive work environment, see that policies are attended to, and strive for equal pay and employment, opportunities for job growth, and ethics in general. We have seen how productivity expectations can be clarified by job models, understood in terms of setting standards systematically, and planned on the basis of the right feedback.

Perhaps the hardest principle to understand is ethics, but even here we can apply an increased understanding of what work is to help achieve ethical behavior. Because ethics has so much to do with increasing knowledge and information around what is right and what is wrong, a common work language can serve as a way to discuss issues in an objective manner without or with a minimum of emotional reactions. Groups can use the model to resolve conflicts such as ethics issues quickly. For example, one can explain that Robin is paid more than Dale based on output, consequences, inputs, and so forth.

Finally, *feedback* for achieving human consonance relates in large part to the communication that will be encouraged or provided. Thus information sharing is encouraged, reinforcement is given, a useful performance review is mandatory, questions can be asked and answers given, and productivity information is provided so that changes can be made before evaluations are given. Let's address the need for human consonance feedback by describing just one of these to see what happens to human consonance when that particular aspect of feedback is not addressed well. In this case we will look at the issue of a "useful performance review."

There are numerous performance review or appraisal systems today in business. However, there is hardly a manager who enjoys the experience or believes that the reviews are worthwhile for improving work performance. They become a kind of paperwork exercise in which various boxes of information are filled out, discussed (or not) in an atmosphere of uneasiness, and result in very little change and growth. It is not surprising that there is a negative human consonance (noise) around the value of performance reviews. The need is there, but the delivery mechanism that matches an understanding of performance and what to do to improve or reaffirm it is not. A greater understanding of work—how to define, measure, and improve it—would help immensely. A performance review method that stands alone and is not tied to a good job model is bound to fail. One that is not tied to how to improve performance in ways that people understand is also bound to fail. The very act of structuring a job model based on the proforma can be used to conduct a performance review and to hire or promote people. This method of performance review and its relation to the job model was described in Chapter 5.

Human Consonance at the Work Group Level

As was the case for work support, there are multiple similarities between human consonance for individuals and for work groups. Some significant differences are also worth mentioning.

The human consonance for *outputs* and *consequences* are pretty much the same; they stress the importance of knowledge of quality outputs and valuing client satisfaction for consequences. For the individual we value the individual and his or her satisfaction; in the work group we value the group and its satisfaction.

One of the key differences for output is the recognition of collaboration. The output, comprised of individual outputs, must have a collective focus by all the individuals who contribute. That old saying, "A camel is an animal put together by committee," is descriptive of what can happen if individuals don't work and think toward a common goal. It is subtle, but a very important distinction is being made here. Parts may not fit together as well as they should when assembled, something can be left out of an order, or repair people may not care about what design people care about. True collaboration achieves a unity of purpose, demonstrated by fine outputs. This collaboration cannot be achieved by mandate, but must come about through support that results in commitment and positive management facilitation.

On the *input* side of work group human consonance, two differences from individual input should be noted (others may be present in your organization): attention to team input and attention to group needs. A mechanism must be provided for the group to get together and generate input or a manager can control when and where input comes from. If the manager is controlling input, it's a negative sign, which we will discuss later.

Attention to group needs as inputs is not so much paying attention to what the group wants to say, as it is paying attention to what the business must do to recognize the group needs. Managers must keep an ear out for signals: Do people need some time off, a party, a continuous improvement process? As simple as it sounds, to ask, request, and provide for group needs is done in the same way as providing for individual needs. As performance consultants, we need to support managers in attending to group needs.

Process element human consonance for work groups relate to the "teamness," the collectiveness of continuous learning and improvement. These are also similar to individual needs. In terms of teamness, if a group is formed in business, the group must know how they are to work together. The business needs to provide the charter, organization structure, and support for this to happen. One cannot simply "bless" a team and expect that teamness will happen. Teams need the freedom to act and be supported. This includes management not getting in the way of the team, but rather facilitating when and where needed. Otherwise, noise is created that prevents teams from being what they could be.

Finally, *feedback* to work groups has perhaps more of the special uniqueness of human consonance than any other work element in the work group proforma. Here we find things like how information is shared, positive client reactions, how individuals get along, information flow, and how questions are asked or answers given. Words like sharing, getting along, and flow are used. Because it is a group, the work group shares communication in common; if it does not, the feeling that only some receive the needed information and rewards deters the building of a team. The element of feedback in this case works counter to another work element (say the process element), which creates nonalignment of work within a work level. If you hear the word "favoritism" or the expression, "They never listen to me," you know something is wrong in human consonance of feedback.

WORK NOISE

The principle of human consonance tailored to your business can go a very long way in setting the business expectations for how humans will be treated, relate to one another, and communicate relative to efficient and effective work behavior, standards, and support. We could simply say that an analysis and provision for these various human elements should be part of a strategic plan. This would go a long way toward achieving human consonance. However, let's discuss the antithesis of human consonance, work noise. Attention to work noise helps us to identify the performance gaps in human relations and focuses attention on needed solutions, especially as they relate to specific instances of noise. We don't want to institute solutions for everyone when everyone is not the source of the noise. That would be like locking everyone in a dorm because a few violated the 1:00 a.m. curfew. It is best to promote the overall need—human consonance—while identifying the specific problem areas and working on them. Both individuals and groups appreciate businesses that can effectively do this without interrupting "getting the work done." Also, they like to see individuals and groups who present problems that can be dealt with.

Figure 9.2 is the Work Noise Matrix of the Language of Work model. On the vertical axis is the usual Language of Work proforma. On the horizontal are the four performance levels of the Business Sphere. The negative indicators of work relations and communication are listed. These were derived from the Human Consonance Matrix by determining what behavior indicates that a human consonance is not present or is not occurring as desired. This was done at a 10,000-foot level, and you are free to add details that fit your business environment. For example, here is a list of the individual input desired for human consonance and the related indicators of work noise:

Human Consonance Matrix	*Work Noise Matrix*
Individual Input Level	Individual Input Level
• Selection by Skill and Experience	• Selection by Relationship
• Client Attended to	• Client Ignored
• Resources Available	• Resources Unavailable
• Management Information Available	• Information Withheld
• Clear Expectations	• No Clarity of Expectations

Here we see a direct relationship between indicators. One is merely the antithesis of the other. We can, of course, be more specific, for example, by determining the specific measures of "client ignored." Items such as not calling, not

Work Noise Matrix

	Input	Conditions	Process Elements	Output	Consequences	Feedback
BUSINESS UNIT	*STRATEGY and BUS. PLANS* 1. Few Business Ideas 2. Customer Complaints 3. Faulty Communications 4. No Strategic Plan	*CULTURE/CONTROLS* 1. Negative Culture 2. Equal Opportunity Lawsuits 3. Little Compliance with Guidelines 4. Adherence to Contracts Minimized 5. Uneven Application of Compensation 6. Little Career Development and Advancement	*MARKET SYSTEMS* 1. Rigid processes 2. Uncooperative	*BUSINESS DELIVERABLES* 1. Low-Quality Work 2. Few Products and Services	*BUSINESS RESULTS* 1. Negative Reputation 2. Little Repeat Business 3. "Customer Is the Problem"	*BUSINESS MEASUREM./EVALUAT.* 1. Positive Client Reaction 2. Bottom-up Information Flow 3. Management Listens and Responds
CORE PROCESSES	*CORE RESOURCES* 1. No Worker/Manager Input 2. Resources Fought For	*REGULATIONS/ POLICIES* 1. Little Compliance 2. Disregard for Rules/regulations 3. No Ethical Standards	*TECHNOLOGIES (SOFT and HARD)* 1. Throttle Effort 2. Blaming Others 3. New Ways Discouraged 4. Sabotage 5. No Learning/Growth 6. Time Equity Ignored	*PRODUCTS and SERVICES* 1. Outputs Are Disregarded	*PROCESS RESULTS* 1. Poor Quality Work 2. Delays	*CONFIRMATIONS and CORRECTS* 1. Feedback Encouraged 2. Suggestions Made 3. Feedback Sought
INDIVIDUALS	*CLIENT NEEDS and RESOURCES* 1. Selection by Relationship 2. Client Ignored 3. Resources Unavailable 4. No Mgmt. Information 5. No clarity of Expectations	*WORK INFLUENCES* 1. Poor Productivity Expectations 2. Negative Environment 3. Policies Ignored 4. Pay Inequity 5. Poor Ethics 6. Job Stagnation	*WORK METHODS* 1. Processes Ignored 2. No Quality Expectations 3. No Learning 4. No Defined Processes 5. Assignment by Favoritism 6. No Personal Productivity 7. Ideas Discouraged	*PRODUCTS and SERVICES* 1. Poor Quality Outputs 2. Disparaging Others' Output and Input	*INDIVIDUAL RESULTS* 1. Client Ignored/Disparaged 2. Individual Disparaged 3. Product/Service Disparaged	*CONFIRMATIONS and SELF-ADJUSTMENTS* 1. Information Discouraged 2. Punishment Given 3. "Dumb" Performance Review 4. "Don't Ask, Don't Tell" 5. Productivity Information Withheld
WORK GROUPS	*CLIENT NEEDS and RESOURCES* 1. Team Ignored 2. Client Ignored 3. Resources Abused 4. Group Needs/ Requests Ignored	*VALUES and PRACTICES* 1. No Productivity Expectations 2. Negative Environment 3. Policies Ignored 4. Ethics Disparaged	*INTERFACE/ RELATIONSHIPS* 1. Teamwork Disparaged 2. Processes Ignored 3. Quality Work Disparaged 4. No Defined Processes 5. Low Productivity 6. No Learning	*PRODUCTS and SERVICES* 1. Individualistic Output 2. Low-Quality Products/ Services Accepted	*GROUP RESULTS* 1. No Group Rewards 2. Client Disparaged/ Ignored 3. Individual Disparaged/ Ignored 4. No Group Satisfaction	*MANAGEMENT/TEAM INFORMATION SYSTEM* 1. Negative Client Reaction 2. Information Hoarded 3. Individuals Fight and Disagree 4. No Information Flow 5. "Don't Ask, Don't Tell"

Figure 9.2. Work Noise Matrix.

responding when called, not attending to expressed needs, and so forth could be specifically measured. Identify indicators as needed for each organization's culture. You can tailor the Work Noise Matrix to the needs of any business.

LAYERING IN HUMAN CONSONANCE

It would be an oxymoron to suggest that we would layer in work noise. Why would we want to layer in negative attributes? Rather, we want to layer in human consonance—the positive human relationships we need for the business. A two-step procedure is described in the next few paragraphs. First, layer in the human consonance to identify the desired (to-be) state for human relations in a business. Then, after a period of time, periodically identify work noise that exists (as-is). The resulting performance gaps between as-is and to-be are the performance consultant's arena for instituting necessary interventions to transition from existing to desired performance state.

When layering in human consonance or identifying work noise, we will use the method we used previously for layering in work standards and support. First, we tailor the Human Consonance Matrix and Work Noise Matrix to the specific business, then layer either of them over each corresponding business unit, core process, individual, and/or work group. A sample application will demonstrate the technique. Let's layer the Human Consonance Matrix over our business case example of the engineering design core process.

First, ask the following series of questions:

1. What provisions has the business made at the business unit level to encourage each human relation need?
2. What provisions has the business made at the core process level to encourage each human relation need?
3. What provisions has the business made and the individual sought to provide to encourage each human relation need?
4. What provisions has the business made and the work group sought to provide to encourage each human relation need?

In the case of business unit and core processes, we see the obligation of a business (primarily in the form of management) to see that provisions are made for each human relation to occur. These manifest themselves in the way of specific interventions that are put into place by management. Some of these should come from already established systematic work support interventions. For example, by having a performance review program in place, and making sure it is good one, we meet one of the needs for feedback to individuals. Other human consonance areas require special programs and management attention.

For example, seeing that employees make suggestions is, in part, a question of management encouragement, even when a work support mechanism is provided in the way of a continuous improvement process. The point is, not every human consonance is met by work support. Indeed, many more are a question of choice, attention by management, the cultural integrity that is encouraged, and so forth. We can have, for example, a suggestion box, but if management doesn't encourage and follow through on the suggestions, the "box" isn't worth the space and intention it was conceived to fulfill.

In the case of the engineering design core process, we would review the entire core processes row of the Human Consonance Matrix. We would look at each human relations need and see what management and work support are planned and in place to ensure the human consonance we deemed necessary. It is basically a checklist approach to assure that we have made a concerted effort to make certain things are in place. When satisfied, we can then use the Work Noise Matrix periodically to test out and identify where things are not working. This is also a checklist approach in which we apply the core processes segment of the Work Noise Matrix to our engineering design core process to determine where the human element is interfering or not reaching its potential for getting work done, either on an individual or on a collective basis. For example, our analysis might reveal that "time is important" as a process element consonance has slipped. Designs are taking longer to complete. We would want to know why this is so and what needs to be done about it. Or, if employees no longer were giving positive, constructive input about the drawings, we would want to know whether they were being asked as they had been before and whether a new management style had any effect. We would attempt to tie down the effect that the noise had on work behavior, reaching standards, and mitigating work support. If we did not, individuals guilty of creating noise might not realize the effect and do nothing to change.

What all this attention to human consonance and work noise adds up to is putting in place an expectation—a culture—of how humans will act in getting the work done. It is also a measure to identify where expectations are not being met. It is the identification of performance gaps in human consonance through the systematic application of matrices that are part of achieving work behavior and standards, and related to work support. It is something managers must learn to do in their own arenas, and workers must learn to value the culture of human relations expected in their business. It is an area of performance consulting full of opportunity.

CHAPTER 10

Achieving
Performance Alignment
in Business

T he previous nine chapters provided a performance-based view of work—
the Language of Work model. In bringing closure to the book, we will tie
together this view of performance with its application to the performance
levels of business (business unit, core processes, individual jobs, and work
groups) and the layers of performance (human consonance, support, standards,
and behavior) to achieve a fundamental goal that can assure efficiency and
effectiveness of work—performance alignment.

Everyone and everything in business should be working in alignment.
If work groups do not support one another, inefficiency and ineffectiveness pre-
vail and improvements are not consistently achieved. If individuals are out of
sync with core processes, the processes are not achieving what they are
intended to achieve. If careful planning at the business unit is not operationalized in core processes and executed by individuals and work groups, performance alignment is out of whack! Today's businesses can ill afford this
situation. They must stay abreast or ahead of others in the global economy. All
work in a business is interrelated and must be seen in relation to dependent
variables. Work is most likely to be successful if the levels and layers of performance are truly aligned. The ultimate operational goal of business, beyond

profit or the welfare of society, is performance alignment. As a performance consultant it is paramount that you have a full and coherent view of performance alignment and how you can help facilitate it in business.

IT TAKES TIME AND COMMITMENT

Understanding what performance alignment is can be relatively easy. To actually achieve performance alignment in a practical way in business can be an amazing feat. It requires discipline, attention to detail, a workable approach, and a commitment of time. Alignment will not happen on its own, and it takes longer to achieve through a fire-fighting mentality. *Performance alignment demands a systematic methodology understood and applied by an informed management, through a disciplined workforce, consistently applied throughout the major performance levels of business, and aided through the facilitation of performance consultant experts.*

Because it is a systematic methodology based on a thorough understanding of performance, the Language of Work model helps make the daunting task easier. It helps operationalize alignment in a practical way, as described in the preceding chapters. The explanation of performance alignment that follows is predicated on an understanding of the 6:4:4 (proforma: performance levels: layers of work) Language of Work model.

Each chapter in this book has been a building block for achieving performance alignment. In this chapter, we will integrate the various blocks to illustrate how alignment can be realized. If the concept is not totally clear at first, remember that learning the Language of Work is much like learning a foreign language; achieving performance alignment will take time, practice, correction, and more practice.

We will begin with a simple simulation game that we, as external performance consultants, usually play with our clients to illustrate two of the three dimensions of alignment; the third dimension will be covered through description and example.

As a word of caution, because this chapter presents the ideal in achieving performance alignment, the task may seem a bit daunting. It requires time and effort to reach true performance alignment. It is important to know that one can begin at any level of business, at any time. The description that follows covers every aspect of alignment as if we were starting from scratch to form and operate or completely reorganize and reengineer a business. In actual practice, we would have the goal of achieving as much alignment as possible. Whichever goal we choose, having a systematic methodology and commitment will help us to achieve it.

PERFORMANCE (WORK) ALIGNMENT DEFINED

Technically, performance alignment, as shown by the Language of Work model, is the relationship of work within and between performance levels of business, combined with the synergistic relationship between work behavior, work standards, work support, and human consonance. It is the harmony of work in all its dimensions within a business.

Performance alignment is difficult because it is a complex, behaviorally based view of work throughout a business. When we as managers and workers operate in only one part of the business, it is difficult for us to see how we could influence and achieve the ultimate goal of performance alignment and still do our work. That is why it is important that organizations have performance consultants to help them achieve the alignment.

Performance alignment is not only multilevel (as in the four levels of the Business Sphere), but also requires a three-dimensional view as four layers of performance (work behavior, standards, support, and human consonance) cut across the levels. To align even a small organization requires great perspicacity, knowledge at several levels, and a paradigm or system that addresses performance in an equal and translatable way. When an organization is large and complex, with many customers and suppliers, alignment may seem to be "an impossible dream." However, any business can achieve alignment. As a performance consultant, you can facilitate executives and managers to achieve the goal through their efforts and the direct involvement of the workforce. As a result, not only will performance alignment be achieved, but everyone involved will gain a far greater understanding of the business and will commit to achieve its success.

Performance alignment is all work-related considerations working together. The fundamental goals are (1) a common good of clients being served and (2) the survival and prosperity of the business and its workforce. At the more functional level, performance alignment is the harmony of all the work elements that must exist for a business to be successful. It is much more than people "working together." Certainly, alignment involves people (individuals and work groups), but it also involves systems (core processes) and the organization (business unit).

Technically, alignment is most often explained as the vertical and horizontal work relationships within a business. This means some kind of interrelated relationship of "work" (however "work " is defined in each business), up and down (vertical) and across (horizontal) the organization. In the case of the Language of Work model, it means the interaction between work elements as defined by proformas at multiple performance levels and work layers. This will be explained and illustrated shortly in greater detail. But first, let's look at another critical dimension beyond vertical and horizontal.

Although we are usually constrained to a concept in a two-dimensional plane (vertical and horizontal) in the Language of Work model, we need to plan and think of alignment as three-dimensional. Vertical and horizontal alignment deal with levels and layers of performance. The third dimension deals with connections between layers. This, too, will be illustrated shortly.

Although it may seem complicated and difficult at first to align performance on so many levels and layers, not to do so is to fail to align much of the business that needs it. For example, goals may be aligned with operational tasks, but not translated to how each individual and work group would operationalize the goal and tasks, what standards would be met, what support would be provided, and how the human consonance would be assured. Multiply this out throughout the business and there are numerous needs in performance alignment.

TENETS OF PERFORMANCE ALIGNMENT

We should be able to align performance company-wide. This is best achieved with a planned, long-term effort in which the business evolves toward a healthy state as each successive level of performance is aligned. It might take only a couple of years or perhaps ten years to achieve alignment initially, then continuous attention to maintain. We have been working with one client for six years to achieve alignment and the business is very close to its goal. Imagine the process that was undertaken to align the organization horizontally and vertically, to install or improve the host of interventions found in the work support matrix (Chapter 8), as well as to define and align its work behavior and standards, plus achieve consonance of human relations. Alignment takes planning, skill, patience, endurance, commitment to the long haul, and continuous attention to maintain and improve the business. It begins, however, with *any* attention to *any* alignment relationship need.

The components of the 6:4:4 Language of Work model are shown in Figure 10.1. They are described in detail in the remainder of the chapter as they relate to achieving performance alignment.

The Tenets of Performance Alignment

1. Achieve *horizontal alignment* by assuring that the proforma for all the four *levels* within a *layer* (as applicable) of performance is complete, accurate, and achievable.

2. Achieve *vertical alignment* by assuring that each of the like elements at the four levels within a layer (as applicable) of performance is aligned with each other.

3. Achieve *synergistic alignment* between the *layers* of work by linking the work *behavior*, as the foundation, to the defined work *standards*,

Figure 10.1. Work Performance Alignment.

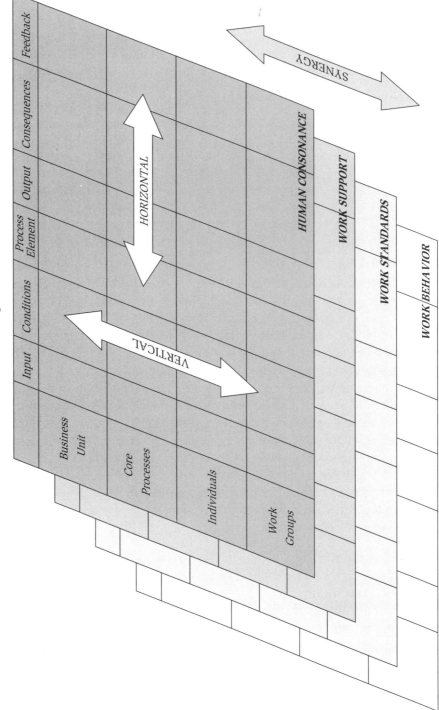

building a healthy organization through work *support,* and assuring *human consonance* to minimize work noise.

We will now see how performance alignment can be established, nurtured, and continued in a business by following the three tenets of performance alignment.

The Work Simulation Game

The first and second tenets above can be best illustrated through a work alignment simulation game. These tenets are related to horizontal and vertical alignment. We often use the game with clients both to introduce the proforma and to build an introductory understanding of alignment. Although the simulation is best played with others to take advantage of group interaction, you can play the game as a reader by taking the time to fill in the information as you go along.

The simulation matrix in Figure 10.2 has twenty-four squares representing the four performance levels of a hypothetical business, the business unit, core processes, individuals, and work groups. The simulated business is a division of a large corporation that provides communications services to both its internal clients and external companies. Thus, the business unit in question has been partially outsourced by its parent company. It is a communication division (business unit) that is to achieve self-sufficiency as a profit center, while still meeting the internal needs of its parent company. The fictitious business unit is called Corporate Communications, Inc. (CCI).

In explaining the "simulation," the president of CCI would say something like:

As your executive officer, I want you to help me make our division more efficient and effective. We need to get our work in order—aligned—to better serve our internal and external customers. If we cannot do this, we will continue to be inefficient, we won't grow, or we may even go out of business. To use specific terms from the Language of Work model we have been learning through our company performance consultant, it means that

- The proforma for each of the four performance levels of our business must be aligned horizontally.
- The six elements of each proforma from one performance level to the next must be aligned vertically.

"After the simulation, we will consider the work standards, support, and human consonance of work and how these can be aligned in the attainment of our work behavior at the four performance levels. For now, we will be concerned only with aligning our work behavior.

With the executive officer's goal in mind, let's see how alignment is illustrated in a simplified way in the simulation. By looking at how work *behavior* is analyzed, we can understand a similar cause-and-effect relationship for work

Figure 10.2. Work Simulation Game.

WORK ALIGNMENT: A Business Simulation Game Worksheet

	Input	Conditions	Process Elements	Output	Consequences	Feedback
BUSINESS UNIT	Business Communication Needs	Stated Company Image	Documentation Production Methods	Company Communication Documents	Positive Company Image	Client Satisfaction Survey
CORE PROCESSES				Printed Document		
INDIVIDUALS				Word-Processed Document		
WORK GROUPS				Various Completed Documents: • Printed Documents • Word-Processed Documents • Posters Produced • Overhead Produced		

standards, support, and human consonance. First, let's see how the company achieved horizontal and vertical alignment. The executive officer continues his instructions to his workforce. See Figure 10.2 for the company's outputs.

I have already defined our major *outputs,* which are various company communication documents. I have shown the outputs for the business unit on a matrix, along with associated work elements at the business unit level. You can see that I have yet to define the inputs, conditions, process elements, consequences, and feedback for some levels of the the business. Of course, our business unit has other outputs, but to keep it simple for now, I've listed only some outputs and will shortly define associated work elements.

In the matrix I've entered one output at each of the core process, individual, and work group levels. Note that each of these is aligned to the output at the business unit level. Thus, we achieve 'company communication documents' at the business unit level by producing a 'printed document' (as one of the communication documents) at the core process level. Then, at the individual level we complete 'word processed document' and at the work group level 'various completed documents.' Again, to keep things simple, I've included only one process, one job, and one work group.

Now notice that there are several blank boxes. I am going to ask you to fill in each box to demonstrate your understanding of what it takes to achieve performance alignment in our company.

"The following is a list of work elements that I want you to place into the matrix. Based on the meaning of each phrase or statement, you are to put each in its appropriate place as a work element of input, conditions, process element, consequences, or feedback for the performance levels of core process, individual, and work group. These statements must align with their appropriate output (horizontally) already shown for the remaining three performance levels, as well as with one another (that is, input to input) as appropriate vertically. Write the number of the work element in Figure 10.2 in the proper box in the matrix. One word of advice: Start at the business unit level, which I've already filled in, and work your way down through core process, individual, and work group. When you have entered each work element in the simulation matrix, perhaps with the help of some other colleagues, return and we will compare your answers with a completed matrix.

Work Elements for Business Simulation Game

1. Error-Free Document

2. Client Requests for Various Communications

3. Reproduction Equipment Specifications

4. Document Review by Client

5. Group Satisfaction with Work Produced

6. Printing

---

7. Document Quality Assurance Report

8. Business Resource Methods: Receive, Log, Assign, Complete, Ship

9. Attractive, Accurately Typed Document

10. Job Assignment to Process a Document

11. Request for Printing

12. Word Processing: Schedule, Type, Print, Proof, Print, Return to Client

13. Division Performance Report

14. Word Processing Standards

15. Copy Editing Standards for Various Communications

Figure 10.3 is a completed copy of the work behavior alignment matrix for Corporate Communications, Inc. The names of the elements are placed in their proper positions and their corresponding numbers are shown. Did you place and align your work elements correctly? If there are differences, some may be due to how you interpreted the words or their context. Some may be because of the need to further clarify what performance alignment is.

To understand the meaning of alignment, let's use Figure 10.3 as a reference point.

Horizontal Alignment
Tenet 1: ◄————————————►

---

1. Achieve *horizontal alignment* by assuring that the proforma for all the four *levels* within a *layer* (as applicable) of performance is complete, accurate, and achievable.

On the horizontal axis of the simulation matrix, viewing work at each of the four performance levels of the Business Sphere, we must make sure that each proforma is complete, accurate, and achievable. We often know this kind alignment is missing when we hear comments such as

- "Nobody pays attention to the rules and regulations of our business."
- "Nobody seems to care what the results of our work are supposed to be."
- "There just isn't enough communication on what goes right and what needs fixing."
- "You know if you tell the print shop something, they don't follow through."
- "I do work the way I think it needs to be done."

One example of horizontal alignment in the case of Corporate Communications, Inc., is shown in Figure 10.4. We see that, at the business unit level, the

WORK ALIGNMENT: A Business Simulation Game

	Input	Conditions	Process Elements	Output	Consequences	Feedback
BUSINESS UNIT	Business Communication Needs (11)	Stated Company Image	Documentation Production Methods	Company Communication Documents	Positive Company Image (1)	Client Satisfaction Survey (7)
CORE PROCESSES	Request for Printing	Reproduction Equipment Specifications (3)	Printing (6)	Printed Document	Error-Free Document	Document Quality Assurance Report (4)
INDIVIDUALS	Job Assignment to Process a Document (10)	Word-Processing Standards (14)	Word Processing: • Schedule • Type • Print • Proof • Print • Return to Client (12)	Word-Processed Document	Attractive, Accurately Typed Document (9)	Document Review by Client
WORK GROUPS	Client Requests for Various Communications (2)	Copy Editing Standards for Various Communications (15)	Business Resource Methods: • Receive • Log • Assign • Complete • Ship (8)	Various Completed Documents: • Printed Documents • Word-Processed Documents • Posters Produced • Overhead Produced	Group Satisfaction with Work Produced (5)	Division Performance Report (13)

Figure 10.3. Completed Work Simulation Game.

output of "company communication documents" is aligned to the work that is needed to achieve the output. It is aligned to the other five elements of its proforma as follows:

Input	Stated Company Image
Condition	Business Communication Needs
Process Element	Documentation Production Methods
Consequence	Company Image Maintained
Feedback	Client Satisfaction Survey

In horizontal alignment the proforma must meet three criteria: completeness, accuracy, and capable of being achieved. We see in the example that the performance is complete in that each of the six elements of the proforma are defined. It is accurate through verifying that the performance reflects the desired behavior. And, it is achievable through actual use. If the horizontal alignment does not meet any of these three criteria, then the performance is not horizontally aligned. The three criteria can be defined as follows:

1. *Complete* means that each of the six elements of work must be present and accounted for.

2. *Accurate* means that each element reflects a verified definition of the performance.

3. *Achievable* means that the work can be performed by those who do the work.

Let's look at a few other examples from the simulation.

In the simulation, if we don't plan for the input of a clear job assignment at the individual level, it is unlikely that the output of a word processed document will be fully achieved. At the business unit level, if we don't properly identify client needs, the business unit will not be aligned to achieve the outputs and consequences. The same would be true if the conditions, process element, and feedback at the business unit level were not accounted for. This is true of any level of performance. If we don't adequately plan to achieve the individual level consequence of attractive, accurately typed documents, they are not likely to occur. Just ask yourself this basic horizontal alignment question (for any level of performance): "If I failed to adequately provide for any one of the work elements in the proforma, what effect would it have on achieving the work behavior the company desires?" The answer may be major or minor. The effect would be failure to achieve horizontal performance alignment.

Now, just as work behavior must be aligned horizontally, a similar horizontal alignment must be achieved for work standards, work support, and work consonance. Horizontal alignment in all these dimensions is illustrated in Figure 10.5a, b. The nature and scope of these kinds of horizontal alignment are discussed next.

BUSINESS UNIT

Input	Conditions	Process Element	Output	Consequences	Feedback
Business Communication Needs	Stated Company Image	Documentation Production Methods	Company Communication Documents	Positive Company Image	Client Satisfaction Survey

Figure 10.4. Horizontal Alignment: Business Unit Example.

WORK BEHAVIOR MATRIX

	Input	Conditions	Process Element	Output	Consequences	Feedback
Business Unit						
Core Processes						
Individuals						
Work Groups						

WORK SUPPORT MATRIX

	Input	Conditions	Process Element	Output	Consequences	Feedback
Business Unit						
Core Processes						
Individuals						
Work Groups						

Figure 10.5a. Horizontal Work Alignment for Performance Layers.

WORK STANDARDS MATRIX

	Input	Conditions	Process Element	Output	Consequences	Feedback
Business Unit						
Core Processes						
Individuals						
Work Groups						

HUMAN CONSONANCE MATRIX

	Input	Conditions	Process Element	Output	Consequences	Feedback
Business Unit						
Core Processes						
Individuals						
Work Groups						

Figure 10.5b. Horizontal Work Alignment for Performance Layers (continued).

As an example of aligning standards, suppose at the work group level the company establishes a quality standard (a condition) that certain documents will always be in three colors. However, the consequences standard for these documents says they will not exceed a certain price. This creates misalignment whenever the three-color copy standard keeps the company from meeting the price for clients who want fewer than one hundred copies. They cannot bid on certain customer requests. Standards for conditions and consequence are thus not in alignment. Either the price will have to be raised or the three-color condition applied to certain circumstances, or both, to bring them into alignment.

The horizontal misalignment of work support is fairly easy to see. For example, if we define a certain workload (as a condition) that the printing business can handle, yet we don't support this by allowing every piece of business (an input) that comes in the door to be accepted with any deadline, there is not an alignment of work support between the condition and the input.

Horizontal alignment of human consonance might be best illustrated by looking at the behavior of a manager regarding expectations about the design and production of a given document. Let's say that the manager has plenty of praise for those who design the document (after all, he used to be a designer), but yells at the printing staff because they are late in producing the document. The fact that the designers usually get the document to printing at the last minute is overlooked. This is a problem in horizontal human consonance alignment.

Now let's move to vertical performance alignment.

Tenet 2: Vertical Alignment

2. Achieve *vertical alignment* by assuring that each of the like elements at the four levels within a layer of performance is aligned with the others.

Just as there is a horizontal relationship in achieving alignment of work behavior, standards, support, and human consonance, performance must also be vertically aligned between each level at each layer. In fact, this is the more traditional view of alignment, although sometimes not well understood. Campaigns to improve the "line of sight" goals, for example, from the business unit to the individual are reflections of this need.

Why is it that vertical relationships often don't exist when they should? The answer is fairly simple. Businesses start with a few individuals and functions, and then add other individuals and functions. A new product here, some new staff there, and some new technology over there. Growth is followed with rearrangement of work and reorganization of work groups. So, too, are standards and support added on an as-needed basis, without necessary attention to alignment need. And on and on. There is, after all, the work to get done!

Occasionally, we need to step back and say, "Hey, let's make sure all of this work stuff we are doing in aligned to achieve what we really need to do to meet our clients' needs!" The fact that this doesn't occur is not because of a lack of noticing or caring (there are plenty of comments that something needs to be done). It is more likely not taking the time or not knowing exactly what work is and how to define and align it. The failure to achieve vertical alignment is largely due to the lack of using a work paradigm by which the various levels of a business may be defined in a common way and thus aligned. Without a common proforma, alignment cannot be conceived, achieved, or tested.

The lack of vertical alignment of performance is commonly expressed in such comments as:

- "Management doesn't know what we do down here."
- "If the print department would just have some appreciation for our needs."
- "If only Mary would contribute to our group."
- "Process, process! I barely know what my job is in relation to my work group."
- "The consequences our business wants and those of my job certainly don't match up!"
- "The executives may think they are communicating (giving feedback), but it doesn't match up with what my manager says."

As represented in Figure 10.6, vertical alignment is the view up and down the levels of each layer in the Business Sphere. This is not the same as the view up and down the organization. That is another issue, and certainly one to be attended to. But here we are addressing the relationship of work behavior (and other layers) as its cascades from work element to work element from the business unit to the core processes to individuals to work groups and back up again.

Note in vertical alignment of performance that there is a direct relationship between each common work element (output to output, input to input, and so on) and within each performance level; that the sequence of this relationship for alignment (and definition) is always from business unit down through core processes, individuals, and ending with work groups; and that the relationship from bottom up is the implementation and achievement of work.

As described in Chapter 6, work groups become the process element of the business unit, closing the loop of work definition and alignment between the four performance levels of the Business Sphere.

Figure 10.7 is a vertical slice of the simulation case for Corporate Communications, Inc., in which we see that the outputs at each level are related to one another. The behavior alignment relationship cascades from the business unit

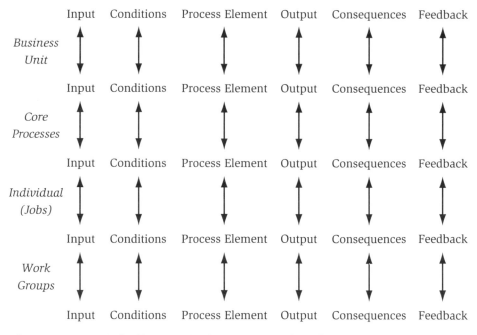

Figure 10.6. Vertical Alignment in the Language of Work Model.

down through the core processes, to individuals, and work groups; during implementation the relationship is from bottom to top.

In the simulation, the same vertical alignment of each level also exists for inputs, conditions, process elements, consequences, and feedback. These relationships must exist in order for performance to be efficient, effective, and congruent within a level of business. If not, things that should happen do not, those things that do happen are less efficient than they should be, or the wrong things happen altogether.

A good example of the lack of vertical alignment occurred at a high-tech company in which we were to improve individual level consequences in collecting data on the repair of equipment. In that instance, the executives of a high-tech company at the business unit level valued different consequences from what the repair people valued at the individual level. The executives wanted certain information, which the repair people did not collect because they didn't see the company's consequences as important. They considered themselves to be repair people for whom the customer's repair was most important. They didn't collect and report the repair data in a form that was useful so that hardware developers could design for fewer repairs and customer complaints. Thus, there was a lack of alignment between consequences at the business unit and the individual lev-

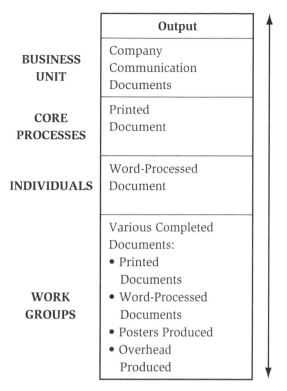

	Output
BUSINESS UNIT	Company Communication Documents
CORE PROCESSES	Printed Document
INDIVIDUALS	Word-Processed Document
WORK GROUPS	Various Completed Documents: • Printed Documents • Word-Processed Documents • Posters Produced • Overhead Produced

Figure 10.7. Vertical Alignment: Outputs Example.

els. Indeed, most of the misalignment in the vertical is in feedback, consequences, and conditions—which is not to say that the remaining three work elements don't have their share of misalignments.

In the simulation we can illustrate, for instance, that the outputs listed at the four performance levels are aligned to one another. We know this because the foundation output at the business unit, "company communication documents," is:

• Manifested at the core process level by "printed document" (as one of the company communication documents);

• Aligned to "word processed document" at the individual level; and

• Aligned to the "various completed documents" at the work group level.

Of course, specifying alignment and achieving it are two different matters. Alignment must be validated during actual implementation. A similar review of the simulation for Corporate Communications, Inc., will show the vertical alignment of inputs, conditions, process element, consequence, and feedback.

In the same way that work standards, support, and human consonance must be aligned in the horizontal relationships of performance, so too must they be aligned in the vertical relationships. This is represented in Figure 10.8a, b. Once we establish a standard at the business unit level for any work element, we know that it needs to cascade its way down through related core processes, jobs, and work groups. For example, if a certain standard in communication for the business is set at the business unit level, this standard must be aligned with the standard to be achieved at the core processes, individual, and work group levels. The same applies to vertical alignment of work support and attainment of work consonance.

Tenet 3: Synergistic Alignment

> 3. Achieve *synergistic alignment* between the *layers* of work by linking the work *behavior,* as the foundation, to the defined work *standards,* building a healthy organization through work *support,* and assuring *human consonance* to minimize work noise.

As depicted in Figure 10.9, perhaps the least attended to aspect of performance alignment is that which needs to exist between the four layers of work: behavior, standards, support, and human consonance. Vertical and horizontal alignment occur within each level and its layer of performance. Synergistic alignment occurs between the layers. Both vertical and horizontal alignment were relatively easy to see on paper, whereas synergistic alignment is a bit more complex because it involves several layers of work.

Managers and supervisors typically worry about and are suppose to achieve horizontal alignment. They are to define and get the work done. By contrast, executives are suppose to achieve and worry about vertical alignment: What will the business be, how will work be done, by whom, and how organized. But who attends to the synergistic alignment in the company? It certainly should be to some degree a responsibility of executives and it should be a responsibility of managers and supervisors. Probably what is really needed is an individual to make sure synergy is being attended to. This is a perfect role for a performance consultant who is charged with looking across, up, and down, and from one layer to the next of business. Perhaps a new role could be created: the "chief performance officer" of a business. The need for continuous attention to alignment in the business and who will facilitate it is not to be answered here, but raises an important issue for the executive management of any business.

The need for synergistic alignment is often found when comments such as the following are heard:

WORK BEHAVIOR MATRIX

	Input	Conditions	Process Element	Output	Consequences	Feedback
Business Unit						
Core Processes						
Individuals						
Work Groups						

WORK SUPPORT MATRIX

	Input	Conditions	Process Element	Output	Consequences	Feedback
Business Unit						
Core Processes						
Individuals						
Work Groups						

Figure 10.8a. Vertical Work Alignment for Performance Layers.

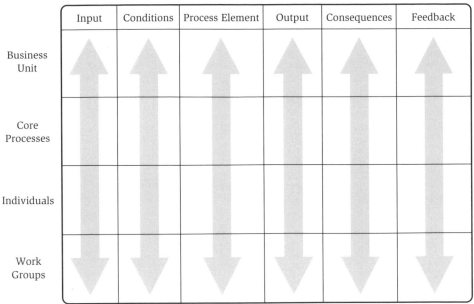

WORK STANDARDS MATRIX

	Input	Conditions	Process Element	Output	Consequences	Feedback
Business Unit						
Core Processes						
Individuals						
Work Groups						

HUMAN CONSONANCE MATRIX

	Input	Conditions	Process Element	Output	Consequences	Feedback
Business Unit						
Core Processes						
Individuals						
Work Groups						

Figure 10.8b. Vertical Work Alignment for Performance Layers (continued).

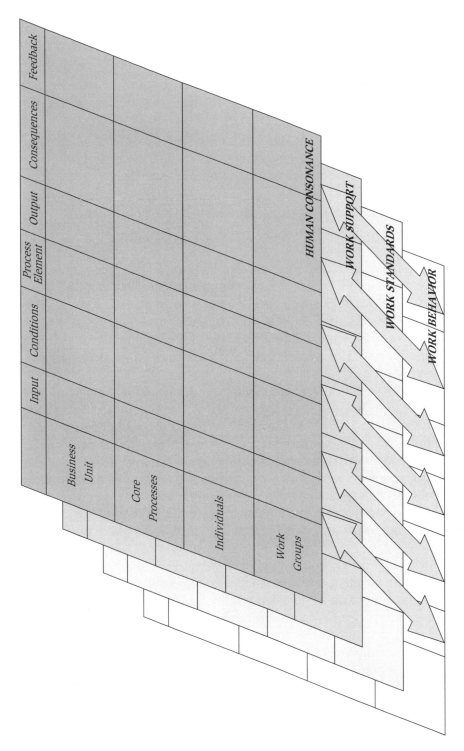

Figure 10.9. Synergistic Alignment of the Language of Work Model.

- "They say mission and vision are important, but you wouldn't know it around here! I can't see it at our level!"
- "It may be a self-directed work team approach we have around here, but the vice president of operations keeps changing the decisions we make as a team!"
- "He may be a great vice president for meeting the profit target in our group, but he is sure a pain to the rest of us who have to work with him, let alone the problems he causes for other divisions."
- "We'd be able to get our process done more efficiently if we just had some computers with the latest software."
- "Standards to that group's work? You've got to be kidding!"

Synergistic alignment calls for a concerted effort to define performance in the proper order, as it has been presented in this book—from work behavior to work standards to work support and establishing human consonance. Furthermore, it requires that the vertical and horizontal alignment of work behavior be established first, and then serve as the anchors for layering in horizontal and vertical alignment within work standards, support, and consonance.

Achieving synergistic alignment further requires that the aforementioned steps be done by using a common model of performance, such as the proforma of the Language of Work model. Without a common performance view, there is no way performance can be equated or aligned within levels and from one layer to another. By analogy, building an organization without attention to alignment is similar to purchasing different computer platforms that cannot exchange data and work together for the common good of the business. To achieve synergistic alignment there has to be a way to connect the layers of performance systematically. The Language of Work proforma is one such way.

As an example of synergistic alignment, when we examined the drawing behavior of the business case engineering example, we saw how the appropriate standards in terms of quantity, quality, timeliness, and cost were layered to the core process of engineering designs. Then, the appropriate support was identified so that the drawings and their standards had the greatest likelihood of being achieved. To further ensure this, the human element was carefully looked at to make sure that positive executive, manager, and worker relations existed to complete the designs to reach the desired consequences. This is synergistic alignment of the core process layer, and the same type of alignment would have to be done for the other three performance layers of a business.

THE DIFFICULTY OF ACHIEVING PERFORMANCE ALIGNMENT

On the one hand, performance is a rather simple thing to define. On the other hand, not everyone has the same perspective of what work is. There is no common work language—and to complicate matters, there is often much emotion involved in just talking about work, before even attempting to reach a basic shared understanding and to resolve the needs of business. One answer involves how we prepare managers and workers to achieve alignment and performance improvement.

In business, we typically devote a great deal of energy to seeing that managers receive the kind of training they need to understand and manage their businesses. However, little of this training teaches how to define, measure, implement, and improve performance itself. Training and education deal with financing, planning, presenting, managing, and communicating. Organizations might well consider putting managers and employees *together* in training to define, measure, improve, and understand their own performance, *with their own work groups.* When trained separately, each can blame the other for what they believe the problems are. Training managers with their intact work groups allows them to work through the issues of performance to common understanding for their own well-being in the business and with other groups. With a common model of work and a common work language, this understanding of performance can be achieved quickly.

If managers and workers had a solid foundation in performance improvement, the business would then do well to have a performance consultant who could facilitate and work with executives, managers, and the workforce to achieve optimal performance. He or she could serve as a teacher of performance for intact work groups, a facilitator of work definition and solutions, and a coach and counselor when needed. Such a person could work across the entire business, seeking performance alignment for the entire business.

Perhaps the most optimistic aspect of alignment is that it can begin today in any business. It does not initially require analyzing, defining, and implementing every work map or job model and installing or implementing every intervention suggested in this book. Each person can start by defining their own job first and making sure you understand your relationship (alignment) to other individuals, your own work group, your customers, and your suppliers. Similarly, managers can see that their groups are aligned in a common work and team effort; managers can use facilitation to lead the work group effort. Executives can see that the "business drivers" are aligned and have in their organization a performance consultant who will help address work behavior, standards, support, and human consonance. Executives also can initiate efforts at alignment by conducting an organizational scan of work support and developing strategic efforts to further develop the support needs of a healthy organization. The interventions (Langdon, Whiteside, & McKenna, 1999) embodied in work support and needed for work improvement can be attended to on a continuous basis, and with the increasing effectiveness that would result, it could reassure employees that their company wants to be the very best.

Finally, if performance improvement and alignment are to be achieved, a common way of perceiving, defining, developing, measuring, and improving work must be understood and used. This is particularly crucial for the understanding of performance, not only within the workforce, but between the workforce and the performance consultant. Otherwise performance alignment is a nice concept but will never become a reality. Now you can use the Language of Work model to help businesses achieve understanding of and alignment of their performance.

REFERENCES

Davis, B. L., & others (1992). *Successful manager's handbook.* Minneapolis: Personnel Decisions, Inc.

Davenport, T. H., & Prusak, L. (1998). *Working knowledge.* Boston: Harvard Business School Press.

Dean, P. J., & Ripley, D. E. (1997). *Performance improvement pathfinders: Models for organizational learning systems.* Washington, DC: ISPI Publications.

Gilbert, T. F. (1996). *Human competence: Engineering worthy performance.* Washington, DC: ISPI Publications.

Hale, J. (1998). *The performance consultant's fieldbook.* San Francisco: Jossey-Bass/Pfeiffer.

Hammer, M., & Champy, J. (1993). *Reengineering the corporation.* New York: Harper-Collins.

Hirsch, S., & Kummerow, J. (1989). *Life types.* New York: Warner Books.

Kolbe, K. (1991). *The conative connection: Undercovering the link between who you are and how you perform.* Reading, MA: Addison-Wesley.

Langdon, D. G. (1995). *The new language of work.* Amherst, MA: HRD Press.

Langdon, D. G., Whiteside, K., & McKenna, M. (1999). *Instruction resource guide: 50 performance improvement tools.* San Francisco: Jossey-Bass.

Phillips, J. J. (1998). *Improving performance in organizations.* Alexandria, VA: American Society for Training and Development.

Rummler, G. A., & Brache, A.P. (1995). *Improving performance: How to manage the white space on the organization chart.* San Francisco: Jossey-Bass.

Tosti, D. (1999) *Global fluency.* Paper presented at the International Society for Performance Improvement International Conference, Long Beach, CA, 1999. Washington, DC: ISPI Publications.

Whiteside, K. (1997). *How to scan the organization to make it healthy: A way for change agents to maximize the investment in HRD.* Paper presented at the ASTD International Conference & Exposition, 1997. Alexandria, VA: ASTD.

INDEX

ABOUT THE AUTHOR

Danny G. Langdon has been an active researcher, model-maker, developer, administrator, and author in the field of instructional and performance technology since 1964. Prior to this he served two years in the U.S. Peace Corps in Ethiopia as a chemistry teacher at the Harar Teacher Training Institute.

While at the Parks Job Corps Center, Pleasanton, California, as an instructor and then supervisor of Instructional Materials Development, he wrote his first objectives, and thus began the inquiry into human and organizational behavior. Two subsequent years with Dr. William A Deterline at General Programmed Teaching, Inc., Palo Alto, California, introduced the skills of programmed instruction and instructional technology.

Ten years at the American College of Life Underwriter's Adult Learning Center, Bryn Mawr, Pennsylvania, were devoted to adult learning research, managing an instructional design and development group, and authoring and editing a forty-volume instructional design series. Eleven subsequent years as the director of corporate training at the Morrison Knudsen Corporation cemented an understanding of business and the expansion into the burgeoning performance technology field. Three years as the director of total quality management for the nation's largest environmental engineering company, International Technology, helped to bridge that technology to business units, processes, individuals, and work groups.

Langdon has been a continuous active member of the International Society for Performance Improvement (ISPI) since 1967, serving as a past national secretary and international president. He has received two international awards for contributions to the field. He has published seven books, as well as contributed chapters in a dozen other works. With his partner in life and business, Kathleen S. Whiteside, Langdon owns Performance International, a consulting firm that facilitates a wide range of businesses improvements using the Language of Work model. Their success in reengineering, job modeling, work group alignment, process analysis, and business problem solutions for national and international firms has repeatedly demonstrated the power of clients learning the Language of Work to solve and commit to performance change and alignment.